Withdrawn from
Sacramento Public Library

SACRAMENTO PUBLIC LIBRARY

3 3029 06059 0767

SACRAMENTO PUBLIC LIBRARY
828 "I" STREET
SACRAMENTO, CA 95814
6/2007

D0731152

The
EVERYTHING.
Managing People Book

Dear Reader,

So, you're a manager. Congratulations! You probab[ly] [have]
ideas about how to do things differently—and bett[er]
already smoothly implemented some of them but have had less success with others. You know you could do more if you knew what to
do and how to do it. Although you've had plenty of training in the
skills your jobs have required, no one's really teaching you how to
be a manager.

You've had your share of bad managers, and you don't want
to become one of them. Perhaps you've been fortunate enough to
have a great manager at some point in your career, someone you'd
like to be like now that you're one. We hope so, because that's the
kind of manager we'd like you to be!

In today's business environment, success as a manager means
directing and balancing multiple objectives. It's not enough to know
processes; you must also know what motivates and supports the
people who make those processes happen. This book is a guide to
understanding how people function within the workplace and to
figuring out how you as a manager can help them grow to be more
productive and successful—so you are, too.

Gary R. McClain

Deborah S. Romaine

The EVERYTHING® Series

Editorial

Publishing Director	Gary M. Krebs
Director of Product Development	Paula Munier
Associate Managing Editor	Laura M. Daly
Associate Copy Chief	Brett Palana-Shanahan
Acquisitions Editor	Lisa Laing
Development Editor	Katie McDonough
Associate Production Editor	Casey Ebert

Production

Director of Manufacturing	Susan Beale
Associate Director of Production	Michelle Roy Kelly
Prepress	Matt LeBlanc Erick DaCosta
Design and Layout	Heather Barrett Brewster Brownville Colleen Cunningham Jennifer Oliveira
Series Cover Artist	Barry Littmann

Visit the entire Everything® Series at *www.everything.com*

THE

EVERYTHING®

MANAGING PEOPLE BOOK

2nd Edition

Quick and easy ways to build, motivate, and nurture a first-rate team

Gary McClain, Ph.D., and Deborah S. Romaine

A

Adams Media

Avon, Massachusetts

Copyright ©2002, 2007, F+W Publications, Inc. All rights reserved.
This book, or parts thereof, may not be reproduced
in any form without permission from the publisher; exceptions
are made for brief excerpts used in published reviews.

An Everything® Series Book.
Everything® and everything.com® are registered trademarks of F+W Publications, Inc.

Published by Adams Media, an F+W Publications Company
57 Littlefield Street, Avon, MA 02322 U.S.A.
www.adamsmedia.com

Produced by Amaranth Illuminare, P.O. Box 573, Port Townsend, WA, 98368

ISBN 10: 1-59869-143-0
ISBN 13: 978-1-59869-143-6

Printed in the United States of America.

J   I   H   G   F   E   D   C   B   A

Library of Congress Cataloging-in-Publication Data

McClain, Gary R.
The everything managing people book / authors: Gary McClain and Deborah S. Romaine. -- 2nd ed.
p. cm. -- (An everything series book)
Includes bibliographical references.
ISBN-13: 978-1-59869-143-6
ISBN-10: 1-59869-143-0
1. Supervision of employees. 2. Personnel management. I. Romaine, Deborah S. II. Title.

HF5549.12.M375 2007
658.3--dc22

2006028206

This publication is designed to provide accurate and authoritative information with regard
to the subject matter covered. It is sold with the understanding that the publisher is not
engaged in rendering legal, accounting, or other professional advice. If legal advice or
other expert assistance is required, the services of a competent professional person should
be sought.

—From a *Declaration of Principles* jointly adopted by a Committee of the
American Bar Association and a Committee of Publishers and Associations

Many of the designations used by manufacturers and sellers to distinguish their products
are claimed as trademarks. Where those designations appear in this book and Adams
Media was aware of a trademark claim, the designations have been printed with initial
capital letters.

This book is available at quantity discounts for bulk purchases.
For information, please call 1-800-289-0963.

Contents

Top Ten Concerns of Today's Managers / x
Introduction / xi

You're a Manager! / 1
Stepping Up to the Challenge **2** • You Set the Tone **3** • Your Role As a Leader **5** • Living Within Your Limitations **11** • It Can be Lonely in the Middle **12**

Finding Your Place / 15
Managing Former Coworkers **16** • Replacing a "Bad" Manager **19** • Replacing a "Good" Manager **22** • Rebuilding a Work Group **23** • Riding the Waves of Change **25**

A Manager's Many Roles / 27
Coach: Bringing Out the Best in Others **28** • Mentor: Trusted Guide **29** • Teacher: Imparting New Skills **30** • Parent: Setting Limits **32** • Mediator: Finding Balance **34** • Cheerleader: Rallying the Troops **35**

What Companies Want / 37
What Companies Care About **38** • Responsibility and Accountability **41** • Keeping Good People **43** • Turning Around Counterproductive Behavior **45** • What Works for Them Works for You **47**

What Employees Want / 49

What Employees Expect from Their Jobs **50** • What Employees Expect from Their Managers **51** • Money Matters **53** • Consistency Is the Key **54** • Stay Connected **56**

What Managers Want / 57

Great Expectations **58** • Your Learning Curve **60** • What Managers Want from Employees **61** • How Managers Succeed **64** • Are You Bridging the Gap or Stuck in the Middle? **65** • Glass Ceilings and Dead Ends **67** • Make the Most of Your Opportunities **68**

Today's Workplace / 71

Flextime **72** • Telecommuting **72** • Job Sharing **73** • Comfort Means Productivity **77** • Workplace Décor and Decorum **79** • Safety and Security **81**

Technology Rules / 85

The Digital Work World **86** • Telework **89** • E-Mail Etiquette **92** • Web Surfing **93** • Confidentiality and Workplace Privacy **95**

Work Styles / 97

Channeling Creative Energy **98** • The Need for Structure **102** • Workaholic: Corporate Culture or Individual Personality? **105** • Running in the Wrong Direction **107** • The Influences of Your Work Style **108**

Work Group Dynamics / 111

Effective Teamwork **112** • Where Do You Fit In? **113** • System Versus People Problems **116** • When Personalities Collide **118** • Resolving Conflicts **119**

Getting the Work Done / 121
A Comfortable Workplace **122** • Realistic Goals **124** • Employee Participation **125** • Support Individual Growth **126** • Managing Manipulation **127** • Job Description Boundaries **129**

Communication and Feedback / 133
Translating Body Language **134** • The Importance of Listening **135** • Daily Interactions With Your Employees **137** • The Open Door Policy **139** • The Feedback Loop **141** • Communication Through Writing **143**

Productive Meetings / 147
Meeting Basics **148** • Who Should Attend? **150** • It's All about the Agenda **151** • Shaping Interactions **153** • Productive Disagreement **156** • Follow Up and Follow Through 160

Performance Standards and Evaluation / 161
The Relationship Between Performance and Evaluation **162** • Performance Evaluation Structures **165** • Identify Performance Issues **168** • Job Performance Coaching **170** • Timely Follow-Up **174**

Diversity, Fairness, and Equal Opportunity / 177
Respect Differences **178** • Generations Apart **179** • Gender Neutrality **181** • What Is Fairness? **184** • Recognizing and Nurturing Potential **187** • The Risks of Playing Favorites **189**

Promoting and Hiring / 191
The Right Start **192** • The Job Description **194** • Applications, Resumes, and References **195** • Interview Basics **196** • The Interview from Start to Finish **199** • The Offer: Let's Make a Deal! **202**

Downsizing, Layoffs, and Firing / 203

When You're the Bearer of Bad News **204** • Big Picture: Restructuring and Downsizing **205** • Small Picture: Individual Failings **207** • The Difference Between a Mentor and an Enabler **209** • The Right Way to Help Out **210** • Firing an Employee **212** • Handling the Fallout With Other Employees **214**

Following the Rules / 217

Why Workplace Policies Are Important **218** • Employment Laws and Regulations **219** • A Safe Workplace **221** • Equity and Fairness **222** • Family Matters **228** • Personal Accountability **230**

Socializing at Work / 233

Workplace Personalities and Office Politics **234** • Where to Draw the Line **236** • Workplace Relationships **237** • Workplace Romance **241** • Office Parties and After-Hours Events **245**

Check Your Baggage at the Door / 249

It's Not Me, It's You **250** • Angry Employees **251** • Angry Managers **255** • Managing Your Stress **257** • Identifying Stress in Your Work Group **259**

Guiding Your Own Career / 263

Keep Your Skills Sharp **264** • Stay Ahead of the Technology Curve **267** • Learn to Read the Writing on the Wall **267** • Change Is the Only Certainty **270** • Keep Looking Forward **274**

Appendix A: Glossary / 275

Appendix B: Resources / 279

Index / 283

Top Ten Concerns of Today's Managers

1. **Rising costs:** Health care and health care insurance; expense of staying competitive

2. **Diversity:** Multiculturism; protecting rights; immigration and legal employment

3. **Globalization:** Competing in a global economy; offshore outsourcing; import and export

4. **Image and ethics:** Perceived dishonesty and greed among top executives; shortage of good leadership; community accountability

5. **Employee management:** Efficiency; productivity; training; motivation; attitude

6. **Technology and communications:** E-mail, cell phones, text messaging, voicemail; offshore support; BlackBerry

7. **Technology and business objectives:** Growth of Internet advertising and marketing; data security; privacy protection; e-commerce

8. **Constant change:** Technologies; business environment; tastes and needs; flexibility and responsiveness

9. **Strategic relationships:** Partnerships designed to leverage skills and products; choosing and developing the right partnerships

10. **Growth versus stagnation:** Expansion or stability; trends and shifts; overexpansion

Introduction

▶ BACK IN THE DAYS of the Industrial Revolution and the advent of automation, "managing" meant "getting product out." Nameless workers stood side by side on assembly lines and in factories, going through the same movements hour after hour, day after day. As mechanization became more sophisticated, managers started paying attention to factors like efficiency. Not only did workers have to do the same thing over and over, they had to do it within specific parameters. If for any reason workers couldn't do the work, they were gone. Job satisfaction? Not even a dream! Managing, from the manager's perspective, was simple.

Then along came laws bringing protections for workers. If managers wanted employees on the job more than forty hours a week, they had to pay extra. Other changes filtered into the workplace, too, as social circumstances evolved. Women and minority groups entered the workforce. Their demands for equity—equal pay, equal rights, and equal opportunities—gave rise to numerous acts of legislation that established standards of practice for affirmative action, worker safety and health, and equitable pay and benefits.

Today, government—federal, state, and local—regulates many dimensions of the American workplace. Labor and employment laws and regulations are so complex they have become specialty areas within the legal profession, and most large companies have their own legal departments to help them remain in compliance. Ignorance of the law carries the risk of lawsuits, not only from employees but also from the communities within which these companies operate. Managing has become very complicated.

Survival and success as a manager in today's business world requires far more than setting productivity goals and enforcing them with ultimatums. People bring different work styles to the job; managers must understand and integrate them to meet department and company objectives. Company goals still require that employees work at their highest level of productivity, but companies also realize that reaching and maintaining such a level also requires attention to employee needs and interests. Employees need creature comforts, vacations, and opportunities for personal growth and career advancement.

No one craves the "good old days," when the primary tool for measuring job performance was a stopwatch. To those days, most of us are quick to say good riddance. But we do often lament the complexities of today's business environment. It's no longer good enough to excel in your field or profession when you want to be a manager. You must also acquire skills and expertise in the philosophies and practices of management. You may not need an MBA, but you do need to know how to conduct performance evaluations, apply government regulations to the functions of your department and company, and motivate employees to work together as a team.

Whether you're a middle manager in a megacorporation or the do-it-all manager in a small company, you must continually balance the needs of the company and the needs of employees. This book offers you key information and real-world suggestions, along with lots of examples. Managing is an exciting opportunity to shape and improve the professional lives of other people, the success of your company, and the path of your own career.

Please note that the examples and stories in this book are composites created from the shared experiences of numerous people. All names, circumstances, and details have been altered. Any resemblance to real people or situations is purely coincidental.

Chapter 1

You're a Manager!

Congratulations! Being a manager is a great achievement, one that many people strive for in their jobs and careers. The problem is that few people are adequately prepared for the rigors that face them once they meet this goal. Does that mean every manager is destined to become the star of a "horrible boss" story? No way! Just as there is opportunity for you to make mistakes (and you probably will), there is also opportunity for you to break the mold and be a really excellent manager whom people truly respect. Read on to get started on the path to greatness!

Stepping Up to the Challenge

As an employee, you had a clear-cut definition of your role and responsibilities. The line around "my job" was fairly solid and easy for you—as well as others—to see. It was fine for you to show initiative by doing more than what was expected of you, of course. But most everyone knew when your efforts went above and beyond the call of duty.

As a manager, you may find that very little is clear cut. Your job description no doubt includes the phrase "and other duties as necessary," which often seems to be the core rather than the periphery of what your daily activities entail. You are expected to wear many hats and to know which one to wear for each circumstance. Don't worry. Odds are good that you will enjoy the diversity of your roles, once you figure out how to play them all.

ALERT!

Not everyone is cut out to be a manager. Many people who are at the top of their professions are among the worst when it comes to managing other people because that's not where their strengths lie. Only by being truthful with yourself can you know if you are one of these people. And remember: It doesn't mean you're less valuable than those in management; a business needs all its constituents to succeed.

One thing you may be wondering about is how to fill your predecessor's shoes. Hold it right there. It's not possible for a new manager to step in and maintain the same atmosphere that existed under the previous manager. Each manager has different abilities, interests, and priorities. The work group will eventually reflect this, and everyone knows it (even you). Even when a change in management is desirable, employees might meet it with resistance. It's frightening and threatening to lose a manager. Even if the new manager is someone promoted from within the company, he or she is still an unknown. People may outwardly agree that the new manager offers new opportunities, but inwardly they feel worried. They want to know answers to questions like these:

- What will happen as a result of the new arrangement?
- Will things be better or worse than they were before?
- If the previous manager was fired, what happens to former allies who still work in the department or work group?
- How will job descriptions and responsibilities change, if at all?

When you step into a new position, be sure you communicate consistently and diligently with all of your employees. You must both talk and listen. You need to hear about what concerns the people you manage. Even if there's little you can do about their worries, listening to them acknowledges that those worries are valid. Explain your perspectives and expectations, and discuss the expectations of your superiors. You can't talk away disappointment, disagreement, disapproval, or fear, but bringing these emotions out into the open gives everyone permission to begin dealing with them.

You Set the Tone

Managers set the tone for their work groups or departments. Employees figure that if the manager acts a certain way, that is acceptable—if not expected—behavior. This is modeling: You are what your employees may strive to become. Seeing yourself through their eyes, are you who you want to be? If you're not, don't panic. Everyone is capable of change!

FACT

Job satisfaction surveys typically place "getting along with the boss" high on the list of factors that matter to employees. Inability to get along with a manager is one of the most commonly cited reasons for leaving a job.

Victoria, the director of a small company, was unpredictable and often abusive. When she was being kind, she could make a criticism sound like a compliment. The rest of the time, she was monstrous. She berated vendors over the telephone in conference calls for not understanding, or not carrying out, her explicit directions. And while she told her employees that she valued their contributions and encouraged their collaboration and teamwork, she was just as quick to single out an employee in front of the others. No one worried about trying to stay on Victoria's good side because she really didn't have one.

It was more than many team members felt they should have to put up with, but to whom were they going to complain? Certainly not to Victoria! So instead they left, sometimes two or three in one month. Eventually Victoria grew tired of spending all her time finding new employees and she left, too.

Her replacement, Clarence, was just the opposite. He was soft-spoken, respectful, and collaborative. He consistently asked employees for their comments and suggestions, in meetings and throughout the workday. He treated vendors as though the company's very existence depended on them. (Imagine that!) Whenever upper management made a decision that Clarence had been unable to influence or that was out of the department's hands, he let everyone know. Then he helped his employees strategize about how to live with it.

When the department received new project assignments, Clarence brought people together to solicit their ideas. He then identified team members and roles and determined how each would contribute and why. Clarence set completion targets, making sure each person was able to identify hurdles and concerns. And he helped the department set up a review process to make sure work that needed approval or input from other employees received it. Everyone knew what to do; there was little discord among team members.

Both managers, Victoria and Clarence, shaped behavior in powerful ways. The difference between them was that Victoria's approach drove productivity down and people away. Clarence's approach built rapport and confidence. The department's members began to work together with efficiency and creativity, boosting productivity.

Managers set the tone and the standards for attitudes toward workload, customers, the company, and coworkers. What messages are you sending? If you arrive forty minutes late, take two-hour lunches, and habitually arrive twenty minutes late for meetings, you're letting your department know that timelines and schedules are arbitrary. If you do things when you get around to them, so will your employees.

ALERT!

Childhood bullies often grow up to become workplace bullies. They constantly belittle and criticize others, often targeting one or two people who are particularly intimidated by such behavior. The workplace bully becomes an especially dangerous individual when he or she is a manager. At a huge expense to companies that must continually recruit needed talent, an increasing number of people are leaving jobs they love because of bully bosses.

Conversely, if you're a workaholic who doesn't see a problem with taking home a couple of hours of work most evenings and going into the office for a few hours on the weekend, you risk establishing this as a performance standard among your employees—formally, informally, or simply by example. Yet your employees might not agree with your version of a work ethic. You might need to modify your expectations to be sure you don't transfer your expectations in this regard onto them. If there is no reason for your employees to work on weekends, that shouldn't be the standard.

Your Role As a Leader

You might get to be a manager because you are a brilliant performer or a great politician, but what keeps you in management is how well you rally your troops and keep them performing. As a manager, you are the face of your company. You represent upper management to your employees. Your bosses expect you to do the following:

- Reflect and support company goals and objectives, even if you don't agree with them
- Reflect and support company policies and procedures, even if you don't like them
- Communicate the company's needs to employees
- Give upper management feedback about how employees perceive and respond to company goals and polices
- Give upper management feedback about what works and what doesn't about how the company does business

If this is your first management position, these expectations can come as a jolt. You've been on the receiving end throughout your career so far. Now, it's your job to help shape and deliver company standards and expectations to employees who not so long ago were your peers, whether you worked with them at this company or with other people just like them at another company.

Learn to Delegate

When you were an employee, among your strongest assets was no doubt your ability to do a lot of things. In the course of the workday you could accomplish numerous tasks and projects. You met people and learned processes that made it easier for you to do more with less, and you excelled. Now that you're a manager, you need to learn to let this approach go. Your bosses expect you to delegate job tasks and responsibilities to the employees who report to you. You are now the one making the assignments. Your task is to make sure other people get them done, not to do them yourself.

At first you may find delegation uncomfortable. After all, when you were an employee, you didn't much like the manager stopping by your desk to say, "Would you get these reports done by Wednesday? I need them for the project presentation." Never mind that you were also working on the presentation—it was now also your responsibility to do the reports. Even when it was within your job description and skills base, it sometimes felt like the manager was dumping on you. Now you might feel that you're dumping on others, especially if you came from within their ranks.

Effective delegation is a craft many managers take an entire career to finally understand and master. It's not easy to know how much you should remain involved. Even if you pass off an assignment entirely, you still remain accountable to your bosses for its completion. Yet you can't hover over the employees now responsible for doing the assignment. Try this approach and you'll find two things: One, it truly is faster and more efficient just do the job yourself; and two, there's no better way to frustrate and demoralize your employees.

An often-overlooked benefit of delegation is that it lets managers learn from their employees. The person to whom you delegate a task or project will undoubtedly approach the work differently than you would have.

You must find a happy balance, which comes through experience. Perhaps you're fortunate enough to have a mentor, a capable and experienced manager elsewhere in the company (or even your own manager) who can offer guidance and suggestions. Every situation is different. As you begin to see former coworkers from a different perspective, you begin to understand how to integrate their respective talents and abilities—and accommodate their shortcomings—to get things done.

Be Present

It's easy to come into work and go into your office—right to e-mail, checking on the status of ongoing projects, and plunging into the day's workload. You could end up going the entire day without talking to the employees you manage, even though they surround you. You could . . . but if you want to stay a manager, you really can't. Instead, make it a point to go from office to office, cubicle to cubicle, and workstation to workstation to make contact with your employees. Don't miss anyone. If you do, people will begin to feel slighted and left out, or they will suspect that something is wrong. If someone's not there for your rounds, catch him or her later in the day to make contact, however briefly.

Be present without being intrusive. Ask questions, and listen to the answers. Walk around and just listen to employees talk as they work. Don't sneak around—you want people to know that you're there and you're interested. But don't hover, either; you don't want people to feel you don't trust them to do their jobs without constant supervision. You can't know what's going on if you're not there. And if you're not there, people will attempt to resolve problems in their own ways, which often results in less-than-ideal results.

Employees are highly sensitive to routine and to changes in it. They learn very quickly to read the moods of their managers and to shape their own moods accordingly. One person's moods can set the stage for a department or even an entire company.

Consistent daily interaction promotes more than just good feelings; it also promotes effective and collaborative teamwork. When the manager takes a few moments to chat, employees feel better about coming to work and about doing the work expected of them. Small-talk matters. When you stop to ask employees what they did over the weekend, chat about how things are going with the kids, or to mention a good movie you saw or your adventures with your new lawnmower, employees feel that you care about them as people and as individuals, not just as cogs in the corporate machine. Not that we need to drag all of our personal problems into work, of course. But we do need to at least remind each other that we are human and have lives outside the office. This is what helps to create bonds.

When providing comments, be concrete. Cite specific, tangible examples, like so:

- "Josephine Hall is a major client, and your follow-up call caught an error in her order before she noticed it. She called me to say how courteous and professional you were over the phone. She received the corrected order by next-day delivery, which averted a potential crisis."
- "Great job getting out that report, Joan. I know you came in early every day this week to make it happen, and I appreciate your effort."
- "You all worked really hard on the Johnson proposal, and we made it to the final round. I know no one likes to work Saturdays, but if we can all give one last effort on these final questions, we can get the phase two proposal done for delivery on Monday."
- "We're short staffed right now, and I know that's not your fault. But we still have customers to serve, so let's give it our best. I'll lead the first team; who wants to lead the second and third teams?"

By commenting on specifics, you show that you're plugged into the daily activities in your department. Even though you have your own job responsibilities, you know what's going on with your employees and their job responsibilities. No one can work in a vacuum for very long; we need interaction and reassurance that what we're doing is right and that it makes a difference. Otherwise, why bother?

Advocate When Necessary

There are times, too, when you need to become an advocate for your employees. An advocate is someone who takes on the cause of another person to bolster the person's position or to use his or her own abilities on behalf of the other person. For a manager, to advocate for an employee means to step up, directly or indirectly, in support of the employee's issues or needs. This may take the form of going to your boss and saying, "We're really overworking this team. We have to give them some relief before they break down and we lose momentum." Such an approach is about getting support to help meet personal and company goals, not getting people out of their responsibilities. And sometimes advocacy takes a less formal approach.

Consider the following example:

In Kevin's department, window offices were at a premium. They were awarded to project managers whose longevity entitled them to move out of the "stable" of cubicles and into the more spacious and private environment of an office with real walls and a door. Having a window was the crowning bonus.

Everyone knew and honored the pecking order for window offices. Then Kevin arrived. Kevin made no secret of his dissatisfaction at having a cubicle in the center of the large room. He complained, loudly and frequently, that he felt like a mouse in a maze. Just as loudly and frequently, Kevin announced his intention to move into the next available window office. He wasn't going to wait around for all the others to move through their paces; he was going to have his cake and eat it, too. A window office opened up, and even though it was supposed to go to Rhonda (who was out of town), Kevin indeed moved in.

When Rhonda returned, she couldn't believe that her manager had simply allowed Kevin to do what he wanted to do. Not wanting to make a big deal out of something that seemed so petty, Rhonda asked her manager, Marge, why she hadn't intervened. "It's just an office," Marge said. "And you spend three days a week out in the field anyway. As long as you have a desk and a computer, what difference does it make? Besides, there's nothing in writing that defines who gets what offices. I can't really kick Kevin out so you can move in and then never actually be there."

Marge let Rhonda down, and in a big and public way. She was right about the amount of time Rhonda spent out of the workplace, but that did not offset the reality that Marge failed to protect Rhonda's right to the informal perks of longevity. Rhonda told Marge that she would have turned down the office, freeing it for the next person in line. But she was hurt and angry that Marge had preempted her generosity. The message Marge sent to other employees was clear: Out of sight, out of mind.

Marge apologized to Rhonda, acknowledging that Kevin should not have gotten the office. Rhonda agreed that since Kevin was already there, it would serve no purpose to make him move back to his old workspace. As a remedy, Marge arranged for Rhonda to use a company car for the days she was out in the field—an perk until then reserved for managers.

Guide Transition

The companies that survive and thrive in the current environment are those that can make quick changes to mobilize to meet the next challenge. Big, successful companies constantly redesign themselves, creating new departments and divisions as well as developing new products and services. Networking, Internet services, wireless communication, e-mail—unknown terms just a few years ago—have become the buzzwords of the business world.

Companies have to redesign their products and services to meet these challenges, which often results in big changes. Departments that once specialized in certain services may become resources for the entire company—or they may go away entirely, replaced by other services and products. As manager, you must guide employees in making the transitions these shifts require. Though many of your employees' work tasks might remain the same, the focus and purpose of their effort has changed.

Living Within Your Limitations

When you become a manager, your work life is no longer about you. It's about your bosses and your employees—what they need and want, and how you respond. Subordinates and superiors alike might expect you to do things like the following:

- Know your own job inside and out
- Know the jobs of your employees inside and out
- Know what everyone needs, and provide it for them
- Maintain both motivation and discipline
- Enjoy coming to work in the morning more than you like leaving in the evening

Are you feeling a little bit like part of your job description reads, "Walk on water"? Don't worry—it's fine if your awkward sidestroke is what gets you to shore. It's okay to have limitations. Everyone does. You can't do everything.

And you can't be everything to everyone. No one can. What matters more is that you know your limits and can compensate for them.

Even with all of the trends in management style, people are still people. It remains a central role of every manager to understand what makes people tick and to know how to use that understanding to motivate and manage them. This is your job, in addition to the myriad other responsibilities your job description specifies.

If you're not a good teacher, or computer whiz, or designer, find out who is and have them do the job. You just need to be able to recognize when it's necessary. You have your talents, and other people have theirs. Your superiors, as well as other managers in your company, might be good resources. And if you need to improve in an area, there's guaranteed to be a book that can help.

The size of your company can also come into play here. If you work for a small company, odds are that you wear many hats and have a broad base of functions and responsibilities. A small operations manager often worries about the details of day-to-day activities, from filling the copy machine's paper trays in the morning to brainstorming new products in the afternoon. If you're a manager in a large corporation, you likely wear a single hat and have a comparably singular focus in your work. A corporate manager might know little about what goes on beyond the boundaries of his or her department.

Whether your company is large or small, its human needs remain the same. What motivates people remains the same. And in the end, the role of managers remains the same. You are the face of your organization, both to employees and to customers.

It Can Be Lonely in the Middle

As a manager, you're not always a welcome presence in the workplace, which is probably not news to you. Employees might resent you, often for reasons that have nothing to do with you personally. Even your superiors might be impatient with what they perceive to be your lack of progress when improvements take longer than expected. You alone cannot make things all better; miracle worker is not among your many roles, although both subordinates and superiors might act as though it is.

What about your superiors, the managers or executives to whom you now report? Being closer to the top means greater visibility. Are they really watching your every move? You bet! Frontline and midlevel managers are the movers and shakers in most companies. Mistakes at your level can be costly, with ramifications that echo throughout the company. This is not meant to scare you but to help you appreciate and understand the significance of your new role as a manager.

This role requires you to maintain a distance from both employees and upper management. Think of this as a "clear vision" boundary that helps you to see both sides without becoming immersed in either. In fact, you might begin to see your job as one defined by boundaries. Without such boundaries and limits, you and your employees might easily lose sight of the real reason you're together: to help the company meet its service, production, and financial goals. You and the employees who work for you can be colleagues, after a fashion, but you can't really be friends.

ESSENTIAL

If you feel like all eyes are on you, you're probably right. Though everyone has enough to do without keeping tabs on your every move, don't think you even sneeze without someone noticing how many tissues you use. As an employee, it was easier to blend into a crowd. As a manager, you're it. You're at the front of the classroom, and everyone is watching you. Mostly they're looking for guidance; after all, this is your role. But they also want to see how you respond to challenges from both above and below you in the corporate hierarchy.

Similarly, as a frontline or midlevel manager, you must keep a safe distance from upper management. Not that you've been invited to join the penthouse club, but as a manager now you have accountability to the powers that be for the actions of others. And you are the one who needs to be able to tell upper management which policies and procedures are working and which ones are counterproductive or even dismal failures.

Maintaining a balanced distance from either layer gives you the ability to support company policies and procedures in front of your employees. Even if you disagree with them, you don't share this with your employees. Instead, you take your disagreements privately to your superiors and express your concerns. This preserves trust and respect on both sides. You can't belong to either side if you are to function effectively as a manager. Perhaps that's why it's called "middle" management!

Chapter 2
Finding Your Place

Though your job as manager may be new to you, having a manager is not new to the people who report to you. You're stepping in to replace someone else. Employees may be relieved and happy to see you in your position, or they may be disgruntled and unhappy that the previous manager is gone. Did you come up through the ranks, or are you new to the company? The circumstances of how you got to be manager greatly influence how successful you will be in your new role.

Managing Former Coworkers

It's exciting to receive a promotion to manager. You're proud of yourself and your accomplishments, and rightly so—you've worked hard to earn your rung on the corporate ladder. Naturally, you can't wait to share your excitement with your coworker friends. They're likely proud of you, too. After all, your promotion is real-life proof that they, too, have a shot at moving up the ladder. You represent possibilities and potential. But they are not your coworkers any more. And whether they remain your friends depends on numerous variables including whether you've moved up and out or just up and your former coworkers now report to you. (See Chapter 19 for more about workplace friendships.)

When an organization's promotion policies are clear and everyone follows those policies consistently, people generally perceive promotions as fair. Those who competed with you for the promotion may be disappointed because they didn't get it, but they will likely be supportive of you in your new role.

It's Monday morning, your first day as manager. You've worked for several years with all the people milling about in the coffee room. But now they return your cheery greeting with cautious reserve. They're not your coworkers anymore. You've moved up, and the ranks have closed behind you. Your former coworkers now report to you and they can't wait to put you to the test. Not in a malicious way, of course—at least not most of them. But they now look to you for answers and action on everything from settling into the day's work routine to customer crises and scheduling snafus. From daily duties to performance ratings and job security, you hold their futures in your hands. They know it more than you do!

FACT

The U.S. military has long prohibited fraternization across rank, such as between officers and enlisted personnel. Though interaction and even closeness among unit members are essential for top performance, the military perspective is that familiarity undermines authority and the performance of duties. The military expects—and demands—that all personnel respect rank, the military management structure.

Use What You Know

Getting promoted within your work group is sometimes the greatest challenge you will face as a manager. Your key advantage is that you already know these people. You know what they like and don't like about the workplace and about the management styles that direct and regulate the work they do. You know what *you* like and don't like. You may even know what changes the employees in your department desire or expect from a manager. You can use this knowledge to start off on the right foot in your new role. The four Rs can help you move from employee to manager within your work group:

- **Resist the temptation to make immediate and dramatic changes.** Unless this is your mandate from upper management, staying the course until you get a feel for what it's like to walk the other side of the line broadens and clarifies your viewpoint.
- **Review existing procedures and practices.** Meet with employees one-on-one or in small groups to ask them what they think works, doesn't work, and why. Ask what changes they would like to see, and keep the focus on the work. Take notes.
- **Revise one step at a time.** Sometimes one small change makes a very big difference. Use a planned approach that includes some sort of measurement system. Incorporate suggestions from employees to the extent possible, even if only parts and pieces of what they've told you they want.

- **Recognize the contributions of your employees.** Always share and spread the credit. All work tasks require some level of collaboration, cooperation, and synergy—teamwork. Upper-level management knows a good team happens only when there is a good team leader.

Handling the Bumps

The transition from peer to superior is seldom smooth. Your former colleagues, now your subordinates, may feel resentment toward you when you give job assignments and evaluate job performance. They may react in one or more of these ways:

- Passive-aggressive behavior, in which they seem to be going along with what you say but in reality are undermining your efforts. Passive-aggressive behavior may take the form of doing only and exactly what you tell them to do, not telling you when problems arise or when they know a particular approach won't work
- Frank anger, in which unhappy former coworkers may be confrontational or give you the "cold shoulder" or silent treatment
- Sabotage, in which one or more employees may intentionally interfere with work flow such as by "losing" files or phone messages
- Insubordination and refusal to do work

These behaviors may be subtle or outright, and there is no single best way to handle them. The most effective approach is to talk with each offender individually. You can work out most grievances by giving people the opportunity to say what's on their minds. It is important to do this in private; nothing fuels disgruntlement like an audience. Hear the person out before you begin speaking. Remember, most of what you hear comes from an emotional base. Say what is necessary to keep the meeting focused on work, but let the person have his or her say.

When it's your turn to talk, acknowledge the person's feelings and then move the conversation to work and a collaborative tone. Do not apologize for your promotion; you have no reason to feel bad about it. "I know you had hoped to receive this promotion, Frank. You've been here a long time and you have a lot of good ideas. I have some ideas, too, and over the next few months I look forward to meeting with you and the others to discuss our department's procedures and direction."

When the behavior is a serious offense—violates company policy, jeopardizes customer relationships, or puts people at risk—you have no choice but to invoke your company's disciplinary policies. Because you are a new manager, you will want to involve at least your boss and probably a representative from your human resources department. Your company may stipulate other processes, depending on the contracts and working relationships (such as unions) that may exist.

ALERT!

Do not slack on disciplinary matters! When an employee puts you to the test by violating company policy, ethical standards, or even laws, you *must* take prompt and appropriate action. Failing to do so at the very least diminishes your authority within your work group and at worst may make you complicit in the violation.

Replacing a "Bad" Manager

What is a "bad" manager? Often, this is a judgment that exists in the eye of the beholder. After all, no one is perfect. But what employees perceive as good or bad in a manager is not necessarily the same as how executive management sees the situation. There are also different levels of "bad" managing. For example, some managers feel such a need for their employees to like them that they gossip with them, even badmouthing the company or its leaders. While this may seem harmless on the surface, these actions end up costing managers from both sides. Employees soon begin to wonder what their managers say about *them,* and executives no longer trust gossiping managers to uphold the company's interests.

Now, gossiping is bad, but there are worse things. Consider the scenario in the following section; although the names have been altered to protect those who wish to remain unidentified, the circumstances are real.

A Truly Terrible Predecessor

Sometimes the former manager truly was bad, no matter whose standards form the measurement. Managers can be dictatorial, disorganized, selfish, unfair, lazy, and abusive. Neither employees nor executives appreciate these characteristics (although nearly everyone has had a boss somewhere along the line who has personified them). When you are replacing a manager who was bad by all accounts and standards, you have both a responsibility and an opportunity.

Jonathan joined Wonder Corporation with rave reviews from the upper-level executives who had hired him. Within weeks, however, his employees were singing a very different song. Jonathan seemed to call in sick every time he had accumulated enough leave time to cover a day out of the office. At least once a week he called to say he would be working from home, although no one answered the phone when employees called with questions. When he was in the office, Jonathan was disorganized, volatile, and unpredictable. He flew off the handle for no apparent reason, cancelled or missed appointments, redefined assigned projects and tasks without consulting those doing the work, and often refused to make decisions about even the most mundane matters (like ordering toner for the copy machine).

Jonathan played favorites, promoting one person and squelching others. It was never safe to be in Jonathan's good graces because his fancy turned faster than a child's whimsy. Without warning, yesterday's favorite became today's scapegoat. Most of the people Jonathan promoted he soon fired. This was supposed to keep the person from showing him up, but it didn't work because everyone in the office was on to Jonathan's game. Fortunately, upper management was on to it as well, and Jonathan was fired. (Upon hearing the news, the employees had a party.)

The new manager, Joanne, started her first day on the job by meeting with everyone. She asked the group to talk about what worked and what didn't, from a process perspective. She explicitly said she did not want to hear names and personal stories. This freed the employees to focus on workflow, assignments, goals, priorities, and other issues related to productivity rather than personality. Over the next two days, Joanne went around to talk privately with each employee, allowing people to express their personal feelings. On Friday of her first week, Joanne called another department meeting. She shared her improvement plan with the group, talking about what seemed to work well and what didn't. She gave everyone a few days to think about and respond to the plan, and then created a revised improvement plan that incorporated many employee suggestions.

Joanne continued talking with employees, both individually and in group meetings. Employees learned they could trust her, and grew to like as well as respect her. Within six months, the department was so far ahead of its goals that it was necessary to revise the plan again.

Cleaning Up Someone Else's Mess

Cleaning up after a bad manager is among the most difficult challenges you can face in your new role. Unless you handle the situation just right, you, too, will look incompetent. All managers, good and bad, have loyal followers. Always assume this to be true. It isn't necessary to treat these employees any differently (and in fact is probably better for you not to), but it is vital for you to know who they are, because your first mission is to get everybody on board, and the loyalists will be the most resistant. (Get out your pom-poms!) Here are the basic steps to follow:

- Express clear and concise goals and objectives. Explain why these are important to each employee, to the department, and to the company.
- Ask each employee for comments and thoughts. Respond to negative expressions without judgment or attempting to refute them. "Yes, that's an interesting point. We'll come back to that."
- Respond directly but nonconfrontationally to efforts to undermine your authority and the process. If an employee persists, quietly and calmly request that he or she meet with you in your office after the meeting to discuss those concerns.
- Continue to gather input and information from every employee. Meet with individuals and small work groups as well as the entire department.

- Listen to what people are saying, and also to what they're not saying. Question, nonconfrontationally, what doesn't make sense to you or seems out of context.
- Integrate employee suggestions into improvement plans. If you can't use a suggestion directly, use it indirectly and credit the employee or employees with providing the impetus for the necessary change.
- Be consistent. If you change direction, have a good reason and present it to your employees.

It's easy to turn the last manager into a bad guy, regardless of whether that was actually the case. You might be tempted to think that by making someone else look bad, you can at least look better—if not downright good. Resist! Although extremes in perception are common during times of transition, eventually the fog clears and balance returns to judgment. When this happens, you're in a much stronger position if your attributes stand on their own merits. On the flip side, turning the last manager into a bad guy can backfire by instead turning him or her into a martyr. It's also human nature to put a halo on the last manager's head. People forget how bad things really were, and they begin to reminisce about the good old times. Before you know it, you become the bad guy.

Replacing a "Good" Manager

What happens when the manager before you was almost superhuman? Those are big shoes to fill. This can be just as significant a challenge as replacing a bad manager. As always, good communication is essential. Here are some key points to keep in mind:

- Listen to employees so you know what concerns them, and talk with them so they know what concerns you.
- Confront the ghosts head-on. Ask what employees liked about the previous manager's approach, and what they would change if they were in your shoes.
- Focus on processes, procedures, and policies. Whether or not employees like you, this is the foundation of the workplace.

- Refrain from presenting your views to change the world at the first meeting. Save your perspective for subsequent meetings, when you can temper your comments with understanding that you acquire by listening to employees' concerns and views.
- Do not comment about the previous manager's ways of doing things. Remain neutral and supportive of the company's goals. Whatever role you're playing, you are above all the face of the company.

Just as with bad, good is in the eye of the beholder. Change doesn't inherently mean the end of good; it can mean a different kind of good. Any good manager can (and should) have an open-door policy in which employees feel comfortable seeking him or her out, an open exchange of ideas, and procedures that support the work group's productivity and happiness.

Rebuilding a Work Group

Sometimes a manager steps into an existing work group or department that remains intact aside from its change of leadership. The employees are seasoned and knowledgeable, and passing the baton is a smooth transition. When the previous manager has been fired, however, there are very likely productivity issues. Other employees might have been fired or transferred as well, leaving some positions vacant. If you are a manager in this type of situation, your mission is to rebuild.

It's important to make sure each person understands his or her role and responsibilities, as well as those of the others in the work group or department. And it's essential to clearly articulate and support new goals and procedures. Ambiguity breeds *mis*trust, and that's not what you need to succeed as a manager.

The need to rebuild can arise from several circumstances. Perhaps there is a new market, making it necessary for a company to revamp its product and service lines to meet changing customer demands. In such a setting, your job as manager is to identify the key strengths and abilities existing employees offer and look for ways to fit them into the new structure. You will need to motivate employees to feel that they are valued contributors in the new order.

Maybe your company has reorganized because of new ownership or to consolidate operations (save money). The employees who remain are likely to be suspicious and reluctant to support (or even appear to support) new corporate mandates. It is fertile ground for resentment, distrust, anger, and fear to thrive. But you're not going to let these negatives grow because you see the situation as a great opportunity. Pull out your parent, coach, and cheerleader hats—you need to mobilize these people. But first, allow for some mourning. While the public view tends to spotlight the people who lose their jobs in corporate shakeups, these have been traumatic events for the employees who remain. It can be more distressing to be among the survivors than to get a pink slip.

People need time to assimilate and adjust. A good manager acknowledges feelings, and then helps employees focus on the future and encourages a positive outlook. After all is said and done, however, your key role is still to craft a cohesive and productive work group. This entails communicating both with the group as a whole and with individual employees to do the following:

- Clarify goals
- Identify roles and responsibilities
- Establish procedures for how people work together
- Get acceptance and support from employees

The sooner you define a clear path, the sooner employees can get on with their work lives. People recover more quickly when there is a plan in place that helps them move forward, toward new responsibilities and broadened abilities. You, their manager, are the one who can—and must—lead them.

Riding the Waves of Change

The turbulent 1980s gave rise to the use of a phrase from Shakespeare's *The Tempest* to describe the magnitude of the upheaval in the business world: "sea change." The new environment was dramatically different from the old one, as were the new ways. Such upheavals are like volcanic eruptions: They blow existing structures to oblivion and construct new ones, often simultaneously. One minute there's a mountain and the next there's a smoking crater. But down slopes make for new hills and valleys and rivers and lakes, a ready-made environment to replace the old one. In the business world, such eruptions take the form of mergers and acquisitions. One day there's a giant conglomerate that dominates the corporate landscape, and the next there's a smattering of small companies scattered all around.

Things change. It's as much a reality of your career as it is of nature. Companies change, people change, needs change. The typical American worker may have as many as seven careers during his or her working life, and three or four times that many jobs—a significant change in the course of a generation. In commerce, as in nature, change results in new and often unexpected growth. Those who thrive are those who can adapt to new needs and demands and respond to challenging or difficult situations with positive attitudes and actions.

Nowhere is this more true—or more significant—than for managers. Not only must you stay current with changes in your field of expertise, you also must remain up-to-date on laws and regulations that affect the workplace, changes in business practices, and advances in technology. Your company may change ownership. Core employees may leave. You cannot influence these events, so you must keep yourself prepared to accommodate them. Chapter 21 provides further information to help you make sure that when you are the manager being replaced (which is inevitable) it's either by your choice or by a means that lets you land on your feet.

Chapter 3

A Manager's Many Roles

Expectations are high for managers today. As a manager, your roles are nearly endless. You might be friend, confidante, advocate, drill sergeant, counselor, sage, and even enforcer. But as a manager, you are always a leader in the end. Leadership means many things to different people. But to you, there is only one meaning: knowing which hat to wear and when. This chapter covers a number of identities you may have to take on as a manager.

Coach: Bringing Out the Best in Others

Odds are, you remember a coach from somewhere in your past. Perhaps it was a track coach who pushed you to run faster or jump farther than you thought was possible, or a swim coach who pushed you to the edge of your endurance. Good memories or bad, these are powerful reminders of the influence a single person can have in the lives of many others.

The other roles you adopt as a manager tend to focus on each individual's needs and capabilities. The role of coach, however, also requires you to bring people of diverse skill levels and backgrounds together to work as a unified team, in such a way that the synergy among them generates a product or result that surpasses each individual's abilities. Sounds like a tall order? It is! But it's really nothing more than ongoing reinforcement of what employees are doing and learning.

An effective coach does a lot of things:

- Provides timely and specific feedback. "Good job!" feels good but says little; "You really nailed the point in your proposal!" lets an employee know what was good.
- Establishes standards and goals that are high enough to make employees stretch, but not so high that they're impossible to reach
- Tells the truth with kindness and caring—but still tells the truth
- Shares ideas and offers suggestions but resists telling employees how to do things
- Teaches people how to cook rather than take them out to dinner, metaphorically speaking

Good coaches inspire loyalty and respect, characteristics that are increasingly rare in the workplace. How do you become a good coach? The most effective way is to watch a good coach in action. If you feel that your workplace is deplorably lacking in such role models, attend some high school or college athletic events. You'll see good coaches, bad coaches, and mediocre coaches, and you'll see how their teams respond to their methods.

Mentor: Trusted Guide

Although we view mentoring as a modern concept, the original Mentor debuted in Homer's classic of Greek mythology, *The Odyssey*. When Odysseus goes off to war, he appoints his close friend Mentor to look after his family and household, including his son Telemachus and wife Penelope. When Odysseus is imprisoned, the goddess Athena takes over Mentor's body to guide Telemachus in safeguarding his mother from the actions of greedy suitors chasing his father's riches. When Odysseus finally returns home after twenty years, Mentor helps him devise the "test" by which he proves to Penelope that he is, indeed, her long-missing husband. Mentor also makes appearances in other Greek myths, often as the disguise for a helpful god or goddess.

FACT

It hasn't taken long for the business world to adapt the concepts of coaching for use in the employment environment. Thousands of consultants offer business coaching services that target motivation of work groups and individuals to improve efficiency and increase productivity. Business coaches charge anywhere from several hundred to several thousand dollars a day for their services. How do you know if they're worth it? Ask around, and check references.

Today's mentors are ordinary people who have achieved extraordinary success helping others reach their goals. Most mentoring is unofficial, though some corporations have structured mentoring programs to groom potential upper-level managers and executives. More typically, a person with expertise takes interest in a subordinate's career and takes that subordinate under his or her wing. A mentor helps an employee do things including these:

- Set long-term goals and short-term objectives
- Explore new directions to achieve goals
- Identify personal strengths and weaknesses
- Find ways to develop and grow

One of the most effective methods of mentoring is shadowing. You put your employee in situations where he or she can observe your actions without participating in them. Your employee might sit in on a conference call or a sales meeting, for example, or read and discuss a report you've written, or accompany you to an event where you are giving a presentation. These lessons are far more effective than any explanations you can offer. Not only do they let your employee see the master in action, but they also show that the master is still human. If you're exceptionally good at what you do, it's because you learn from your mistakes as well as your successes. The better you are, the smaller the increments of measurement. These are subtleties that are difficult to convey in any other way.

Consider this valuable bit of advice offered by General George S. Patton of the U.S. Army: "Never tell people how to do things. Tell them what to do and they will surprise you with their ingenuity."

Mentoring extends beyond teaching in that it relies on establishing a relatively long-term relationship that revolves around sharing and mutual respect. A mentor shares knowledge as well as wisdom—a fine line, perhaps, but a crucial distinction. While knowledge can be learned, wisdom must be acquired. Knowledge is having the right words; wisdom is knowing when and how to say them—and when to keep them to yourself.

Teacher: Imparting New Skills

A teacher is someone with expert skills and knowledge who has the ability to share this expertise with others. A good teacher—one whose students learn—improves both the individual and the company. But it isn't always easy to find a balance between "Let me show you" and "Get out of the way, I'll do it myself!"

A small software company hired Miguel to do its PR. The company chose Miguel because he was good at explaining technical concepts to nontechnical people. But Miguel had never used his skills to write marketing materials, and his debut in his new job was less than spectacular. In fact, it was a bit of a dismal spectacle.

After bleeding all over Miguel's first few attempts with her red pen, Miguel's manager called him into her office. For the rest of the afternoon, she became his journalism teacher. She explained and demonstrated the basic principles of journalism. She showed him how to establish those principles—who, what, where, when, and why—in the first paragraph of virtually anything he might write. She showed him how to make up quotes that would pass muster with corporate executives, how to put words in their mouths that they would wish they had actually said (and would say, after reading the stories generated by the press release).

Now, Miguel's manager could just as easily have reamed him out. After all, Miguel had been hired to write press releases and he wasn't doing a very good job of it. Miguel's manager could have counseled him for his unacceptable job performance and placed a memo in his personnel file.

But she didn't. She put on her teacher hat and turned her office into a classroom. She not only showed Miguel just what she wanted him to do, she also taught him the skills he needed to apply the same lesson to other situations. For a few weeks after, Miguel's manager met with him to strategize the approach for each new press release. Miguel went to his desk to do the writing, then sat down with his manager to review the results. Within a few months, Miguel was getting compliments from senior executives. Not only did Miguel's skill level improve tremendously, but his self-confidence grew as well. He even enrolled in an evening continuing education class at a local community college to further hone his writing skills.

Not all situations end in such success, of course. Some people resist the suggestion that they need to clean up rusty skills or learn new ones. Some managers lose patience when improvements fail to be immediate and dramatic. Some managers know what they want from their employees but don't know how to express their needs in ways their employees understand. If the teaching hat doesn't fit you very well, consider alternatives (as your budget allows):

- Hire consultants to conduct workshops or seminars for your work group or department.
- Send employees to training courses (all expenses paid, of course).
- Reimburse or otherwise compensate employees for taking classes that directly improve their job skills.

Parent: Setting Limits

Many people view the workplace as an alternate home and the people there as surrogate family members. After all, you spend more waking hours at work than at home or anywhere else. Coworkers are pseudo-siblings or pseudo-spouses. And managers become—you guessed it—pseudo-parents.

ESSENTIAL

Just as parents need to set limits and structure at home, managers need to establish boundaries and organization for their employees at work. As a manager, it is your job to tell employees what they can and cannot do.

Just as you might have to tell your ten-year-old son to stop spitting out the car window, you might need to tell a thirty-two-year-old administrative assistant that she can't swear on the telephone or a fifty-year-old sales representative that he can't shave during the morning staff meeting. It seems petty and counterproductive—and sometimes it is. But people push limits just to be sure those limits are still in place. Everyone needs to feel there's a certain level of stability in their lives, and limits allow them to do so.

In the role of parent, you are often training your employees in basic behaviors. This differs from teaching them skills. You might find yourself repeatedly reminding employees to ask clients if there is anything else they can do for them before rushing to the next call, just as at home you might find yourself repeatedly reminding your kids to unball their socks before putting them in the laundry basket. And your parent role might frequently compel you to reinforce core values and the behaviors that support them, such as prioritizing client requests even when that requires interrupting other work.

Sometimes being parental also means providing a listening ear. It might mean listening to complaints, even some whining, and being able to listen between the lines to understand the real issues. And sometimes wearing your parent hat means being firm and saying, "Yes, I understand this is a lot to do."

FACT

A study reported in the February 2000 issue of *Entrepreneur* magazine found that having managers they could respect ranked at the top of the list of what employees want in their jobs. The survey concluded that the relationship employees have with their managers is a key factor in whether employees stay or leave.

When you are functioning effectively in your manager-as-parent role, your employees can be expected to do the following:

- Know and follow established guidelines and procedures
- Understand that there are clear and consistent consequences for stepping outside the boundaries
- Accept accountability for meeting project timelines rather than pointing the finger of blame at others if things go wrong
- Be comfortable in coming to you with problems or concerns
- Respect you, but not fear you

Remember, though, that you are not, of course, really a parent to your employees, and the work group is not really a family. There are important differences, many of which are performance based. Your employees are adults, and they have adult rights and responsibilities. It does not serve them well, in the long run, for you to make decisions for them as you might for your children. They have been hired to perform specific tasks and accomplish particular goals. You might be wearing your parent hat too long if you find yourself doing any of these things:

- You look at the employees sitting in your office airing yet another dispute and realize that if they were younger and shorter, they'd be tattling.
- "Nobody told me I had to do that" is a familiar chorus in staff meetings.
- Employees ask permission to go to the restroom or take a break.
- No assignment gets completed without repeated visits to your office to be sure it's being done right.
- You make excuses to your superiors when your employees fail to complete projects either on time or correctly.

Mediator: Finding Balance

Acting as a mediator is familiar territory for many managers who feel that all they do help people find common ground. You might help employees resolve disagreements among themselves, investigate disputes between clients and employees, or negotiate differences between the priorities of upper management and the needs of employees.

QUESTION?

What is mediation?
To mediate is to be in the middle or intervene to settle a dispute between two parties. Mediation is the process of finding common ground, of seeking win-win solutions to differences and disagreements.

Mediation is most effective (and successful) when it is a process of collaboration rather than compromise. This is more than just word play. Collaboration comes from the Latin *collaborare*, meaning "to labor together." Compromise, despite its core word "promise," implies giving up something of value, or conceding a cherished point, to reach agreement. These implications are important because they set the tone for the discussion. Few people are happy when compromise means they get less than they hoped for or expected, yet most are pleasantly surprised to get more.

Mediation is most effective when you aim to do the following:

- Focus on common goals and look for common ground to help you reach those goals
- Treat all parties, and their viewpoints, with respect
- Propose win-win solutions
- Remain interested but impartial
- Establish a process for assessing the success of the agreed-upon solutions

Cheerleader: Rallying the Troops

People worry about their jobs and their abilities to complete new tasks and assignments. They need someone (you) to rally them back to believing in themselves. It's a major part of your job to motivate and excite your employees. Leading the cheering section demonstrates that you believe in your team and its ability to succeed. But you have to have those pom-poms always at the ready. It's not acceptable to sit in your office all week, and then pop out when a productivity report tells you your department is in jeopardy of missing its deadlines. Cheering on the troops is only effective when the troops know that you truly care—not just about their projects and assignments and meeting your department's goals, but also about them as people and individuals. And they won't know you truly care unless you're involved in what's going on every day.

When companies begin involving employees in identifying problems and designing solutions, there is a dramatic leap in buy-in. Once employees feel they are owners in the process of improvement, they become enthusiastic supporters of improvement efforts.

Do you watch sporting events? Do you watch the cheerleaders? (It's okay, you can admit it.) They're always interacting with the crowd, no matter what's happening on the field or the court. They're chanting and dancing and smiling, working to stay engaged with the spectators. Their mission is to create a roar of support beyond what they themselves can generate, support that motivates the players to give the proverbial 110 percent. But the players know that the cheerleaders are always there. And they know that even when the crowd boos, the cheerleaders are still there, cheering.

This is your role, too. Even when your superiors—or your clients or customers—are unhappy with your team's work and productivity, you need to stay right there on the sidelines, cheering your team on. If you've been there all along, they will respond.

Chapter 4

What Companies Want

Managers make things happen, and that is precisely what companies expect from them. Upper-level executives want managers to see the big picture—the corporate vision, if you will—and to structure the processes, within their fields of expertise, to bring the picture to life for the prosperity of the company. Your bosses want you to motivate the employees who report to you to meet the company's needs as well as the needs of employees. Sometimes, it seems, this means a smoke-and-mirrors approach—doing much more with far less. But that's what companies want, too!

What Companies Care About

The cynics say that companies care only about profits. And of course, companies must care about whether they are earning or losing money. Unless companies can stay on the plus side of the balance sheet, nothing else will matter. But good companies—those with staying power—are the ones whose corporate visions reach beyond earnings statements. Good companies try to involve employees at all levels of the corporate chain in decision-making. They emphasize and practice open, two-way communication. And they provide opportunities for learning and advancement. They understand that employee productivity relies on numerous factors, key among them being the following:

- Personal satisfaction
- Opportunities for self-expression
- A feeling of having some control over personal destiny
- Having a voice in what happens within the company

Contrary to popular perception, most companies *want* employees to succeed. Corporate leaders are, after all, employees, too. They like their jobs, so why shouldn't you like yours? Job satisfaction ranks high on the list of factors that go into a desirable lifestyle, even higher than salary.

Each day is an adventure for Carolyn. When she steps through the doors of the software company where she works as a team manager in the fantasy game division, she never knows what she will encounter. Employees often dress up as the characters they are creating. There are toys everywhere, from collectible movie figures to toy swords and lasers. Sometimes all the light bulbs are red or green or yellow; sometimes black lights give off an eerie glow. It isn't unusual for Carolyn to walk into the middle of a "battle" or other scene enactment. Often, a hail of soft foam arrows greets her arrival, flying at her from behind doors and under desks. Boisterous laughter follows.

This work group has fun. So much fun, in fact, that some employees work around the clock when creativity is hot. And their fun pays off. The computer and video games they develop rank at the top of the market. Of course, this environment is a bit extreme for other kinds of work groups. But it supports the needs of its members, and that's what matters most.

Enjoying what they do at work ranks near the top of the list of job satisfiers for most people. Employees—including managers—should want to come to work each day. Many companies have implemented casual dress policies (such as "casual Fridays") and minimized formality, especially if there is no direct interaction with customers. Numerous studies conclude that employees who are relaxed and comfortable are better able to concentrate on job tasks.

A Productive Work Environment

The work environment needs to support the work being done within it. Do employees spend a lot of time on the telephone, or do they need quiet to help them concentrate? Then they might need office space with walls that go to the ceiling and doors that close. Do projects require employees to discuss possibilities and brainstorm ideas? Then a more open floor plan is probably better. Of course, these elements are not always within your ability to control. But if you do reshape what you can control to meet employee needs and requests, we're willing to bet that your work group's productivity and efficiency will improve.

FACT

A study conducted by the University of Missouri-Columbia revealed that when it comes to what determines happiness on the job, Americans like to feel independent, good at what they do, and close to others. Money becomes an important factor only in times of uncertainty.

The Challenge of Balance

The challenge for managers is to balance the needs of the organization, the demands of customers and clients (internal and external), and the desires of employees. To be consistent and effective in supporting a company's principles, managers must also be committed to them. This doesn't mean you live or die by the rules, but you must feel enough commitment that you can and do use them as the guiding force in your interactions with employees. If you deeply resent certain corporate policies or goals, this commitment will be difficult for you. Ask yourself these questions:

- What is it, precisely, that I don't like?
- Why do I feel so strongly about it?
- Do other managers share my feelings?
- What have I done to attempt to change the policy or goal?
- Could I live with this policy or goal if I understood the reason it was in place?

Often, simply exploring the reasons for how you feel brings your concerns to the surface where you can examine them to decide if they truly have merit. Sometimes your feelings about certain policies or goals have little to do with the principle, but instead relates back to some personal baggage you're still carrying around. If you think about it, companies don't have anything to gain by implementing policies and procedures that are unreasonable. Sometimes the original purpose for the guideline gets lost in the process of moving it through the process of approval. Once someone points this out, it's possible to correct the flaws.

ALERT!

As a manager, you need to let your superiors know when there are problems. Who knows better how to make improvements than the people who do the work—the employees who report to you? Listening to them is more than just good business. Employees who feel there is no audience for their concerns work in frustration and may leave in anger.

Successful companies create working environments in which employees and managers feel welcome to share their views and concerns. This kind of dialogue helps companies avert potential problems. After all, the company doesn't exist solely for the purpose of creating rules. Rules are in place to support the company's mission and goals, whatever those are. Like nearly all other dimensions of doing business, rules must be dynamic to remain effective. This means that a company must continually review and reassess its policies to be sure the policies are keeping up with changes in the business environment.

Responsibility and Accountability

As an employee, you were responsible for completing job tasks and work projects. You may have had limited authority to delegate certain responsibilities to others, but for the most part the line of authority ran in the other direction. Your manager delegated to you, and you carried out the assignment, though your manager bore the brunt of accountability for how well you did your work. When you succeeded, your manager got the bulk of the credit. When you failed, your manager took the fall.

You're a manager yourself now. Though you undoubtedly have a heavy load of responsibility, you have the authority to assign tasks and actions to the employees who report to you. You also accept accountability for their performance. We hope that when things go well you share the glory (along with any tangible rewards) with those who did the work. We also hope that when things turn out not so well, you have the fortitude to suck it up and take the hit. This is why you get paid the big bucks. Afterward, of course, there'll be time enough for constructive review of what went wrong. Accountability summarizes the concept of "The buck stops here."

The common perception is that accountability is related to negative consequences, the fallout from circumstances that go awry. But accountability also encompasses the positive consequences. When a project comes through and accomplishes its objectives, as its manager you are the first and most prominent to receive accolades. When things do go wrong, it's more effective and productive to look at the circumstance as an opportunity for learning—for employees and for you. How you handle responsibility and accountability is often the single most important aspect of your position as manager and the key to your future success in management.

Lewis toiled long and hard as a computer programmer before his superiors finally took notice and promoted him to manager. The promotion was long overdue, Lewis felt, and he threw himself into his vision of a manager with great zeal. He felt important, he acted important, and most of the time, he rushed around looking important. Now that he had a real office, he closed the door whenever he was in it.

Not sure whether they should knock or just walk in, employees took to waiting for Lewis to emerge—which he did mostly when he needed something or to grandstand about his latest accomplishment (which always happened solely because of his extraordinary abilities, not because of any contributions from the department, to hear him tell it). When Lewis communicated at all with employees, it was through e-mail or Post-It notes left on their computer screens.

Lewis's behavior turned out to be self-sabotage. With no human bond to him, people in the group short-circuited him. They failed to rally around projects. They fulfilled their responsibilities, but they did only what they had to do and nothing more. They made it clear to upper management and to Lewis's counterparts that they really had minimal interaction with Lewis. Ultimately upper management restructured department lines, which eliminated Lewis's department and job. While Lewis's employees all received transfers to other jobs within the company, Lewis got a severance package.

When it becomes necessary to resolve a problem with an employee who reports to you, always offer the opportunity for a fresh start. The person should not feel compelled to continue a certain pattern of behavior with you. No matter the trail of angry words that follow the person into your office, let it stay at the threshold. This lessens the pull of past behavior (however immediate that past is) and allows you to break off on a new path that hopefully leads to resolution.

Keeping Good People

Once, perhaps back when you first entered the workforce, it was enough to land a job. It wasn't so long ago that working people were happy to simply have paychecks, and employers were glad to have productive employees. Then it becomes apparent that there's a difference between a job and a career. People no longer stay in the same job or work for the same company for all of their working lives. On average, people have three to five different careers and work for a dozen or more companies from the time they enter the workforce until the time they leave it. More of either is not uncommon.

Encourage employees to come up with two or three personal goals. An employee might set a goal to complete a specialty training program, undergraduate degree, or graduate degree. This accomplishment would clearly benefit the employee, but it has benefits for the company as well by making the employee more promotable or, at the very least, more knowledgeable.

Your company entrusts you with its most valuable resource—employees. It expects you to help your employees develop their skills and careers. Sometimes you want to do this anyway because they are good people who have really worked hard and you want to see them grow. You don't want to lose them, and you know they might quit without appropriate support. Sometimes you need employees to grow so that they can take on more responsibilities—and free you up for the same reason. If employees don't feel like they are growing, they become stagnant. Over time, the department will grow stagnant and so will the organization. It often doesn't require that much for you to provide the opportunities your employees want and need. You might try the following:

- Create a departmental training committee so employees can assess training needs and present ideas for meeting them

- Ask employees with particular proficiency in certain areas to conduct short workshops for other employees
- Sponsor brown-bag lunch training sessions in which experts from other parts of the company or outside sources conduct short presentations during lunch breaks
- Establish a mentoring program in which employees pair up to learn from each other

Use regular feedback to help employees improve their skills and performance. (See Chapter 13 for more on this.) Suggest different approaches to achieve better outcomes. Make sure that feedback is relevant to the employee and how he or she approaches job tasks and work responsibilities, not a comparison or criticism because the employee's work style differs from yours.

It might be your preference to work on an assignment without having your superiors checking in with you all the time and telling you what a good job you're doing. And that's fine—it works for you. From there, it's easy to assume all people are the same way or should be the same way, particularly if you have some employees who are like you in terms of work style. Being among people who share your characteristics reinforces your attitudes and behaviors.

FACT

With the shift in today's business environment from a domineering management approach to one that is more collaborative, managers often benefit from training in conflict resolution and mediation techniques.

Your perspective and work style might set you up to think that employees who need a lot of feedback are just brown-nosing to stay in good with the boss. Although of course office politics come into play with all people (even you) at times, there's a strong likelihood that these employees are just people who need the sense of structure that constant feedback provides. For such people, the manager is the one who defines the work group and its functions and thus is the most logical choice to go to for feedback. After all, you set the standards, and ultimately it's you who must be satisfied with the results.

This is reality—for you and for your employees. Make sure they each have the same opportunities to showcase their successes and achievements for you. Just be sure you know whether that apple-polishing employee is advancing the goals of the team and the company or feeding the beast. Take the time to ferret out the true objective before you come to a conclusion. When an employee attempts to communicate with you at the expense of the team leader or coworkers, send the employee back to the group to communicate appropriately. Sometimes the employees doing the most communicating have the most time to do so because the real performers are too busy doing the work.

Turning Around Counterproductive Behavior

Employees represent a significant investment on the part of companies. Though the media makes it sound like employees who mess up or hit a trouble spot are immediately fired, most companies are more interested in trying to resolve the situation to protect their investment. Companies and their managers (like you) often genuinely care about the happiness and well being of employees.

Consistent, regular feedback is the most effective means to keep most employees on the right track when it comes to job performance and compliance with company rules and policies. Consider this an incremental process; no one makes major changes overnight. If you see a pattern of behavior emerging, focus on one facet of it at a time. If the issue is time management, you might cover establishing timelines this week and prioritizing next week. This is a work in progress, and results won't necessarily be consistent. But be patient. This is the most important kind of shaping, and it's well worth the effort and time you put into it.

Sometimes inappropriate behavior at work reflects problems outside the workplace, such as at home. A spouse or child may be ill or a marriage breaking up. There may be financial difficulties or substance abuse. Sometimes inappropriate behavior is a warning sign of deeper personal issues, such as drug use or psychological problems. Many companies offer employee assistance program (EAP) benefits or other services to get troubled employees the help they need. Employees who have a lot of personal problems or who aren't a good fit with their jobs or work groups often end up becoming self-destructive. Clearly this is not good for them, for other employees, or for the company. Signs that this is happening include these:

- Not getting work done on time or even at all
- A generally negative attitude
- Yelling and angry outbursts
- Engaging in passive-aggressive behavior (actions that appear legitimate or helpful but really are not)
- Trying to rally other employees to side with them
- Going from cubicle to office to cubicle, stirring up trouble
- Tuning out or being argumentative at staff meetings
- Showing up late, leaving early, or taking excessively long lunches
- Staying on the phone for a long time, often on personal calls or discussing personal matters with coworkers or customers
- Flagrantly violating or ignoring company policies

Inappropriate behavior may be nothing more than the actions of someone who doesn't really know how he or she is supposed to behave in the workplace. Sometimes the employee's work style is the primary factor in performance and production matters. And sometimes people simply have trouble finding their bearings, particularly in times of major change such as corporate restructuring. New employees as well as seasoned employees for whom these job responsibilities depart from previous experience might be struggling to find a good match between their personal work styles and their new job assignments.

Employees need to know that they really can come to you whenever they feel they need to, not just when you determine it's appropriate for them to do so.

What Works for Them Works for You

If it feels extremely generous of you to work so hard to support training and skill improvement activities for your employees, go ahead and take a minute or so to enjoy the feeling. Then take a few steps back and look at the bigger picture. Unless you're a working manager with job responsibilities similar to those of the employees you manage, it's probably not necessary for your skills to match those of your employees. Still, you need to know enough to know whether your employees need additional training and if so, in what. Subscribe to newsletters and magazines that are relevant for your industry or field. Ask employees what publications they would find useful. Web-based resources are abundant, too, and becoming increasingly sophisticated.

FACT

Many companies require managers to have at least a bachelor's degree. Though experience within the industry is also crucial, the market for managers has become so competitive that education level is often a screening criterion for job candidates.

Does your company have an education support program that provides tuition reimbursement and other benefits for employees who go back to school? Many colleges offer evening classes and distance learning programs by computer, targeting working adults who want to advance their formal education. Many companies have education requirements, such as a graduate degree, for managers. This is most likely the case if you work in an industry where the people who report to you have advanced degrees or levels of education. Even entry-level positions that are on the company's promotion track are likely to have minimum education requirements that may not have applied to you when you before you joined the management team. If your education is in a specialty field, you may desire further education in another field or in a broader area.

Progressive companies support ongoing education and training for employees at all levels. Larger companies may have their own programs to teach management skills or be willing to send new managers to outside programs. Even if your company has a human resources department that handles the legal end of employment, it doesn't hurt for you to know the basics. As a front-line manager, your accountability may be limited when it comes to such matters. As you progress upward in the management hierarchy, however, you must learn more of the details. In small companies, midlevel managers may conduct all human resources functions. Encourage yourself to update and expand your skills and expertise the way you encourage the employees who report to you. You can never know too much!

Chapter 5
What Employees Want

Though you may not believe it, what employees want from their managers is fairly simple. They want to work under clear and reasonable expectations, they want to receive honest and constructive feedback, and they want to be treated fairly. Just like their employees, of course, managers are only human. They can't do everything and be everywhere at once. At the same time, managers do need to be acutely aware of the way their actions affect others. When managers act inappropriately, unpredictably, or inconsistently, it has a negative impact on the entire organization.

What Employees Expect from Their Jobs

People work for myriad reasons, but most of these reasons figure into three core factors: They want to be entertained, feel appreciated, and earn money. The job description that covers these needs might read, "Our company offers challenging work, opportunities for career growth, and a comprehensive compensation and benefits package." The excited employee who applies for the position might think, "Finally—a job that will let me use my skills and knowledge in ways that make me happy, a company that will see how good I am and promote me, and a paycheck that will cover payments on a new car!"

F A C T

Employees often expect their jobs to provide a certain level of social interaction. Going to work is a chance to reconnect with friends and acquaintances. Human beings need this interaction. In most situations, this need is not necessarily incompatible with productivity and efficiency. People work better when they're happy, and interacting with other people is a way to be happy. The challenge for managers is to keep such interactions appropriate for the workplace.

On the surface, an employee's expectations are often brief and clear. He or she wants a reasonable paycheck, reasonable work assignments, reasonable hours, and a reasonable level of respect. The definition of "reasonable," however, is different for each employee and changes over the course of an employee's career. A young, single person at the start of his or her working life might be eager for opportunities to travel and willing to work long hours to complete complex projects. For a married person with a family, however, travel and overtime might be resented intrusions.

Though expectations vary among individuals, three basic needs are common to most people:

- To engage in work that is interesting and that provides a sense of accomplishment

- To feel that the job offers economic stability
- To grow toward personal potential

An employee's expectations begin with the job position posting or advertisement. Someone—hopefully a person who intimately knows the job's technical skill requirements and work environment—attempts to summarize the position's needs in 100 words or less. This can be a considerable challenge, even for the entry-level jobs employees might apply for to gain experience. Most job descriptions include a certain amount of "planned ambiguity" to accommodate the rapidly shifting needs of the business world.

Usually, this benefits both the company and the employee. Employers need to be able to change a job to fit new needs. Workers generally appreciate the opportunity to learn new skills and have new experiences. Managers and employees alike who establish rigid expectations based on the job description in place at the time of hiring are likely to resist changes that arise. This can lead to angry confrontations and dissatisfaction on both sides of the management line.

What Employees Expect from Their Managers

What do you think your employees expect from you as their manager? Put a checkmark in front of the statements you believe are true for you.

My employees expect me to . . .

- ❏ Know what they want, even if they don't say anything

- ❏ Understand that they have lives away from work that sometimes interfere with work

- ❏ Pick up the slack for them or intercede in some way when they aren't able to get their assigned job tasks completed on time

- ❏ Be available at any time of the day to answer questions and resolve problems

- ❏ Treat them fairly, which they define as considering any and all extenuating circumstances before passing judgment or taking action

❏ Help them acquire new skills, even if that means they will then become qualified for different jobs

❏ Advocate for them when they have needs that require upper management decisions

❏ Occasionally take them to lunch or bring in goodies as a show of appreciation for the good work they do

❏ Give them full credit for the department's successes and take full blame for the department's shortcomings

❏ Always remember that they are only human but to never reveal this about myself

Most managers will check off seven or eight of these expectations, chuckling over some and groaning over others. Some are not very reasonable or realistic, while others are essential. Some seem selfish—and they are. But all, at some time or another, are valid.

Here's another area of responsibility you may not have considered: While your employees will certainly expect you to advocate for them with regard to upper management decisions, they will also expect you to be attentive to problems that arise between employees. If one employee is causing trouble for the others, you must immerse yourself in the issue until an acceptable solution is reached. Consider the following scenario, for example:

Eve was a brilliant computer programmer. She had the ability to listen to a client's needs, and then produce exactly what the client needed. But Eve wasn't much of a team player. She preferred working alone; she wanted to go away to do her work and return with the finished product.

Eve's department was organized into teams around a structure that encouraged and supported collaboration. When her colleagues confronted her about taking on projects and not telling anyone what she was doing or letting anyone else become involved, Eve swung to the opposite extreme and started delegating everything. She was either on top of her game or at the bottom of the heap—there seemed to be no middle ground.

Responding to complaints from other employees, Eve's manager began documenting the problems. He sat down with her, identified the difficulties, and outlined a way to fix the problems. Eve agreed to the plan, and for a while everything went smoothly. Eve attended staff meetings, presented her projects to her work team, and even seemed eager to work in collaboration with her colleagues.

Unfortunately, the agreement soon broke down. Instead of discussing her ideas, Eve stormed out of meetings. Within weeks, Eve was again at one extreme or the other. Her manager had to make the critical decision of whether to keep her or fire her. The company would sorely suffer to lose her skills (especially if she were to take them to a competitor). But keeping Eve would likely mean losing other employees, and that wasn't a particularly enticing option either.

Finally, after consulting with the company's executives, Eve's manager offered Eve the opportunity to work from home. She received specific assignments and deadlines, and the manager and Eve's colleagues worked out a foolproof system for staying in close communication. Eve came in to the office periodically, usually to meet with clients, and it turned out to be the perfect solution. Eve was happy, the company was happy, the work group was happy, and the clients were happy.

There had never been any issues around the quality of Eve's work, just around her style of working. Innovative thinking and the willingness to try something different salvaged a highly productive and talented employee, giving the company a strong competitive edge in its market. At the same time, Eve's manager paid attention to the concerns of the other employees. It was a win for everyone.

Money Matters

The harsh reality in the business world is that companies have to make a profit. (Even not-for-profit organizations must still meet financial goals and keep their constituents happy.) Businesses must balance profitability, customer or client satisfaction, and quality products or services. While high-level money matters can create tensions in the office, remember one thing: Your employees care about profit, too. Though they try to choose jobs they enjoy, most people work because they need to earn an income.

FACT

Sometimes money talks and employees walk—to competitors who offer deals too good to refuse. But for the most part, money moves up and down on an employee's list of dissatisfiers (things he or she does not like about the job) rather than on the list of satisfiers (things he or she likes about the job).

It used to be that there was a set salary range for a position, and it established the boundaries for negotiation. It was a range that didn't vary much from company to company for positions at the same relative level of management. Most people started at the lower end of the scale, ostensibly so there would be incentive for them to improve (which really meant there would be money to give them raises for staying in the job). Those with exceptional abilities or unique skills might start at the middle of the range. Few started at the top; those who had the qualifications to do so were probably overqualified for the job in the first place, and would soon move on when it became clear that there was no room for advancement within the position. Money and ability were like twins, seldom separated. Today, salaries are often open territory.

Consistency Is the Key

In the workplace, it's all about consistency. If you're not consistent in your practices, employees won't trust you—or each other. One way to make sure everyone is on the same page is to distribute documents outlining the company's policies and guidelines. If your company doesn't have such documents already, don't just leap to your keyboard to begin writing your own policies. Talk with your superiors first. A written policy, even something you send out as an e-mail or a memo, represents your company. Its content can have legal ramifications. Many companies even have policies that outline the process for writing new or revising existing policies and procedures.

It's not very glamorous, but in the end, consistency scores big points with employees because it shapes as well as supports their expectations.

Larisse was a manager for a company that gave bonuses for completed projects. When the company first implemented the policy, the procedure was simple: Each employee had one project at a time, and each project had a timeline. Each time the employee met the timeline, he or she received a bonus.

The company grew and its market became more sophisticated. Projects became increasingly complex, and employees often handled several projects at the same time. To meet timelines, employees started working together, collaborating and cooperating to finish projects. A manager's dream come true, right? Only until bonuses were due, and then it turned into a nightmare. At first, the company tried splitting bonuses among the various employees who worked on the project. This worked only until employees began complaining that two of them did most of the work, while the others made only token contributions.

Because there was no formal company policy about shared bonuses, Larisse became a frazzled wreck. There was no way she could be consistent because there was no structure to support her judgments and decisions. Employees began to feel that she was fickle and arbitrary, even though she often spent hours pouring over project time logs to determine which employees had made what contributions.

Though the last thing Larisse wanted was yet another set of rules, she finally felt compelled to ask her superiors for a more comprehensive policy. Within a month she—and every employee—received a copy of the new, detailed guidelines for bonus payments. There was the usual grumbling as everyone dissected the new policy. Even Larisse found guidelines that she thought were unfair. But she enforced the policy anyway, because as a manager that was her job. In the end, that consistency restored peace and productivity. And Larisse found great peace of mind, because she no longer had to remember how she had handled a bonus on a previous project and try to figure out if this project had a similar set of circumstances.

Consistency is crucial not only because it establishes standardized procedures but because it also affirms fairness. Even if employees (or managers) disagree with human resources (HR) policies or department procedures, they will accept them when they know everyone else must, too.

Stay Connected

There is no substitute for effective communication. If you don't know how life is for your employees, you can't know how they're doing. And if employees feel like you're not in tune with their needs, they'll soon come to distrust and even resent you. This can be the kiss of death for a manager; you don't want to look around one day only to find that all the members of your team have quit. You must roll up your sleeves and get your hands dirty, metaphorically speaking, to stay connected to the daily grind.

While it sounds rough, this job is not as thankless as you might think. In fact, the rewards are pretty impressive. For starters, your employees will respect you. They'll work more efficiently and effectively, not just because they know you're watching but also because they want to earn your respect. While they might never name their firstborn after you, they will go the extra mile for you because they know you'll do the same for them. When your employees do well, you do well. And when they look good, you look good. It doesn't get any better than that.

Chapter 6

What Managers Want

As much as people look forward to promotion, management is often a thankless job. This reality catches both new and experienced managers by surprise. It's human nature to expect others to appreciate your efforts on their behalf, but somehow in today's corporate culture it has become the norm to view what a manager does on behalf of his or her employees as just part of the job. So why, then, would anyone want to be a manager? Well, being a manager has its rewards, even if you have to dig a little deeper on some days to find them.

Great Expectations

Despite how it may seem, managers aren't charity workers who continuously give and get nothing in return. There are various tangible rewards of management: higher salary, an office of your own (or at least a work area with a wider frame of space separating it from everyone else's space), and perhaps other perks such as stock options or parking privileges. Being a manager is also an opportunity for you to take your knowledge and the skills you have learned and leverage them out over a group of people to achieve collective results that transcend the capabilities of each individual. The sense of accomplishment can be a real rush, as can the recognition that follows.

Without such rewards, your job would soon become drudgery. Perhaps you had already reached that point before your promotion, feeling that you knew pretty much all there was to know about your job. Now as a manager you have the opportunity to test your knowledge by putting it to work at a different level, where the higher stakes make the challenge more exciting. For most managers, the thrill exceeds personal gratification; there is also the satisfaction of taking your employees, your department, or even your company to the next level.

Your Salary

Of course you care about your salary. To a degree, salary is the universal language that identifies how much a company values your abilities and contributions. If you earn significantly less than other managers in your company, all other factors being equal, read the writing on the paycheck. It should be telling you, "You're not meeting our expectations." If you are this manager, it's time to meet with your superiors, with an open mind and nonconfrontational approach, to find out where they feel you're coming up short. There are situations in which companies use salary to drive someone out of the organization or take advantage of a manager who won't challenge salary decisions. For the most part, however, the current competitive job market forces companies to pay competitive wages. Doing so is just good business.

Recognition and Reward

Who's not familiar with the carrot-and-stick image of fable fame? There's the hapless donkey, trudging around and around to grind grain on a millstone or pull water from a well. A stick fastened to his harness hangs over his head, a carrot dangling from it. He's worn a deep tread into his circular path as he plods on, eternally chasing the carrot just out of reach. He never gets it, but he sure keeps trying. Why? Because every night when he's put to pasture, his owner pats him on the back and tells him what a good job he's done. Of course, people are not donkeys (not most of them, anyway). But in many respects they come to work each day to do the work that grinds your company's grain, motivated by both tangible and intangible prospects.

Recognition is important to everyone. In a recent Gallup poll, 62 percent of people who reported dissatisfaction with their jobs also said they felt that their managers failed to recognize and appreciate their efforts and accomplishments. The most effective managers have a word of praise for each employee, every day.

Loyalty and Job Security

There is a risk associated with being a manager that differs from the risk of taking a job as a regular employee. If your management job doesn't work out, what do you do? You might be able to go back to your old job, and even be the high performer you were before catching the attention of your superiors. But chances are that both you and the company would find this regression too embarrassing to be effective. Coworkers might resent you, if you had been in a position of authority over them for any length of time. And human nature being what it is, it would be hard for you to become a subordinate again. When you become a manager, the only place you can go is up. If you can't meet your goals and responsibilities as a manager, your opportunities are seriously limited. It's fair to say that managers have less job security than their employees do.

Lee started working for the Great Gizmo Company as a customer service representative. A few months after he was hired, there was a major reorganization in his department and Lee was promoted to manager. Over the next six months Lee seized on a few well-timed political opportunities and became the department's vice president. He angered a lot of people during his rapid climb to the top, and once he got there it quickly became apparent that he was in over his head. By now the company had invested a lot of time and money in Lee, and it didn't want to just let him go. So Lee was offered a job as a sales representative, where he at least had the opportunity to make good money. But he failed at that, too, and a few months later he was out the door.

Most companies are loyal to employees and managers, but that loyalty has limits. Once you stop being productive and are no longer contributing to the organization's goals, that loyalty ends. Yet, ironically, managers are expected to demonstrate extraordinary loyalty to the company. It is up to managers to promote loyalty among their employees, even when they don't feel the company is being loyal to them. Though it seems they have it made, managers are on the line more than anyone else.

Your Learning Curve

Managers don't instinctively know how to manage. You probably went to school or studied in an apprenticeship program to learn what you know about your job. You relied on the expertise and knowledge of others to show you the way to proficiency. Managers, too, need training. In some respects, however, the situation is similar to the familiar lament about parenting—it's one of life's most vital responsibilities, yet there is no training program to teach new parents how to shape and nurture the young lives that are now their responsibility. Most people learn about parenting from their parents and grandparents and from friends who became parents before them. They might learn methods that are ineffective, yet they lack the knowledge or insight to identify them as such. Similarly, most managers learn about managing from the managers they've had through their careers. They absorb the good, the bad, and the ugly. Without a framework for understanding the intricacies of human relationships, they might perpetuate methods that are ineffective or even damaging.

Being the best at what you do doesn't necessarily qualify you to manage. It takes a very narrow, intense focus to excel as an employee—a dedicated, almost single-minded concentration to complete the tasks at hand. It takes a much broader, though equally intense, focus to excel as a manager. As a manager, you must manage a process, not produce a product. It's no longer your job to write computer programs or assemble components. It's now your job to manage the people who perform these tasks. You can't step in to rescue them when they become overwhelmed; instead, it's your job to find ways to help people help themselves. In fact, a manager's rescue efforts are likely to alienate employees, who often interpret them as not-so-subtle suggestions that they can't do the work themselves.

What Managers Want from Employees

How would you describe the ideal employee? Go ahead and take a few minutes to think about this, and jot down some of your thoughts if you like. Managers seldom have the liberty of considering what kinds of employees they'd like to manage. Instead, as a manager, you typically inherit a work group whose members span the "Why is this person still working here?" continuum. Some employees barely do enough to count as contributors, working as though they're using teaspoons to dig their way through mountains of work. Others bulldoze right through, clearing multiple projects with apparent ease and even taking on the responsibilities of other employees in the process.

Most managers would be satisfied to manage a work group in which each employee completed his or her assigned tasks correctly and on time. This would allow them to be what they are—managers—instead of what circumstances often force them into—hall monitors, babysitters, scoop patrol. "If only these people would act like the adults they should be!" is a common manager's lament. Are your expectations simply too high? No. In fact, they might not be high enough. As a manager, you have the ability to shape the attitudes and behaviors of the people you manage. Don't misunderstand—

you can't change them. True change comes from within. But you can set and model the standards of acceptability. (Are you reaching for your parent hat? Good!)

FACT

The tendency to use promotions as rewards has given rise to a concept known as the Peter Principle, put forth in 1969 in a book of the same title. In that book, Laurence J. Peter asserts that people rise through organizations to the highest level of their competencies. The final promotion a person receives is to a level beyond his or her competency, and it is at this level that the person remains. Though Peter's observation of this phenomenon was somewhat tongue-in-cheek, the Peter Principle has become part of the modern business vocabulary.

People establish patterns of behavior based on conformity. No one likes to be the odd one out. The department with one truly bad apple (or one outstanding performer) is rare; far more common is the work group bound together by mediocrity. The peer pressure that was so molding in high school simply metamorphoses into new forms in adulthood. If there are no incentives to complete work on time and correctly, nor any consequences for failing to do so, why bother? People need reinforcement to do the right things. Your job as a manager is to provide that reinforcement.

Articulate your expectations to your work group as a whole and to new employees who join it. Be specific but not restrictive, like so:

- "I expect you to be at your work station and ready to work when your shift starts." (Not "Everybody is to be sitting at their desks, pencils in hand, when the clock strikes eight.")
- "I expect you to complete projects by their deadlines. If this is not going to happen, I expect you to tell me about it as soon as it becomes clear to you." (Not "For your monthly report, do an outline, then your research, then your draft, then your final.")

If you want people to act responsibly, you have to give them responsibility—and hold them accountable for meeting it. Most people work best when they understand what you expect from them and when you expect it, as long as they have the necessary knowledge, tools, and resources to complete their assignments. If they don't, then the issue is not one of personal but rather organizational responsibility.

If there is a problem or things have gone badly, discuss the situation with employees without pointing fingers or placing blame. Focus on processes, not people. You can accept accountability without taking the fall; seeing you do this helps your employees see that they can do so as well.

Be generous and consistent with feedback and recognition. Some managers hold meetings at the end of the week to recognize completed work and discuss problems and challenges. This method holds employees accountable before their peers as well as before you, and it also gives them the opportunity to shine in front of their coworkers. Give credit to everyone who participates in bringing a project to completion, and compliment teamwork.

What if your employees consistently fail to meet your expectations? Ask another manager whom you trust to casually observe your work group and your interactions with employees at different times over a week or so, then give you feedback. Objective observation can reveal attitudes and behaviors that give messages counter to the ones you articulate. This is somewhat like watching yourself in the mirror or having someone play audience as you practice a presentation or speech. It's a method that performers, athletes, and others who are in the public eye use as one of the many tools to help them improve their abilities. Once you can see yourself as others see you, you can shape your behaviors to reflect the attitudes you want to convey.

How Managers Succeed

Managers succeed by putting other goals before their own agendas. They succeed by placing the company goals first, and they succeed by helping employees achieve their goals. When employees are functioning at their best, then the department is, too. And that is what makes the manager succeed. For this chain of events to occur, however, managers must understand what makes different employees tick.

Most mentors have in mind the goal that the employee will become as good at something as they are—perhaps even better. This benefits your employee, of course, by providing opportunities for growth and advancement. But it benefits you, the mentor, as well. If you can create and shape your own replacement, you are freed to pursue new opportunities yourself.

To hear all the talk about meeting employee needs, you'd think companies don't consider managers to be employees. Of course, you are just as much an employee as are the people who report to you. But an odd thing happens on your climb up the corporate ladder: Your expectations are supposed to become more global. While upper management hopes that line-level employees care about the company in some way, it expects that you, as a manager, care about the company at least as much as you care about yourself. Fair or not, that's the way it is. As the company invests more in you—salary, training, responsibility, perks—it expects more from you.

When Doug got his first job in management, he could hardly wait to share the good news with his family. After everyone congratulated him, his older brother took him aside. "I know you got a raise with your promotion, but let me tell you something," he said. "Your hourly rate just went down."

Doug soon learned that his brother was right. Doug was a working manager, accountable for his primary position as a corporate trainer. And he was responsible for the four employees who now reported to him, watching over their work and providing the guidance they needed. Sometimes Doug's day-to-day responsibilities were so demanding that he couldn't break away from them, so he worked late, and even on weekends, reviewing the work of his subordinates. He felt like he had ended up with two jobs—and no appreciation.

Even before Doug received his first paycheck as a manager, reality shattered his expectation that he would cheerfully delegate work to a staff happy to take on new responsibilities, grateful to Doug for making such a positive difference in their lives. Instead, Doug found himself mediating often-petty disputes and telling people what to do. The people who had last month been his peers and who had joined with him to discuss solutions for work group problems now expected him to have all the answers. And of course, he didn't.

Are You Bridging the Gap or Stuck in the Middle?

Sometimes being in the middle leaves you feeling left out. The demands managers face today can be overwhelming, causing you to wonder if accepting this promotion or position was such a good idea after all. For some people, the answer will be no, it wasn't such a good idea. On the other hand, many people do enjoy or even thrive on the challenges that come with being a manager.

Organizations, whether for-profit or not-for-profit, must be in a constant state of development. The market requires this in response to new technology, changing trends, and shifting opportunities. Managers must be ready to adjust to these demands as well. Sometimes your role is to interpret the change for employees and help them adjust to it, especially when it results in corporate policy that directly affects them. Sometimes your role is to listen to employees, collect their suggestions and reactions, and interpret those for upper management.

ALERT!

People spend more of their waking hours at work than anywhere else. If you aren't having any fun when you're at work, those are long hours indeed. As a manager, it's your responsibility to cultivate a work environment that employees find supportive and pleasant.

A savvy manager sees change as opportunity and is able to actively bridge the gap. To do this effectively, you must be a good listener and a good diplomat, as well as able to get things done through prioritizing and implementing action. Unfortunately, managers often shy away from bridging the gap. This reflects their insecurity with change. They don't want to expend the extra energy required to be an active rather than a passive manager.

Jolene was a manager whose hands-off yet supportive style engendered tremendous loyalty among the employees who reported to her. The work group was open, fun, and hardworking. But Jolene's style wasn't as popular with the superiors to whom she reported, who felt uninformed about her work group's activities. As the company grew, upper management wanted all managers to establish better procedures to account for staff time and resources, and to shift assignments among employees for improved efficiency. Jolene resisted these efforts, believing they were unnecessary intrusions into her work group's operations. As a result, the company put a new manager in place between Jolene and upper management, in effect curtailing Jolene's authority.

The new manager, Marilyn, was more formal and procedure-oriented, and Jolene didn't like her. Though Marilyn's approach was much more consistent with the direction the company was headed, Jolene continued to resist. She badmouthed Marilyn to her employees and encouraged them to resist Marilyn's changes. The tactic backfired. Jolene and her most loyal employees lost their jobs when Marilyn, implementing upper management directives, reorganized the department. Instead of stepping up as a leader and bridging the gap between employees and the company, closing the distance between the old ways and the new ways, Jolene allowed herself to become trapped in the middle and ultimately squeezed out.

It can be difficult to be the bridge, especially if you disagree with the company's new direction or methods. But resistance is generally futile and ends up tainting your reputation. Jolene was, overall, a good manager. She just couldn't respond to the demands of change, and it cost not only her but also her employees. If your disagreements about upper management directives are strong, you have an obligation to discuss them with your superiors. But as a manager, you have an equal obligation to support those directives in dealing with your employees. By doing so, you help them change and adapt if that's what they choose to do, and you keep yourself well positioned to move on to other opportunities.

As a manager, you may wonder what difference, if any, you make in the work lives of the people who report to you. It's a greater difference than you think, reports the January 2006 *Gallup Management Journal*, especially when it comes to satisfied employees. An employee is most likely to decide whether to stay or leave a job based on the extent to which his or her manager provides regular positive support and encouragement.

Glass Ceilings and Dead Ends

Not all promotions are upward movement. Appearances can be deceiving. Sure, you're a step above where you were yesterday. But where is that step taking you? One of the harsh realities managers face is diminishing opportunity. There are simply fewer positions at the top. Competition for them can be fierce and sometimes unfair.

The term "glass ceiling" came into use in the 1970s, in the early days of women's push for equal opportunity in the workplace. It defines a "lip service" approach in which the promotion looks like a major leap up the corporate ladder but in reality is the top of the ladder for the person. Like watching the activity above through a glass window, opportunities exist but are out of reach. The general premise of the glass ceiling is that its basis is in personal factors other than the person's qualifications, such as gender, race, or ethnicity. Though federal laws in the United States make such discrimination illegal, the glass ceiling remains a fixture in the American corporate culture.

A dead-end promotion similarly has no future, though it's more like a wall than a window. There's usually little question that the promotion leads to nowhere. Perhaps the company is small and upward movement can carry managers only a short way along their career paths. Moving up, in such circumstances, means moving out. Sometimes the "dead end" exists within the person, such as when skill needs change within an industry. A person might be highly qualified in the old ways but lacks the education or knowledge to participate in the new ways. Often we see such walls at times of sea change in a particular industry or following a significant advance in technology. Computer technology, for example, continues to create dead ends even as much as it generates opportunities. Dead-end promotions are not usually personal but rather reflect changes in the ways of doing business.

FACT

According to a 2005 Gallup poll, 53 percent of Americans believe men and women have equal opportunities for jobs and promotions. However, the 2000 U.S. Census reports that women continue to earn less money for comparable work—81 cents for every dollar a man earns.

Make the Most of Your Opportunities

You, of course, could be among the fortunate ones who have had positive role models to guide your development as a manager. Or your company might have a training program for new managers. If neither of these is true for you (or even if they are), there are other ways for you to learn how to be a manager. You could do any of these things:

- Enroll in continuing education courses. Many universities and community colleges offer noncredit programs that cover a wide range of management topics, from legal issues to communication techniques. (Your company might pay, or reimburse you, for this.)

- Ask a manager you respect and would like to emulate for suggestions and advice. You might be able to "shadow" this person for a day or so, to see him or her in action.
- Ask your company to pay for you to attend management workshops, or at least allow you paid time off from work to go.
- Find out what professional magazines your company's executives and human resources staff subscribe to, and borrow them. This will expose you to the many dimensions of management from varying perspectives.
- If there are management certifications available in your industry or profession, find out what it takes to meet the requirements. Ask your company to sponsor your certification efforts, in full or in part.
- Read books like this one, as well as those that present specific management methods or issues. Read about your industry or profession as well as beyond it.

As an employee, your outstanding job performance convinced your superiors that you were worthy of promotion. As a manager, you must demonstrate your ability to transcend daily details and visualize the bigger picture. You can't learn too much about management, people, or communication. The broader your base of understanding, the better equipped you are to handle the unexpected.

Chapter 7
Today's Workplace

Until the 1990s, the workplace was a world of its own where most people spent most of their waking hours. You arrived at a certain time, stayed a certain amount of time, and clocked out at a certain time each day. Then technology liberated workers from that routine. Today, work is something you do. Where you do it—and sometimes even how you do it—is often not so important. The people who report to you may work in satellite offices in different locations, telecommute from home, or share jobs. It's a brave new universe out there!

Flextime

From an average of sixteen minutes each way in Corpus Christi, Texas, to more than thirty-eight minutes in New York City, American employees spend a lot of time traveling to and from work. Those thirty-eight New York minutes add up to more than 300 hours a year navigating traffic. As a way of reducing traffic and traffic-related pollution, many state and local governments began offering incentives to employers who encouraged their employees to work alternate shifts that let them commute during less busy times—the birth of flextime. Though required to work a specific number of hours, employees choose which hours to spend in the workplace. Companies like flextime because it allows them to have the most employees working during their busiest times. Employees like flextime because it permits them to schedule work around other activities, such as children's school events.

FACT

The U.S. Bureau of Labor Statistics reports that 28.8 percent of Americans—29 million—work flexible hours or shift schedules. Of these, just about the same percentage have children (28.9 percent) as don't (26.8 percent). About 45 percent of managers work flexible hours compared with 35 percent of support workers.

Telecommuting

What if you never had to come into the office? Would that be a dream come true? Millions of Americans live just such a dream! They work from home (usually), connecting to the office via e-mail and the Internet. Many companies have sophisticated intranets, elaborate internal computer networks that give telecommuting employees access to customer databases and other relevant electronic data. Even meetings may take place from a distance, using Web cams, microphones, and other electronics to connect work groups. As a manager, you may meet in person with your telecommuting employees once a week, once a month, or when they or you determine such a meeting is necessary. Telecommuting also allows companies to hire or work with people whose qualifications are ideal but live too far away to come to the office every day.

The number of Americans who telecommute at least one day a week jumped from 15 million in 2000 to more than 44 million in 2006. Nearly 5 million Americans telecommute four days or more a week.

In the early days of telecommuting, employers sometimes worried that employees were not working as hard as they would were they in the office. It was a derivation of the "out of sight, out of mind" philosophy. But all data since supports the theory that people are more productive when they're happy in their work environments. Not having a regular commute, wearing what's comfortable rather than what's fashionable, and regulating one's own work pace are all factors that make most people happy, a key factor in job satisfaction. And job satisfaction translates to productivity.

Job Sharing

Job sharing is a creative approach to flexibility that has grown in popularity, particularly among new parents who want to work fewer hours but still stay on track with their careers. People who want to go back to school, pursue intensive hobby activities, or simply remain plugged in but not tied down may also find job sharing an appealing option. Though some jobs are easier to share than others, in most situations where two people want to share a single position, there is a way to make it happen.

In most companies, the important or career-oriented jobs are full-time positions. It's just too much for companies to invest in training lots of people to do pieces of jobs that are critical to the company's success. But these jobs are also demanding. It might be necessary to meet with clients outside regular work hours, or to travel. These demands are difficult for people who also want to spend time with their families or doing other things.

While job sharing primarily benefits the employees who participate, it offers advantages for companies as well. Job sharing can help companies do the following:

- Retain qualified and experienced employees who would otherwise quit or move into part-time jobs
- Improve employee job satisfaction and morale
- Maintain, and in some situations improve, productivity and efficiency
- In some situations, save on benefit expenses

Job sharing is really about sharing time. In exchange for less time spent at work, job-sharing partners gain more time to be with their families, go to school, or enjoy personal interests such as artistic or athletic pursuits. Job sharing can permit employees to care for children or aging parents, return to college or graduate school, take up watercolor, study piano, train for marathons—whatever is important to them.

QUESTION?

What is job sharing?
Job sharing is when two people share a single position, including its tasks and responsibilities, salary, workspace, and other elements. Usually the division is equal, though sometimes one person may have a larger share than the other.

Job-Share Arrangements for Employees

Generally, an employee who wants to job-share will approach you with a partner in mind. If your company already uses job sharing, there are probably procedures already in place. If job sharing is new to your company, there are numerous books and Web resources on this topic (see Appendix

B). The following are some key points to address when considering a job-share request:

- **Job tasks:** Can the job's tasks and functions be reasonably divided? Will dividing the job create any overlaps or duplication that would not exist if one person did the job? Who responds if there is a problem—the partner "on duty" when the problem arises, or the partner who did the work?
- **Communication:** How will the job-sharing employees communicate with each other? How will they stay in touch with other work group members, if this is important? Is one of the partners the primary contact, or must each person receive memos, e-mails, telephone calls, and other communication?
- **Flexibility and availability:** Can the job-sharing partners trade off if they choose? How will this affect their working relationships with you, with other coworkers, and with clients or customers? Will one partner cover if the other is sick or on vacation? Are both partners willing to attend meetings if other team members or customers want them to be there?
- **Compatibility:** How well do the prospective partners get along with each other? Are their work styles similar? If each does half of a project, will the pieces join seamlessly or will someone else (you!) have to put them together?
- **Pay and benefits:** How will the job share partners share the job's salary and benefits package? (If your company provides benefits for half-time employees, this might not be an issue.)
- **Work space:** Will the partners share space in the workplace? Usually this is the case, since they are two people sharing one job and presumably its accoutrements as well as its responsibilities. Each is then responsible for leaving the workspace and its equipment ready for the other to use. Occasionally a manager has the resources to give each job-share partner a separate desk in the same office or even separate computers, but this is often not the case.
- **Performance evaluations:** How will you evaluate productivity and performance? Are the job-share partners willing to be evaluated on

the basis of their work as a team rather than as individuals? Do your company's human resources policies support this?

Ask prospective job-share partners to discuss these and any specific issues relevant to the job they want to share or to your company, first with each other and then with you. Once everyone agrees to the details, put them in writing and have each employee, and you as their manager, sign the agreement. If you are unsure whether the arrangement will meet the needs of your work group or company, establish a test period of three to six months. (Less than this probably won't be enough time to work out any wrinkles so you can get a fair assessment.) Include in the agreement the steps you and the employees will follow to measure the arrangement's success.

Job-Sharing Pitfalls and Risks

Job-share arrangements that fall apart usually do so because the division of responsibilities between partners was not clear or because the partners fail to get along. Some people have trouble giving up decision-making authority, for example. If one job-share partner continually overrides the other's decisions and actions, other employees will become confused about which one of them to talk to. People who have worked in the same work group for a year or two before entering into a job-sharing partnership are more likely to be successful, although some challenges are difficult to see until they hit you in the face. One partner might be fastidious to a fault, while the other is comfortable with a fair amount of disorganization.

Can Managers Job Share?

Job sharing can work at nearly any level within an organization. Whether it will or not depends. It's essential for any job-sharing partners to be compatible. When these partners share a management position, that compatibility must extend both downward (to employees) and upward (to upper management). Employees tend to be leery of situations that make them accountable to two different managers. So a key element of structuring a job-sharing arrangement for a management position is to emphasize the position, not just the people who share it. Some managers find that job sharing works best if they divide the work group into members for which each has responsibility. This way, the work group functions as two teams, each with its own leader. Employees know the nuances of the manager to whom they report, and they worry less about reporting to someone who doesn't know theirs. The drawback to this arrangement is that neither manager is in the office full time, so one must "cover" the team of the other.

ALERT!

Sometimes circumstances beyond the partnership cause it to fail. A job-sharing partnership is a lot like a marriage. Sometimes two people who seem to be compatible and get along discover that they have vastly different perspectives when it comes to how things get done.

Everything that applies to employees who want to job share also applies to managers. Because you are accountable both to the employees who report to you as well as to your superiors, it's critical that you work out every detail of the arrangement before putting it into practice. As a manager, you aren't likely to have the luxury of letting some details work themselves out. It's important that your actions support consistency and cohesiveness within the work group, not jeopardize stability.

Comfort Means Productivity

When our middle-management fathers left each morning for work, they wore polished shoes, slacks, collared shirts, ties, and sports jackets. A meeting with upper management often required a suit. Women who worked wore dresses and high heels. It wasn't that the workplace was making a fashion statement; it was just the way things were. Dress was a sign of respect, an indicator that what went on in the office was serious work. What you wore to work also signaled your station in the work world. Ties and jackets or skirts and heels were the uniform of middle management. Work was hierarchical; it was important for everyone to know who had what status.

While some companies maintain formal dress in executive offices, most have gone decidedly casual. This reflects the recognition that people who are comfortable are also more productive. It also demonstrates a much-diminished emphasis on status and its inherently divisive qualities, as well as a redirection to focus on collaboration and teamwork. Many middle managers today are working managers—not only do they manage a work group or department, but they also share in the team's workload. The manager of a training department often designs and delivers training programs as well as provides guidance and support for employees doing the same kind of work. Clothes still symbolize status, of course; that will never change. But the symbolism is far more subtle and less directly related to job or occupation. The man or woman striding down the corridor in jeans and day hikers could be the mail clerk or the vice president of finance.

FACT

The move toward casual attire in the workplace gained momentum in the late 1980s, when companies began implementing "casual dress Fridays" to build employee morale and reward hard work. The idea was to create a not-quite-a-day-off atmosphere. As it became clear that employees worked no less productively on casual dress days (and in fact, often more productively), casual dress became the standard any day of the week. Some companies now invite employees to participate in "formal Mondays."

For managers, the casual office can raise some issues. While some companies have explicit policies that define the workplace environment, many do not. This leaves department and work group managers responsible for setting and upholding standards. How do you determine what attire is appropriate? Here are some questions to consider:

- Does the work environment have special safety concerns? Loose clothing, long hair, jewelry, and even long fingernails can present hazards in work areas where there is moving machinery.

- Do employees have direct contact with customers or clients? If so, the rule of thumb is to dress as the customers dress, within reason.
- Are employees dressing in ways that are distracting, inappropriate, suggestive, or offensive? Older customers (internal or external) might not consider a young person wearing jeans to be competent or to have the appropriate authority, for example.
- How do employees want to dress? A standard that your work group mutually agrees upon is much easier to monitor and enforce than one that "management" imposes.

What employees wear to work and how they conduct themselves can be concerns for managers even when there are detailed policies in place. It's human nature to push the curve of individuality. As much as possible, it's usually more productive to support that curve. Do your employees wear uniforms? If so, why? Some companies like their employees to present a homogeneous image. This makes it clear, to employees and customers alike, that each employee represents the company at all times when wearing the uniform. In such situations, individuality is not as important (for the corporate good) as consistency. Compliance is fairly easy to monitor and enforce. Other organizations such as medical facilities require uniforms because clothing can become contaminated or damaged. In such situations, there is often greater latitude in accommodating individuality—some people might prefer plain colors, others like bright patterns and designs, yet all can be in compliance. And in some work environments, regulations and rules (federal, state, and industrial) dictate attire.

Workplace Décor and Decorum

What about personal space? Many employees like to decorate their offices, workspaces, or desks with family pictures and small personal items. Most companies find that this is not a problem as long as the decor doesn't interfere with job tasks and doesn't offend other employees or customers.

Is music appropriate in the workplace? Many businesses allow employees to play music or have music playing over a loudspeaker system, though some employees find this distracting. Different kinds of music can influence the moods and behaviors of employees as well as customers. Again, consensus is often the deciding factor. Generally people who work in enclosed areas or individual offices have greater freedom to listen to music while they work.

Can employees have food and beverages at their desks or work areas? Decisions on whether to allow eating and drinking depend on what kind of work employees are doing. Sipping coffee or munching a snack is less likely to interfere with job tasks for employees who work at desks and are in contact with clients by phone or electronically than for those who deal with customers in person.

FACT

Marketers have used music to influence customer behaviors for decades. Music with a hard, driving beat makes people feel excited and impulsive. Such effects influence people to make spontaneous purchases and leave rather than linger—ideal behavior for fast-food restaurants. Soft, soothing music makes people feel relaxed and thoughtful. This helps improve mental focus and muscle coordination, and it also makes people feel that they want to stay and be comfortable (desired behavior in luxury restaurants, bookstores, and expensive boutiques).

There are some behaviors that are inappropriate in just about any workplace, including these:

- **Profanity:** Swearing is everywhere today, so much a part of common conversation that many people scarcely notice it. But profanity is offensive to quite a number of people, and its frequent presence implies discourtesy and lack of professionalism.
- **Smoking:** Many cities and states have laws restricting indoor smoking to reduce the risk of exposure to secondhand smoke. Some companies have smoke break rooms that are separately ventilated, while others ban smoking on the property entirely.
- **Offensive clothing:** Many people in the working world are offended by clothing that is tattered, torn, dirty, sexually suggestive, or derogatory. T-shirts with slogans often fall into the latter categories.

However casual the environment, the workplace is still the workplace. Managers sometimes must explicitly—and endlessly—describe what is and isn't appropriate for employees to wear, say, and do.

Safety and Security

As much as it is casual, today's workplace has become cautious. Workplace safety is a perpetual issue. Most safety concerns relate to work hazards—falling objects, exposed blades, relentless gears, fires, fumes, toxins, and other dangers. These days there is yet another workplace risk: violence. Our times might have no more negative, angry, frustrated people than any other period in history, but they are more apt to take their feelings out on others. Everyone has bad days, of course. Maybe it's because the pace of modern life is so hectic—even frantic—that people sometimes feel they've lost control of their lives. Maybe it's because the line between work and the rest of life has become less defined. Maybe it's a consequence of global warming. Whatever the reasons, angry people are more likely to vent their ire at work—and at coworkers.

ALERT!

Only motor vehicle accidents claim more lives and cause more injuries than incidents of workplace violence. Sometimes the connection is personal, such as a spouse or significant other who also works at the same company. Sometimes the association is symbolic, such as when a boss behaves in the same way an abusive father used to. Most often, there is no link at all: Two-thirds of all workplace violent deaths occur during robberies and other acts of apparently random violence at the hands of strangers.

Workplace Violence

The potential for workplace violence is frightening for employees and managers alike. No matter how rare deaths resulting from such violence may be, the U.S. National Institute for Occupational Safety and Health (NIOSH) estimates that 1 million people a year are victims of workplace violence—accounting for 15 percent of reported acts of violence nationwide. "Desk rage" is both a familiar term and a familiar experience to many employees. Experiences range from threatening language to acts of aggression.

NIOSH recommends that all companies develop policies for identifying and addressing the signs of potentially violent behavior, as well as procedures for dealing with acts of violence if they occur. Unfortunately, this is not as easy as it sounds. Attitudes and behaviors are often subtle and difficult to discern as "across the line." Studies of recent workplace violence incidents have given psychologists new insights into early warning signs. Would you recognize these warnings in your workplace? In the following situations, which do you think poses the greater threat?

- The person who slams things around when he's angry, or the one who believes federal agents read all of his e-mail messages?
- The person who brags about his bar fights, or the one who continually complains about the idiots who make his life miserable?
- The person who has a restraining order against a spouse, or the one whose spouse has a restraining order against him or her?

Though it's impossible to know with certainty which people are blowing off steam (a healthy response) and which people are about to blow (decidedly unhealthy for them and potentially for others), in each of these scenarios most experts would bet that the second situation is more likely to lead to violence. Aggressive attitudes and behaviors are often subtle and easy to dismiss, at least in the beginning or at first glance. These become warning signs when they become a pattern that emerges over time. Psychologists say managers should be alert to employees who do the following:

- Are chronically late or frequently miss work
- Speak with and show contempt for authority and people who have positions of authority
- Are paranoid or cynical (believe others are watching them or are out to get them, or that events such as economic downturns, layoffs, or even computer problems happen because "they" planned them)

- Are hot-tempered, easily fly off the handle, argue when given directions to do something a specific way, or walk out of meetings when others disagree with them
- Talk about how nobody appreciates their abilities, dedication, knowledge, or power
- Delight in the misfortunes of others, laugh inappropriately, or fail to laugh at jokes and situations that others find humorous
- Are awkward in social situations to the extent that they make others uncomfortable or others make fun of them, or create environments of isolation for themselves

If your company has policies and procedures for dealing with potentially violent employees, know what they are and follow them. It's essential to document your observations, including comments and complaints that other employees bring to you. The earlier there is intervention, the better.

The potential for workplace violence is a tricky issue for managers. It's hard to know when and how to take action. The Occupational Safety and Health Administration (OSHA), the U.S. National Institute of Occupational Safety and Health (NIOSH), and many employee assistance programs (EAPs) offer advice, materials, and even workshops about recognizing and handling aggression in the workplace. Take advantage of these resources.

Many companies have employee assistance programs (EAPs) that can provide advice for managers as well as counseling for employees. Is the employee someone new to your department or company? If so, is the person still on probationary status? Or is this someone you inherited when you became the work group's manager? In either case you need to step in, but the circumstances could influence what you do and how you do it.

Some states have laws that regulate how companies may approach, discipline, and fire employees based on how long they've been working in the job or for the company. Research the laws, regulations, and company policies that might apply to the situation so you know what you can and cannot do. Talk with your HR department and your manager so they know what's going on and can support your choice of response.

ALERT!

Companies often fail to recognize when a situation crosses the line of the law. Notify the police if an employee hits or in any other way physically assaults someone, makes specific threats or threats that are particularly scary to you or others, or damages property.

Then, meet privately with the employee to discuss your observations and your concerns. Do this in a calm and nonconfrontational manner. If you are concerned that the employee might become violent toward you, have this meeting where others can see you or have another person (such as an HR representative or your manager) present. Explain, explicitly and clearly, what behaviors are problems, why those behaviors are unacceptable, what it will take for the employee to rectify the situation, and what will happen if the problems continue. Offer the employee consultation with your employee assistance program (EAP) consultation or other forms of assistance.

Information Security

Other issues of workplace caution involve safety of another sort: information. The underground market in stolen identity makes customer data a hot commodity—and electronic storage systems make its theft alarmingly easy. Personal information about employees and proprietary company data may also be at risk. Many companies are implementing internal tracking mechanisms and access safeguards to help prevent theft of data. Employees must wear identification badges and use security codes to gain access to computer records. Unfortunately this is an area of continuing challenge for managers, who must balance the need for employees to access and work with sensitive data with the needs to protect that data from inappropriate use and outright theft. You'll read more about electronic security in Chapter 8.

Chapter 8
Technology Rules

Do you check your company e-mail from home before you go to bed or in the morning with your first cup of coffee before you shower? Do you commute via public transportation and work on your laptop during the trip? Do all your calls forward to your cell phone? Do you know where your desk phone is, or do you even have one? It's both a blessing and a curse that technology lets us work from anywhere, any time. Digital devices can extend the workday and blur the boundary between professional and personal lives like nothing ever has.

The Digital Work World

Ours is a technology-driven society. Professionals ranging from doctors to hairdressers use computers to schedule appointments, order supplies, and communicate with employees and customers. In less than a generation, America leaped from room-size to desktop computers, party lines to cell phones, Day Planners to Palm Pilots. The transformation has revolutionized not only the way we work but also the way we live. As a manager, you need to know how to use technology to improve your staff's productivity and efficiency—and to know when technology is not the answer.

Computers have replaced typewriters and calculators, graph paper and ledgers, address books and calendars. Cellular telephones and wireless modems make it possible to work from literally any location. Facsimile machines, e-mail, and the Internet have greatly reduced the need for surface mail and courier deliveries. Software programs make it easy for people with modest skills to perform sophisticated tasks, from word processing applications that allow you to integrate text and images into formatted documents to financial applications that let you track and report any accounting functions.

FACT

The Commodore 64 and the Apple computers debuted in 1977, forever changing the technology landscape of the world. IBM entered the market in 1981 with the personal computer, or PC, which catapulted to the lead in market share in only four years and quickly became the generic term for any kind of small computer. Today, few work environments are without PCs.

Managers have to make numerous decisions about technology. They need to know the technology related to their fields as well as general technology in use in the workplace. Even in companies that have information technology (IT) departments, it's department managers who will need to know what software is most appropriate for their needs. Employees love to be on the leading edge, and they generally recognize the value of technology in keeping their own careers up to date (and their daily tasks easier).

When you, the manager, are a well-informed advocate for the technology that simplifies the work lives of your employees, you encourage loyalty among those employees. They feel that you have their best interests at heart and are willing to take action. The increased productivity that results from the right technology makes the company feel more loyal toward you.

Making Technology Decisions

Which financial software should the company purchase for the accounting department? The manager of accounting will get that question first. Is he or she keeping up with technology? What direct marketing database software should the marketing department use? The marketing manager needs to know and also must be able to justify the department's need to computerize these kinds of functions. What image should the company's Web site strive to present? Should it be humorous, sophisticated, or eye-catching, using the latest whiz-bang animated graphics and streaming video? Should the company produce materials in formats that can work on the Web as well as in print? If you're a manufacturing manager, you'd better know about CAD/CAM and ERP and just-in-time and all of the other buzzwords, and be able to talk about what software products might be best used within that environment.

Nearly from the onset of their use in the workplace, computers took the rap for carpal tunnel syndrome, a repetitive motion injury of the wrist. According to the conventional wisdom at the time, continuous keyboarding put the wrist in a strained position. However, a large research study in the early 2000s failed to prove the connection.

And then there is worker productivity. Do you need to think about a networked system? Does it need to serve your department alone or to link all departments? Do the sales representatives need handheld organizers, or can they get by with laptops? What productivity software should you consider for the sales reps? Do they need to have promotional literature with them, or should they be able to do PowerPoint presentations from their laptops?

ESSENTIAL

Read professional journals within your field and join professional associations and organizations to keep yourself abreast of relevant technology. This will serve you well in your current job, and could be the key to other jobs.

Technology is relentless, whether you dread it or embrace it. Professions and the world of work constantly change, and much of this change is driven by technology. Those who don't keep up get left behind—companies as well as people. There are plenty of ways you can update your knowledge level, easily and fairly effortlessly, like these:

- Make a friend in your company's IT department and learn what criteria the "experts" use to assess new equipment and software.
- Ask questions when sales representatives come calling. Find out why a change is really an improvement—or if it's not. Sometimes what's touted as an upgrade is nothing more than the current version in new clothes, with a lot of flash that turns out to be nothing but fizzle when it comes to functionality.
- Ask experienced users what they like and don't like about the computer equipment and programs they use. Get a variety of opinions to see what patterns emerge. Although anecdotal, this kind of information helps you weigh marketing hype against real-world experience.

Staying Current

You need to be able to adapt, if not to be one of the leaders in adopting current technology. You can only sit back for so long—maybe long enough to take a breath. The technology you laugh at today might crunch out your pink slip next week. Managers who really excel in their organizations often do so by introducing or supporting new technology. This contributes to others—the employees who report to them as well as their superiors—perceiving them as innovators and leaders.

Even though it can seem that computers and software are already obsolete by the time you get them installed and configured to meet your needs, it's crucial to remain current with technology. New software is only backward-compatible (meaning that newer versions can work with data from older versions) for a short period of time. You might be able to squeeze five years from your PC system, especially if your needs are basic. But soon enough you'll have trouble finding software that will run on older computer systems.

Telework

Technology has opened many doors in the work world over the past few years, and one that is gaining in significance is the option to not leave home at all to go to work. This is telework, or telecommuting. The U.S. Department of Labor (DOL) estimates that 10 percent of the employees in the private sector, or between 13 and 19 million people, participate in telework arrangements and projects the number of teleworkers will grow as technology continues to improve. Some jobs don't require the employee to be in a particular location, or they require the employee to be out of the office more than in it.

QUESTION?

What does telework mean?
Employees who telework (or telecommute) work from home or other locations, connecting with coworkers via computer and telecommunication. According to a 2000 report from the U.S. Department of Labor, workers telecommute in 70 percent of American companies with more than 5,000 employees and in 43 percent of those with fewer than 1,000 employees.

When teleworking, the employee works at a location other than the company's site, usually at home, and is connected to the workplace via digital technology—computer, telephone, e-mail, Internet, and even televideo conferencing. Telework is an ideal option for people who are strongly self-motivated and can work productively without continual supervision. Teleworking can improve productivity by removing common distractions such as office socializing. It also reduces the expenses associated with providing office space for employees.

If your state has significant traffic problems in urban areas, state law may mandate that employers over a certain size participate in commuter reduction efforts. Look into alternative forms of transportation for your employees, such as carpooling or public transportation, or eliminate commuting altogether by supporting telework options.

But out of sight can mean out of mind—and that's not a good thing, especially at work. In the work world, it often means lack of communication, lack of control, and potential disaster. When communication lapses, the benefits of teleworking can become liabilities. Other employees begin to wonder what the teleworker is really doing. They might complain that the work-from-home employee isn't pulling a fair load or has special privileges by not being subject to office policies and standards.

Absence allows people—coworkers and managers alike—to create their own scenarios about what the teleworking employee might be doing. They begin to envision the teleworker lounging around in pajamas and slippers, enjoying a walk in the sun, or running errands at the mall. It's not easy for employees who have never worked from home or a distant location to understand that teleworkers put in the same amount of hours (and usually more) that they would were they in the office.

Some managers find it difficult to have teleworking employees. It's essential for others to know when the teleworker is available and for the teleworker to be available when expected. Ways to keep teleworkers in the loop include these:

- Hold regular in-person meetings if the teleworker is in the same city. In most situations, meeting once a week is enough to maintain connections and communication.
- Hold regular conference or video calls when the teleworker is working from a distance. This at least keeps the person's voice familiar.
- Schedule occasional visits to the office if the teleworker is in another city or state. Even when there is regular voice contact, it helps to keep a face attached to the voice.
- Maintain diligent communication about availability and variations from schedules.

Managers should expect employees who are teleworking to let them know when their e-mail is down or they're going to be out for a doctor's appointment—just as they would if they worked in the same office. Likewise, managers need to keep teleworkers informed about schedule changes, shifts in priorities, employee vacations, office meetings, and other matters that teleworkers would know about if they were in the office.

Having employees who telework requires companies to stay current with technology. An employee who is working from a distance is most efficient when he or she has the equipment to support the job tasks. This might mean updating computers and modems or even improving infrastructure elements, such as installing digital phone lines. And, of course, not all jobs will support telework. Telework is not a good option when the job requires close and constant integration with the tasks and projects of other employees.

Managers who want to keep productive, creative employees need to be open to finding solutions that balance individual and company needs. Our society is changing, and so is the business world. People have always had private lives, of course, but until the 1980s, companies functioned as though they wore blinders that kept them from recognizing this. Now things are different. Personal needs are as important as career needs, and people will move around in jobs and among companies until they find what fits. The manager who can be flexible is the manager who will retain top talent—and earn the respect and loyalty of employees as well as superiors.

E-Mail Etiquette

Paper memos and letters are at risk of following the typewriter into oblivion. The vast majority of office communication takes place today via e-mail or its transient cousin, instant messaging (IM). These forms of communication have the advantage of instant delivery, and an ongoing exchange of e-mails feels more like conversation than correspondence.

When e-mail first became available, computer technology limited the number of characters that could appear in a line of text. This led to the development of a sort of e-mail shorthand, a system of abbreviations and symbols that convey messages. E-mail correspondence was quite cryptic: "gr8t 2 c u, g2g" was shorthand for "Great to see you, got to go." Though the technology has improved and nearly all e-mail programs now automatically accommodate line length through a feature called word wrap, some people continue to use the cryptic shorthand. Don't be one of them! Write e-mails in full sentences as you would write memos printed and distributed the old-fashioned way.

Think before you write. E-mail and other forms of digital messaging are instant, and once you hit "Send," that message is gone. You can't take it back to say something a different way or to delete something you shouldn't have said. Keep your comments brief and to the point without being terse. If what you're saying requires more than a few paragraphs, consider making a phone call instead. And don't type your e-mails in all caps, either. In "netiquette," this is the equivalent of yelling.

ALERT!

It's not unusual for managers to exchange several hundred e-mails a day. Use the subject line to provide a clue about the nature of your message. This makes it easy for you to remember why you've e-mailed someone. It also helps your e-mail make it through antispam filters on the e-mail servers and on your own computer.

Keep in mind that the instantaneous nature of e-mail gives a false sense of presence, as though you're engaged in conversation. But other important dimensions of communication that add nuances of meaning are missing. The other person can't hear your voice or see your facial expressions. Words on the screen can appear harsh when what they're saying is not. Especially when giving assignments and schedules, ask rather than tell or provide a few sentences to soften the message.

Spam

Little is as annoying in the digital environment as spam—those unsolicited messages distributed by the millions primarily as marketing efforts. Most Internet service providers (ISPs, the companies that serve as the "switchboards" for Internet traffic) use filters to intercept as much spam as possible before it reaches your company's network or your computer. Internet experts estimate that 40 percent or more of Internet traffic is spam. What can you do about spam? Beyond making sure you have effective filters to screen it out, not very much. Whenever possible, do not even open spam e-mail messages. In particular, you should never open attachments from unfamiliar senders! Delete them. Sometimes spam carries viruses.

Viruses

Computer viruses are the bane of the Internet. Viruses are malicious structures of computer code that implement some sort of action on your computer. Many viruses are more annoying and time-wasting than harmful, but others can steal or destroy data, hijack your computer and use it for Internet activity, or damage programs and files on your computer. Always use antivirus software, and keep it current.

Web Surfing

The Internet is a virtually endless beach that connects people across cubicles, company sites, and continents. As a manager, you are the lifeguard on this beach. Your company has rules about how its employees surf the vast waters of the Web, and it is your job to make sure the employees who report to you follow these rules. When you were a kid, swimming rules were simple:

No running at the water's edge, no diving in shallow water, and always swim with a buddy. Would that the Internet was such a simple environment!

FACT

A 2005 survey of 10,000 workers revealed that 44 percent of them use time when they should be working to surf the Web and send e-mails. On average, they spend one to two hours of the workday engaged in personal activities on the Internet that range from checking stocks and online shopping to planning vacations and looking for other jobs.

These days, it's less important to have a head full of facts than it is to know how to use the Internet to get those facts quickly. You and your employees may spend significant amounts of time surfing the Web for information relevant to job tasks and projects. Most people who regularly use the Internet in this way have favorite search engines that locate a specific key word or phrase, then display a list of the Web sites that contain the word or phrase. The technology behind Web searching is complex but the interface with the user (what you see when you request a search) is astonishingly simple and straightforward—and fast. What might have taken hours, days, or even weeks to find through "hard copy" methods now is at your fingertips in seconds.

The business applications of the Internet are endless. Many companies use Web sites to convey information about the company or to sell products and services (e-commerce). Web sites provide instant access to numerous business resources, government agencies, reference sources, and even competitors. The challenge is to keep information current. Large companies have information technology (IT) departments that handle such tasks. Other companies may contract with outside experts.

Off Limits

The Internet is unrestricted and worldwide. There is no general oversight for what gets onto the Internet. You have no way to know whether the information you get from Web sites is true or correct other than to surf only sites you know to be legitimate. Your company likely has policies and guidelines to keep Web use on the straight and narrow—and legal. The worldwide reach of the Internet brings products and services available in other countries but not in the United Stares virtually into your office. Doing so with certain of these—prescription medications, banned or controlled drugs, gambling, pornography—represent criminal actions in this country. You are accountable for how you use your computer.

The Company Intranet

An intranet—sometimes called a network—is like the Internet, but it is confined to content and services your company makes available through it. It allows you to share files, gain access to databases you need to do your work, and send e-mail messages within your company. An intranet uses the same technology for its structure, and you access and use it in the same way as the Internet. People outside your company cannot use your intranet, however, or can only use certain areas. Passwords give access to data, files, and information.

Confidentiality and Workplace Privacy

A hot issue in today's workplace is that of personal privacy. When communication was limited to telephone or in-person conversations, we had a sense that our discussions were limited to those participating in them. Sure, others in the office might overhear, but the discussion itself was private. No one recorded it (unless it was a voice mail message), and it wasn't likely to come back as evidence in a lawsuit. There was even a sense of immunity about telephone calls; if no one else heard the conversation and it later became an issue, it was one person's word against another. This had the potential to create some ugly scenes, to be sure. But for the most part, there were few tangible ramifications.

Federal and state laws limit the level to which a company can intrude on telephone calls, voice mail, and real-time e-mail (e-mail messages as you're sending and receiving them). Though companies can monitor business-related calls and messages, in reality, it's often difficult to distinguish them from personal calls and messages. Telephone logging systems may keep records of all received and dialed phone numbers. Other forms of electronic communication—notably Internet activity and e-mail—create similar records with the internal numbers assigned to all computers that link to the Internet.

FACT

Internet and e-mail are the top reasons for computer use in the workplace, the U.S. Bureau of Labor Statistics reports. Over 55 percent of the American workforce—77 million people—uses computers on the job, and two in five have Internet access.

We sometimes have the perception that because e-mail and Web surfing are digital activities, electronic communications somehow disappear when we're done with them. But they don't. They travel, as bits of electronic data, through a network of computers that store them. This process is for efficiency, not to spy on you. But the bottom line is that while what you do on your computer may appear invisible, someone somewhere has a record of it.

Does your company have the right to read your e-mails? Under laws in effect at the time of this writing, yes. Your e-mails can resurface in ways too numerous to cite, and can have any imaginable consequence. Companies also have the right to track Internet traffic, block access to Web sites, and censor content. Your company has a legal obligation to prevent its computer networks from being used for illegal activity, and can be held accountable for such activity. Employees also are accountable to companies for the way they use company resources. Most larger companies have written policies for Internet use (including e-mail, which travels via the Internet).

Does your company routinely read your e-mails and review your Web surfing activities? Probably not, unless you've done something to raise suspicion. But it's in your best interest to act as though every action you take on your computer is under observation—because it might be. This may include your personal computer, too, if you use it for work or for work-related e-mails.

Chapter 9

Work Styles

Work style blends personality, knowledge, skill, ingenuity, and creativity into the package you know as an employee. Each person's work style is unique, although there are common traits that identify general types. Some people are absolutely true to type, but many adopt various elements from different work styles, creating a blend of approaches. These differences are all good in the workplace, where jobs and tasks require different work styles and approaches.

9

Channeling Creative Energy

Nearly every job involves some aspect of creativity, from jobs we consider to be creative (such as media or teaching) to those we think of as more mundane (such as accounting or cleaning). Creativity covers the spectrum of innovation, from the ability to see new ways to accomplish familiar tasks to the capacity to envision entirely new processes or products.

ALERT!

Some people require constant direction, feedback, and redirection. Others are better left to a general framework within which they are free to structure the job's tasks, flow, and progress measures. Consider how each employee works most productively, and then shape your oversight and interactions to be appropriate within the context of the employee's work style.

Creativity and productivity are not mutually exclusive, although channeling creativity into productivity can be a significant challenge for a manager. You just need to identify people who are naturally creative thinkers and make sure they have the flexibility—in terms of assignments and environment—to express their creativity. How can you stimulate and support productive creativity without squelching the creative process? You might try these ideas:

- Present assignments in general terms, explaining the desired end result but allowing employees the latitude to find their own ways to that result. Establish timelines to keep productivity on track, but don't structure the work process.
- Allow people to express risky ideas without immediately shooting them down. "Let me play devil's advocate" is the surest way to cut creative thinking off at the knees.
- Let people work through mistakes to find their own solutions, and allow time for this as part of the creative process. It takes a lot of coal to make diamonds.

- Learn how to praise someone's efforts without focusing on the result or product you want those efforts to generate.
- Ask employees what you can do to provide a stimulating and supportive environment. You might be surprised at how simple some of their requests will be.
- Sponsor workshops conducted by outside resources. Creative people are always looking to broaden their base of knowledge and expertise. New faces bring fresh perspectives. Employees are sometimes more willing to question and raise issues with outsiders than they are with internal trainers or consultants.

Remember, though, that new approaches are sometimes threatening. Everyone's neck is on the line these days, and managers don't like to take risks that will stretch theirs. Too many people, up and down the corporate ladder, notice. Many managers take the easy route and stay with the tried and true, no matter how tired or even nonproductive that approach has become. This reflects an insecurity that employees pick up on, even if you yourself don't. But it's critical to take risks now and again, to explore new ways of doing things. Familiarity breeds repetition, which soon becomes complacency and stagnation. No company, no matter what its products or services, can thrive (or even survive) without fresh ideas.

Creative Jobs

Although you can find them in just about any job, creative people tend to gravitate toward creative jobs—work that requires them to come up with new processes or products. These jobs are often in fields such as advertising, marketing, electronic media, publishing, design, and architecture. You might define these people as writers, artists, or programmers, or they might have a combination of talents that defies definition.

Creative people tend to make managers a little nervous—it's hard to tell sometimes whether they're working or goofing off, and they seem a bit, well, unleashed. Creative types can often be characterized as follows:

- They appear to have little regard for authority, rules, structure, and routine, viewing these as elements of the work world that do not apply to them.
- They establish surroundings within their work environments that support and feed their imaginations.
- They have unorthodox or eccentric methods for stimulating their productivity.
- They appear disorganized and to "fly by the seat of their pants" when giving presentations.
- They find humor in, and even make fun of, just about everything (and might not understand why others don't or why others may find these "funnies" offensive).
- They work in spurts of intensity that can last for hours, days, or even weeks, then go into a "down" phase, when they appear to accomplish very little.
- They arrive late or even fail to show up for staff or other general meetings that don't apply directly to their projects.

FACT

According to U.S. Bureau of Labor (BLS) figures, nearly 100 million Americans—70 percent of the workforce—work in jobs that provide services. BLS projects that another 19 million workers will join the service sector by 2008, bringing the level of service jobs to 75 percent.

People in creative professions require tremendous flexibility in management terms. Emotion, not logic, rules the creative process. The result is often behavior that goes beyond what others might consider conventional business behavior. The office of a creative person might look more like a preschool classroom or a toy store than a workstation. Creative types also need to be able to shut themselves away, to get away from the structure of rules and decorum, to give their ideas space and time to evolve.

Companies or departments that rely on creative people, such as advertising agencies or media companies, often use brainstorming sessions that to the uninitiated (or those who require structure) might appear to be wild free-for-alls. People laugh, yell, throw things, draw pictures, and tell jokes as they toss about ideas. Political correctness stays in the hall; there's plenty of opportunity later to run the censor filters. The entire mission is to let brains wander freely through the vast seed bins of ideas until some start to sprout.

Appearances Are Deceiving

Despite appearances to the contrary, most creative people are highly organized. It's just that the organization doesn't necessarily take the form of neatly labeled files and calendars that record meetings and commitments—the standard trappings of structure. Those "seat of the pants" presentations often reflect not lack of preparation but instead a deeply assimilated knowledge of the topic acquired through intense and often extended research or observation—sometimes with a dash of intuition thrown in. This less tangible organization can have the appearance of chaos, but it's not. For the creative individual, it's as close to logical as it gets.

Many companies in creative businesses have lounge areas with pool tables, coffee bars, video games, bean bag chairs, and other diversions to get people relaxed and thinking. Such an atmosphere creates an oasis from the reality of business (which is of course why the creative professionals are employed in the first place). Once ideas take on viable shapes, creative types retreat into the cocoons of their offices. They re-emerge when they've created something from those shapes that they're ready to share with others or that now needs feedback.

Not surprisingly, too much structure stifles creativity. As a manager, this can be a difficult balancing act for you. On the one hand you have a creative genius (or even a team of creative geniuses) whose ideas generate most of the products that make your company successful. On the other hand, you have the company, which wants to make sure the time it pays for is productive. Perhaps you are also responsible for managing other people whose work is more traditional and who might believe that anyone who's having so much fun at work isn't working hard enough.

The Need for Structure

Not all people, no matter how creative, function well in an environment with minimal structure. Some people don't know how to channel their energy into productive tasks with measurable outcomes. Other people crave—and excel under—close and specific direction. And occasionally you'll encounter a person who must have external structure because without it he or she simply won't do any work at all.

Employees who need a lot of structure need a manager who is willing to be more hands-on. Structured people tend to have the following characteristics:

- They are often tidy and organized. Their desks and workspaces are neat and functional. Nearly anyone could step into a structured person's environment and find a file or project.
- They arrive and leave on time, and at the same time every day. If they are early, which many tend to be, they are consistently early.
- They follow obvious routines. Other employees almost always know where they are and what they are doing, just by knowing what time or day it is.
- They know what work is due and where in the process the work is, and they deliver on time unless circumstances beyond their control intervene.
- They handle complex projects by breaking them into smaller, logical steps. Structured people often keep status and progress logs of their projects.
- They appear disciplined and goal-oriented.
- They seldom knowingly break rules, and they might take offense with those who do.

Every company, regardless of its products and services, requires a certain amount of structure. Some functions and departments, such as accounting, are bound to established procedures for conducting their work. People who work in these areas generally (but not always) have work styles and personalities that are compatible with this level of structure. Other functions and departments require structure that supports project timelines and productivity targets. Such structure might require you to precisely establish priorities, goals, and tasks.

Structured Jobs

The backbone of structure is clear communication. Employees need to know what they are expected to do and by when. What is more important? What is less important? What happens when tasks compete for people, time, and resources? Some people are good at establishing priorities, while others struggle. Sometimes employees have trouble prioritizing because they are unfamiliar with the department, the company, or the industry. They have no context for the work they do, so they don't know what to tackle first. *Everything* becomes critical in such an environment, and as a consequence what gets completed is often frustratingly trivial. The important stuff gets left undone or missed completely.

ALERT!

A key challenge for a manager whose personal work style is structured is letting go to let others find their own way—but let go you must. Employees will rebel if they feel you have a "my way or no way" approach. Rebellion against excessive structure often takes the form of passive-aggressive behavior such as remaining engaged in a task without answering a ringing phone.

As a manager, your role is to help employees who need structure establish priorities and processes to support them. Once the base structure of priorities is in place, most employees can then build additional structure around those priorities. Generally it's most effective to meet with employees one-on-one, so you can gauge just how much structure each employee needs.

Start by laying out specific tasks and the small goals that must be accomplished by the end of the day. Be sure the employee has the necessary tools to complete the tasks and knows how to use them. Next, identify common problems that might arise, and establish a procedure for dealing with them. Some employees find it useful to have a chart or diagram that outlines priorities and procedures, while others might just take notes.

Schedule a follow-up meeting with the employee to discuss how he or she approached the tasks and what actually got finished. Communication about expectations, and what worked and didn't work, is critical here. Establish procedures for identifying and addressing emergencies and unexpected changes in priorities. At first, this might mean having the employee come to you whenever work deviates from the planned schedule. As the employee becomes more skilled in structuring and adjusting priorities, the procedures might shift to general guidelines for when to contact you and when to proceed without assistance.

ESSENTIAL

Be willing to revise and adapt. People grow and needs change, and it's essential to keep up with both. What an employee self-monitors and what you monitor should evolve over time so that you as manager play a less direct role in sculpting the employee's daily activities.

Over time, and as the employee's comfort with the structure progresses, designate daily tasks as part of the employee's routine, with the employee responsible for making them part of the work week with less monitoring from you. Schedule brief but regular meetings or other processes to provide feedback and reinforcement. You might stop by the person's desk every Tuesday at 3 P.M., have employees generate daily or weekly progress reports, or hold staff meetings.

Work Overload

Sometimes an employee's apparent inability to complete job tasks reflects an overwhelming workload rather than a structure problem. In such situations, you might need to reassign job tasks to lighten the load. This could mean realigning work responsibilities among your current employees, hiring temporary employees to help out, or creating new positions to accommodate a growing workload.

Each employee has a slightly different need for structure. It's important for you as the manager to remain in close contact with all employees so you can adjust various elements of structure to support their highest levels of productivity. Asking each employee how he or she feels is the most effective way to structure the workday. By tailoring structure to each of your employees, you help them buy into the process. They feel an investment in it because they helped create it.

Workaholic: Corporate Culture or Individual Personality?

How many hours do your employees put in each week? The standard forty, or more? People who are committed to their professions or who enjoy what they do are willing to spend more than the required number of hours at work. People who are overburdened feel compelled to stay late, even though they know the attempt to catch up will ultimately be futile. An occasional need for extra time and effort is certainly not unreasonable. But the employees who are the first to arrive and the last to leave, day in and day out, are headed for burnout. They are the ones who are addicted to their jobs, by choice or by default. And this, like all addictions, will eventually turn destructive.

You Set the Example

When employees are at work too long, they burn out and then they resent their jobs and other employees, as well as their managers, who either haven't rewarded them as much as they thought they deserved or don't seem to work as hard. This kind of commitment isn't dedication—it's lunacy. Are you setting the example? Then stop! Right now, today. Take out a piece of paper and write, "Today I will leave work at 5 P.M." Sign it. There—it's a contract. Be gone at five, period. Pack your briefcase and head out the door. Let your employees see you leaving.

FACT

In a recent Gallup poll, 44 percent of those surveyed considered themselves workaholics, to the extent that work activities interfered with or prevented a life beyond their job. More than half of those who worked full time said they put in more than forty hours a week; the average number of hours worked was forty-six.

It is important for you to set the example you want your employees to follow. If you are a workaholic, most of them will be, too. It's fine if you don't have a life beyond work—that's your choice. But don't establish the expectation that your employees can't have personal lives. They might go along with you for a while, but eventually they'll rebel or burn out. Neither is pleasant.

Helping a Workaholic Employee

Do you have an employee who regularly burns the midnight oil? It's time to assess the reasons and get ready to find a comfortable way to discuss it with the employee. Make some observations and ask yourself a few questions to get to the bottom of the situation:

- Why is the person working so many hours? Does this person have too much work, use his or her time during regular work hours inefficiently, or not want to go home?
- If there are work-based problems, try to identify viable solutions. If the workload is too intense, how can you lighten it? If the employee has trouble prioritizing, what can you do to help?
- Be supportive and nonjudgmental, yet firm. Make it clear that while you appreciate and respect such dedication, no one expects anyone to stay at work all the time.
- Express your concern that the person might burn out, leaving you in dire need of the skills and talents only he or she can provide. What happens then? Neither the employee nor the company comes out ahead.

While the personal lives of your employees are none of your business, it is your responsibility to be sure they have the freedom to pursue them. No one should feel that a job owns any employee (not even you).

Running in the Wrong Direction

Some people are just not good fits for the jobs they hold, which raises a number of issues for both employees and managers. As a manager, you hope that good hiring practices and regular performance evaluations catch these situations before they become problems, but you also know that even in the most ideal circumstances things sometimes don't work out.

The employee might have misunderstood the job's actual responsibilities; sometimes condensing a job description into 100 words or less to fit in a help-wanted ad or position posting leaves out vital details that no one detects during the interview process. Sometimes an employee is desperate to have a job and convinces himself that this is the perfect one.

Managers can also find themselves wanting to hire someone for reasons other than compatibility with the job; perhaps the job has been vacant for a long time, or the person strikes the right note on the personality scale and has the desired skills, even though there are signals that he or she is really overqualified or views the job as a stepping stone to more interesting positions. Sometimes the result is an employee has the skills the company needs but a work style that's not compatible. Then the manager has to decide whether those skills are needed enough to accommodate the person who has them—and how to do that.

As a manager, it's up to you to be sure you—and your department and company—are doing everything possible to help an employee be successful. It's your responsibility to do all of the following:

- Provide adequate and appropriate resources, including workspace and equipment.
- Clearly articulate goals and priorities—for the employee, for the work group, and for the company. Put them in writing, so you each have a copy.

- Ensure that the job tasks are consistent with the job advertisement (and vice versa). The best time to establish that you are all on the same page is during the interview. Then affirm understandings and expectations within the first few days of employment.
- Give clear instructions when tasks must be performed or completed in a certain way or by a specific time, and monitor workloads to be sure employees are working to capacity but are not overwhelmed.
- Communicate clearly and regularly with all employees to see how a new employee fits into the work group.
- Carefully document problems that you notice or that other employees bring to you, and meet with the employee as soon as you can clearly define that there are problems.
- Work collaboratively with the employee, and with coworkers if appropriate, to find mutually agreeable solutions.

ESSENTIAL

Someone who excels at innovation is not likely to do well at maintenance. Someone who thrives on detail isn't likely to do well conceptualizing. Your role as manager is to identify the work styles among the people who report to you and encourage processes that support those work styles in ways that balance individual strengths with department needs.

In some situations, you'll find ways to work things out to keep a valued employee on your team. In other situations, the challenges will be insurmountable and you'll have no choice but to let the employee go. If you have done all you can do to give the employee the best possible chance to succeed (including discussing the situation with your superiors as well as your HR department), then you truly have done all you can do.

The Influences of Your Work Style

Although it's important for you to understand the different work styles of your employees so you can support them, it's also critical for you to understand your own work style. Are you creative? Structured? Wedded to your job? Resentful of the time your job keeps you from other activities? If you're not sure, look around you. What do you see in your employees? While each person has a unique work style, like attracts like. People tend to be drawn to people who are like them, which is as true in the workplace as anywhere else. All other qualifications being equal, you're more likely to hire someone you feel has something in common with you than someone who is clearly your opposite.

ALERT!

You might be a creative free spirit overseeing the work of people who prefer structure, not well-suited for the level of detail managing these employees requires—or the reverse. Be honest with yourself about your work style and your expectations. If you are not a good fit for your managerial duties or are in over your head, you and your employees will suffer. Pursue options that better match your abilities.

Sometimes remaining fair across work styles means separating out the accomplishments, both real and potential, of employees from your own values and standards. You might be pretty loose when it comes to the structure of your workday, content to work late all week and then take Friday afternoon off. Yet you might have employees who insist on leaving right at the stroke of five, regardless of what activity engages them when the workday officially ends.

As frustrating as this may be within the context of your work style, it's important to shift your perceptions into the employee's work style. If this person is incredibly productive during the workday, then it's only fair for you to acknowledge this. You can't expect your employees to behave like you do, or only reward them when they do. Fairness also means being able to respect and reward people for what and who they are, not what you want them to be.

Your personal work style forms the platform from which you accommodate other work styles. Yes, it's a bias. But it's where we all start. The key to being successful as a manager is to move beyond square one. Once you understand what your work style is, it's easier to understand differing work styles. The only way to appreciate differences is to understand them. Then you can truly manage by building on people's strengths and minimizing their weaknesses. And you can learn from your employees, so you too can grow and evolve.

Chapter 10
Work Group Dynamics

Some groups come together or "click" from the first time their members meet, while others labor for months or longer to be something other than separate and competing personalities. Creating an effective work group is part planning and part luck. Just as mixing chemicals produces different results depending on the substances and their quantities, combining personalities and work styles results in varied effects. Indeed, we often talk about the "chemistry" among group members as critical to the group's success. Changing just one member often alters the group far beyond that one member's role and responsibilities.

Effective Teamwork

A work group exists because a company hires a number of people to perform specific tasks and jobs. A team develops when those people work together in ways that enhance their efficiency and productivity. A team is a complex organism that exists as an entity in its own right and also as a collection of the individuals that comprise it. Individual personalities and work styles significantly influence the team's collective identity. The most effective teams contain complementary, not necessarily similar, personalities and work styles. In such a setting, the whole truly becomes more than the sum of its parts: a team. Each person's strengths overlap the others' weaknesses.

Sometimes teams form around job responsibilities. Certain people in marketing, like the PR group, are a natural team, as is the production control or quality control group in manufacturing. Teams also form that slice across responsibilities. For example, managers can pull together people from different jobs or departments to look at morale issues, evaluate new technologies, or help the department get ready to implement a new procedure or methodology. Such teams get people interacting in new ways by forming relationships that cut across the usual functional boundaries, especially when those boundaries also separate groups that compete with each other in some way. And when managers constantly bring different people together on various teams, employees learn to adapt better to change because they have to quickly become cohesive and then accomplish something.

Teams develop not only a way of operating, but also of interacting. A culture forms that establishes the team's expectations and standards. Each team member has a role; this defines and distributes responsibility. In some teams, one person surfaces as the leader, often emerging naturally, although sometimes the manager designates the leader. In other teams, the members share leadership roles and responsibilities. While shared leadership is generally more effective, much depends on the team itself—its goals and purpose as well as the personalities and work styles of its members.

Where Do You Fit In?

As the work group's manager, shouldn't you be the team's leader? Well, yes and no. You are the leader in that you're the one with the authority to make decisions, and usually the one held accountable for the group's actions, performance, and productivity. But in most situations, the manager isn't a team member. It's nearly impossible to be a team member and an authority figure concurrently. Teams function most effectively when there is a relatively even distribution of power so each team member feels he or she is making an equitable contribution. As manager, it's your role to stay on the periphery. It's your job to be sure everyone knows his or her role and responsibilities, and the roles of other members. And you'll need to be available to serve as facilitator, mediator, teacher, mentor, cheerleader, coach, and parent—whatever the group needs.

FACT

Generally, strong individual productivity generates strong group performance. When each member is pulling his or her load, the work gets done. Also, people feel that their contributions are both valued and valuable. Even with one or two weak members, most groups can maintain strong productivity. But the more pronounced the disparities in workload and contribution, the less satisfied all group members become—and then the group's performance suffers even though some individuals within the group are outstanding producers.

Guiding the Team

When teams are working, there is nothing more exciting. But even teams that seem to come together well on their own need guidance and occasionally intervention to help them grow and develop. It's a balancing act that requires constant attention and adjustment. Just remember that this is about the team, not about you.

Acme Industries was a mega-corporation. Employees often joked that it was like its own little city; the corporate campus covered several square miles and included a day-care center, health clinic, fitness center, several cafeterias, and even a private security force that patrolled the grounds and facilities. There were many rules and restrictions—some company-wide, others specific to particular divisions, departments, or work groups.

Sheila was the education department's manager. Her department was both a microcosm of and a haven from the company's bureaucracy. On the one hand, Sheila had to enforce corporate rules and policies as well as keep the department on track with corporate goals and objectives. Daily policies such as leave time and working hours had to be consistent with the company's procedures.

Sheila recognized that it was important for people to feel that they had some control over their work and work environment. Although the corporation was enormous and complex, her department could succeed in meeting its goals only when its members could feel that they were more than just work units. Sheila encouraged both independence and teamwork among her employees, and gave them the latitude this balance required. Employees had to follow the company rules, but they could bend them on occasion to fit the needs of their assignments and projects. Team members could work off campus, for example, or order in lunch when work tasks became intense. The department was, in many ways, a haven from the rigid corporate culture.

Employees formed tight working relationships with one another. They had a high level of trust and a strong sense of belonging. They knew Sheila believed in their abilities to handle complex training projects as well as to resolve challenges that might arise within the group. And they knew Sheila was available to them when they needed her—to help with problem solving, to commiserate when stress levels escalated, to be a sounding board for new ideas. As a result, the department excelled in meeting its goals as well as helping the corporation to meet its goals. Absenteeism and turnover were extraordinarily low, and the department maintained a training schedule that would have swamped a less effective team. Sheila praised her department's efforts and contributions, both within the department and in her meetings and contacts with others in the company—her superiors as well as her peers. Her employees knew she, and by extension the company, valued them.

Traits of an Effective Team

Effective teams share certain characteristics. First, they have a clear sense of mission or purpose and clear goals. To be productive, team members need to know why they're working. When a work team knows its mission or purpose (reason for existing) and its goals (desired accomplishments), its members are more likely to focus on activities that move the group closer to completion—of tasks, of projects, of products or services.

QUESTION?

Do team members have to like each other to be effective?
As much as we'd like to think professionalism transcends petty matters like popularity, the reality is that people who like each other get along better. Certainly a team whose members provide complementary skills can function competently and even productively without friendship to bond them. But when team members consider themselves friends as well as colleagues, they have a heightened investment in the team's activities.

Second, effective teams foster mutual respect and support. It's hard to be innovative when you're never sure how others will react to your ideas. In effective teams, members know that even if coworkers disagree, they will focus their objections on the idea, not on the person presenting it. Each member feels he or she has the fundamental right to a level of trust that precludes backstabbing, gossip, and other negative behaviors. Members instead provide positive encouragement and work cooperatively to achieve common goals.

Effective teams demonstrate open communication. Team members are comfortable sharing ideas and concerns with each other as well as with you. Communication happens on numerous levels, from casual chitchat to structured meetings. While each level has its protocols and norms, openness is an essential foundation. Inherent in such communication is the ability to resolve disagreements, conflicts, and problems. No group (no matter how small, tight-knit, or productive) gets along all the time. The ability of team members to work through their differences to renewed understanding and cooperation is crucial to the group's success. There will be squalls and occasionally storms, but conflict is a normal part of human interaction. The most effective groups have processes in place for airing grievances and working out problems.

Lastly, effective teams receive appropriate external support. Even the most self-sufficient, effective work teams can't function in a vacuum. They need you and your superiors (often viewed collectively as "the company"), and sometimes other departments or work groups, to provide the resources required to achieve their goals. Team members need the proper equipment and supplies, an appropriate workspace, adequate administrative support, and suitable environmental amenities (such as lighting and temperature control). It's your role as manager to be sure all of these elements are in place.

System Versus People Problems

Problems within a team can result from personal issues, system issues, or both. Sometimes the source of the problem is obvious. The design team can't complete the final drawings because the software update they need to install first is backordered from the manufacturer. The customer call center can't improve call wait times and dropped calls because there are too few lines to handle the volume of incoming calls. The production department is ready to roll, but the templates were cut wrong and the manager had to send them back to the supplier. These are clearly system problems. The people are ready and eager to do what needs to be done, but they don't have what they need to move forward.

Sometimes the part of the system that's not functioning optimally is its people. Personal issues may arise from personality conflicts or performance problems. Employees may not understand their job responsibilities, or they may not like them and so attempt to pass them off or simply not do them. People have personalities, and personalities sometimes rub the wrong way. Counterproductive behaviors can destroy even the strongest teams, sometimes in a surprising manner.

Sometimes people simply don't get along with each other. Though we like to believe that adults can put aside their differences to work toward common goals, this doesn't always happen. The challenge is to isolate the personalities that are clashing—not always as easy as it sounds—so they can try to work out their differences. In other situations, people might get along fine (or even too well) but lack the skills or the competence to do the job.

In general, ruling out system problems points the finger at people problems. Sometimes it's difficult to tell where the lines are drawn. In fact, it might be a combination of the two that is causing issues. Consider the following example.

Wacky Widget's customer call center had a telephone tree that routed calls, no matter what time of the day or night, to an extension where a "live body" could answer the phone. The sophisticated switching circuitry relied on computerized records that identified employees as they signed onto their computer terminals. The telephone tree identified them as "live" and routed calls according to a priority structure based on job function.

For months, the customer service desk fielded complaints about calls not being answered between 8 A.M. and 11 A.M. on Tuesdays and Thursdays. Technicians checked all the wiring, circuits, and connections. Systems analysts checked all the computer algorithms to verify personnel routings. Finally a consultant from the telephone company helped set up a process for tracing call paths. This narrowed the problem to a phone in the middle of the call-forwarding sequence. Although technicians were unable to find any equipment problems in the office or with the phone, they replaced wiring and installed a new telephone that tracked all calls that rang to it, whether or not they were answered.

Astonishingly, the phone logged no call activity on Tuesday and Thursday mornings, even though the customer service desk continued to receive complaints. So a technician decided to sit in the office and observe. After an hour or so of sitting in silence, the technician asked the employee working in the office if the phone was always so quiet. "Of course!" he said. "I unplug it as soon as I sign in, so I can work without interruptions."

The rest of the story quickly unfolded. The employee was a temporary filling in for another employee who was on maternity leave. Although he had his own log-on ID, the computer station itself was registered to the employee who usually worked there. So when the temporary employee logged onto the computer, the telephone tree routed calls through the office's number because the computer showed it as manned. But the temp using the office was doing special assignments, not filling in for the employee who was on leave. He worked in three different offices during the course of a week, but this was the only one with a direct-ring phone. So he did what he thought made sense to keep calls that he couldn't handle from interrupting his work: He unplugged the phone.

So, is this a system problem or a people problem? The answer, unfortunately, is both.

When Personalities Collide

Friendship and liking one another at work are important to many people. So important, in fact, that some will take or leave jobs on the basis of the other people who work there. You probably know who these people are in your workplace, and as a manager you have likely been called upon to mediate their problems with coworkers. These employees need to get along with their coworkers; it's as much a part of their personalities as of their work styles. There's nothing wrong with this, as long as it meets their needs (and doesn't interfere with productivity, theirs or yours).

You can work with people you don't particularly like and still be happy in your job. It's unrealistic to expect you'll like everyone in the group. The more friends and interests you have outside work, the easier it is to work with people you don't consider to be your friends.

Whether employees like each other or not, it's still important for them to be able to work together or to share a project. This can be a challenge (which could be the understatement of the year!). The most effective way for a manager to bring people together in collaboration and cooperation is to stay focused on the job and its tasks—what the job requires and how well the employees do or don't complete those tasks. This helps them—and you—tolerate differences in personality. Employees expect managers to "protect" them, to watch out for their interests and to be involved enough to understand the personalities in the group and put protections in place to assure that equality is maintained. When this doesn't happen, employees grow resentful and frustrated. Morale slides, taking productivity with it. Sometimes the issues that drive employees away seem minor, yet they reflect an underlying problem with trust and betrayal.

ALERT!

Putting people on project teams to force them to cooperate can backfire. Don't jeopardize other team relationships and the integrity of the project by trying to engineer the impossible.

Many managers do not want to involve themselves in issues such as these because they are uncomfortable with feelings and emotions and don't like conflict. But failing to become involved can cause tension that disrupts teamwork and productivity. Employees feel their managers don't respect them when they fail to look out for their interests (it's that parent hat again). You can be proactive, and avoid conflict, by building in a structure that helps employees work together.

Resolving Conflicts

The workplace forces people into relationships with each other that otherwise might not exist, and while they often get along just fine, sometimes there are problems. It's important for you, the manager, to always have your finger on the pulse of your team so you'll immediately know when things are out of sorts.

Once a situation escalates, it can be too late to salvage the group, at least in terms of restoring it to its previous level of collaboration and productivity.

Depending on the nature of the problem, you might meet first with the entire team or with members individually. Take action as soon as you figure out what's going on. Don't wait for the right time—the right time is now. Intervene with individuals who seem to be having personal or individual performance problems. It's usually also a good idea to meet with the group to talk about the problem in general—its nature, how it's being addressed, when you expect to see things change, what changes you expect to see, and what role, if any, other group members have in resolving it. Avoid naming individuals unless there is no other way to talk about the situation. If you must use names, be sure to focus on behaviors and events, not the people.

E ALERT!

It's not enough to peek in at people a few times during the day to see if things look all right. You need to consistently monitor both output and attitudes. If there are problems with either, deal with the situation right away. Such interventions are not always comfortable, but they are essential.

Put on your parent, mediator, and cheerleader hats—it's time to become a multiple personality. You need to take decisive action and at the same time help group members see each other's perspectives. Sometimes the involved member will have to transfer to another department or leave the company entirely. You might need to introduce a new communications process to force employees in complementary but competitive positions to communicate more effectively. The team might need to establish a new approval process to ensure that members know about, and have the opportunity to discuss, product or service promises before anyone makes them. And when the problem is system-based, you must be willing to stick your neck out by advocating for employees. These responses build teams and create loyalty, among group members as well as toward you (and sometimes even the company). Who wouldn't want to go the extra mile for a manager who at least tries to go the extra mile for them?

Chapter 11

Getting the Work Done

You're the manager. Now it's your job not only to do your own work but to make sure others do theirs. You must integrate the functions of your department with the needs and goals of your company. You must be both motivator and taskmaster. When things go wrong, all eyes turn to you. You may need to identify and resolve performance issues and problems. Remember the exhilaration you felt when you first got your job? Good! It will cushion the bumps of the road.

A Comfortable Workplace

There's no doubt about it—the workplace's physical and social environments are key factors in whether employees are satisfied and content or dissatisfied and stressed. With so much attention focused on trimming costs to hold down prices, many companies find themselves struggling to define what's essential and what's extravagant. It's a shifting line. Often, creature comforts ebb and flow with the economy. When times are good, companies lease or build enough space to accommodate niceties such as employee lounges, exercise rooms, recreation areas, and snack counters. When the economy tightens, the employee lounge might become cubicle heaven (or hell, depending on your perspective) so the company can consolidate its employee force and lease space to other businesses. When people are happy to just be employed, they don't complain about not having free popcorn or bottled water.

Swings in formality also affect the workplace environment. In the 1980s, most large companies were very formal. They had stringent, almost uniform-like dress codes that even stipulated shoe styles, grooming standards, and whether men could wear facial hair (usually not). People weren't allowed to have personal items displayed in their cubicles or work areas, and they couldn't eat or drink at their desks. The philosophy behind this was that such structure kept the employees and the workplace focused on work. Without distractions, management gurus of the time believed, people would be more efficient and productive. Clients and customers could feel that anyone within a company could provide identical service.

Twenty-some years later, "open market" offices are the trend, with large rooms filled with desks or sometimes with three-sided cubicles. Business gurus now believe that people are most efficient and productive when companies encourage individual talents and abilities. Most experts agree that it's important for employees to be able to personalize their offices, to feel comfortable, and to bring some sense of home, or their personalities, into the office. This gives people a sense of control.

Psychological comfort is important as well. Managers need to be willing to look at the emotional and the psychological dynamics in their departments. They need to acknowledge that people have feelings, and they have to be able to talk about feelings. They also have to be able to both support and confront so they can maintain an environment where people can be productive and grow. Although "therapist" is not a hat managers should wear, they do need to look for symptoms of discord and dysfunction so they can take steps to minimize the impact before it gets out of hand.

It is important to allow some flexibility to allow for differences in personal style as well as scheduling start and end times, lunch breaks, and other activities. Unless there are practical reasons for everyone to follow the same time structure, the work environment is most functional when it offers some flexibility, some sense of individual expression, and some sense of control. When people have too many rules, they either look for ways to break them or they leave.

This often means encouraging employees to get enough rest and to take breaks and vacations to recharge and reinvigorate their bodies and their spirits. Most companies should be able to permit employees to occasionally take an afternoon off or to come in late after working late the night before. Although the way employees use benefits such as vacation time is really up to them, managers should encourage every employee to take some extended time off. This is good for the employee, and it's good for the company. Not even a machine can keep running without occasional downtime.

Psychological comfort also entails taking an interest in each employee's life beyond work. Take the time to understand each employee as a unique individual, and develop a way to appreciate them for who and what they really are. Share your interests with employees so they can see that you, too, have a human side. You need to be a resource for your employees when they need to express concerns and receive guidance; this happens only when employees perceive you as a person who cares about them and their needs. In the end, it's this human touch that creates an environment where the real tasks—getting the work done—can be carried out.

Realistic Goals

How do you determine whether someone is putting an appropriate level of thought or creativity into the job? And with people working in teams, how do you figure out what each person should be doing? Every job has specific, core tasks as well as general responsibilities. Most jobs require interactions among employees to generate the products or services that are the company's reason for existing. Though the job description specifies such functions, it is your role as manager to establish the criteria for completing them. Such criteria vary widely among jobs but often include project timelines, production schedules, and unit of completion goals.

Managers often have high expectations for their employees, and they become frustrated, disappointed, and angry when employees fail to live up to those expectations. That's because these expectations are as much about the manager as they are about the employee. When your employees excel, you look good, too. Employees also often feel grateful to their managers for providing opportunities and encouragement. All of this strokes the manager's ego. When employees fail to meet expectations, managers feel hurt and let down.

ESSENTIAL

In some companies, it might be useful to divide the department or team into groups, each of which tackles a specific company goal, department goal, or job responsibility. If the process represents a major overhaul, consider starting with a task force that comes up with the initial take on what the standards should be.

Sometimes you might identify too closely with an employee. Perhaps the employee reminds you of yourself in an earlier stage of your career or is at risk of going down a path that you believe will be a mistake. You want this person to do well or even better than you have done. So you invest in this person—you provide opportunities, recognition, support, and encouragement. You may have high expectations for comparable investments in return, such as the willingness to arrive early and stay late to meet deadlines or accommodate a heavy workload. Such expectations are often unrealistic and become distortions. You might interpret an employee's unwillingness to work day and night as an attack on your values and authority rather than seeing it for what it is—an infringement on the employee's life beyond work.

It's not always easy to see that you're doing this, and it's even harder to stop when you make the recognition. Ask yourself: Is this about them or me? Be honest. It's not always a bad thing for your expectations to be about you even when they involve others, but it is essential for you to know when this is the case.

Establish boundaries, within the framework of specific job requirements, around your expectations. Performance evaluation standards and job descriptions, as much as they may feel intrusive and bureaucratic, can help save you from yourself. When problems do arise, take two steps back to identify them clearly. Are you angry because the employee failed to complete an assignment, and now others can't complete theirs? Or are you upset because you now you can't showcase the project at this afternoon's staff meeting as you had planned? Put your effort into addressing the real problem.

Employee Participation

People are most likely to accept and comply with performance standards if they have a role in establishing them. In many companies and industries, certain standards are carved in stone—set by regulation or outside authority, or inherent in the work. Hospitals, colleges, universities, and other kinds of organizations are subject to quality expectations established by accrediting bodies. Without meeting these, they cannot remain in business. Standards that apply to the organization trickle down through all levels, becoming imbedded in job descriptions as well as performance evaluation procedures. Within these standards, there may or may not be room for variation, depending on the industry.

Even when it appears that there is little latitude for employee participation, there are usually small areas open to influence. For example, a hospital must require employees in patient care areas to wear certain clothing and protective aids to safeguard them against exposure to infectious diseases. Allowing employees to choose clothing in various colors, patterns, and designs gives them a dress code they can live with because they developed it.

Implementation and Adjustment

There's more to meeting performance standards than personal satisfaction. Salaries, as well as any bonuses, generally depend on how employees meet the performance standards. Some companies assign a percentage value to each standard. While sending follow-up notes might be worth just 2 percent, this function is essential to client satisfaction which, in turn, might be worth 25 percent of the total points. This kind of a system gives weighted importance to key functions, yet makes all activities essential to the whole.

ALERT!

Whatever system your department or company uses to set performance standards, as manager it's your job to make it work. If employees suspect that their participation has been an exercise in futility, it's all over for collaboration and teamwork. This is an invitation to frustration, disappointment, and office politics.

Support Individual Growth

Employees are not at jobs simply because they have nothing to do all day or because they want to save the world. They want to grow or at least to make more money. And they want you, their manager, to show them how they can do this. Any performance evaluation process should include short- and long-term personal goals. These goals, perhaps more so than department and company goals, change and evolve. For each employee, consider the following questions:

- What steps does the employee need to take to grow in the job and the department?
- What reward can the employee expect for achieving such growth?

- Where can the employee expect to go next in his or her career?
- What are the employee's prospects for a few years down the road?

Of course, it's essential to have the employee participate in formulating personal goals, since manager and employee will need to agree to these goals. It's also important for you to help employees identify their strengths, where those strengths can take them, and how they might change or improve their options by taking certain training courses or learning special skills. (Are you wearing your mentor hat?) If you can't help an employee honestly define his or her next career goal, you're showing the employee a brick wall.

Performance standards, while somewhat bureaucratic are also a way of ensuring both the perception and practice of fair treatment—which is something managers and employees alike desire.

With employees whose abilities shine, this is an easy as well as enjoyable part of your job. It's exciting to watch people grow and develop and reach their potential. But some people choose career objectives that their skills and abilities don't support. As a mentor, you can help such employees find paths that are better aligned with their talents—or find ways for them to successfully pursue the directions that interest them.

Managing Manipulation

Not all is as smooth as the workflow you design. People are dynamic, always thinking and feeling something different. They may disagree with the approach you've put in place, even when they were part of developing it. Some don't intend to be disruptive; they've learned counterproductive habits through the years that are hard to change. But just as you must shape, direct, and nudge the flow of work, you need to accommodate and remedy the challenges the behaviors of others can bring to bear.

Manipulation is one such challenge. When employees try to wiggle out of assignments, the work group's productivity is disrupted. Most manipulators learn their behavior patterns early in life, and they receive reinforcement each time they use them with success. They tend to shift into manipulator mode when conventional efforts fail to produce the desired results. Manipulative behaviors target people rather than processes and present generalities rather than specifics. They may include threats, demands, insults, and efforts to make you feel guilty. Manipulation may also take the form of compliments, kindnesses, treats, and other attempts to be ingratiating.

ALERT!

Anger is sometimes a presentation of manipulation. Most of are so uncomfortable around anger that we'll do just about anything to stop it. Manipulators know this, so anger often becomes a staple in their behavior arsenals. Like other manipulative behaviors, anger works only as long as other people let it.

It is important to confront manipulation with facts and specifics. Give the person a fair opportunity to present a specific concern or complaint. Always, never, everyone, no one—these are all terms of generality. If you can't put a finger on it, you can't do much to fix it. Separate the facts of the concern from emotions and intent so you can examine them in context. Be detailed and tangible. Then, break issues down into manageable components. Throughout history, armies have used this "divide and conquer" tactic with great success, and it will work for you, too. If you can engage the employee in the process of identifying components, suddenly the two of you will be on the same side.

Keep your emotional responses in check. If the employee is in tears, hand over a tissue box—without comment. If the employee is yelling, wait for the noise to stop and then speak softly so the person must remain quiet to hear you. If the employee is using an audience of other employees for support, ask the employee to come to your office or give the other employees a coffee break.

FACT

According to the U.S. Bureau of Labor Statistics, an employee's salary represents about three-fourths of the company's direct compensation costs for having the employee on staff. Benefits (such as insurance, paid time off, and retirement plans) account for the remainder.

If your efforts to focus on processes and solutions fail to influence the employee's behavior, summarize your response in a single sentence and repeat it each time the employee broaches a new tactic. Keep the tone of your voice even, firm, and friendly—not easy, as master manipulators will see what you're doing and try to break your resolve. Think of a broken record and let your tone and the message just keep repeating.

Job Description Boundaries

Sometimes employees feel that all do is repeat the same tasks over and over again. They want a break from what has become tedium. They might want to branch out into new territory, but they are afraid to or feel they can't because their existing job descriptions confine them. For others, the desire for change is really a form of manipulation that successfully gets them out of what they don't want to do.

Joan's official job was to collect, analyze, and report customer service complaint data. She entered information from customer comment cards into a relational database, then once a month she generated a series of inquiries, summations, and reports. All departments in her company used the information Joan provided to identify problem areas and design solutions that would improve customer service. Joan's manager presented the monthly reports at the executive staff meeting; one month, she could not answer the questions top managers had about the data and what it indicated. It wasn't her area of expertise. So she asked Joan to attend the next executive staff meeting to present the reports herself. "No way!" Joan said. "That's not in my job description!"

Now before you charge what you see as a red flag, take a deep breath. What is Joan actually saying? That she feels put upon, or uncomfortable? It often requires an extended dialogue to figure out the meaning behind the negative response. In some circumstances, this is the ultimate passive-aggressive behavior from an employee who uses "no" as the ultimate weapon in the battle for power. In other situations, it's an overwhelmed employee's cry for help, a last-ditch effort to stem the flow of work before it completely swamps the boat.

ESSENTIAL

Most employees welcome the opportunity to stretch beyond the confines of their routine tasks, as long as they don't feel that the real motivation is to take advantage of them somehow. Whenever possible, present additional tasks as optional and in such a way that employees feel comfortable declining.

As annoying as it can be to hear "That's not in my job description," it's often a message to you that things are not quite right with at least one employee. You need to take the following actions:

- Initiate a private conversation with the employee. Invite him or her to meet with you in your office or in a conference room. Ask, in a nonconfrontational manner, what the employee meant.
- Listen actively and openly. Such employees do not come to the point quickly, and they may not fully understand the point until they talks their way to it.
- Try to understand the employee's framework and background, as much as this is possible. Perhaps the person comes from another

department or company where the division of labor was clearly defined and no one crossed it.

- If this is a situation of control, see if there are other ways to address the underlying issues.
- If the employee believes another employee is getting away with a light workload, address the matter with the other employee.
- Explain the expectations that you and the company have of this employee and others. Sometimes it's necessary to revisit and update expectations, particularly if the employee has worked for the company for several years.

If you want the person to do something that truly is beyond the scope of the job description, explain why. Make it clear that you respect and value the contributions he or she is already making to the work group and to the company. Help the employee to see that there is a benefit in taking on the additional tasks or responsibilities.

QUESTION?

Can an employee legitimately refuse assigned tasks not within his or her job description?
Of course anyone can refuse an assignment. But not without consequences, which may range from re-evaluation of the job's requirements to disciplinary action, including dismissal. In most circumstances, employment is a negotiation that starts and ends with an employee's ability to meet the needs of the company.

It's a rare job where there aren't unexpected circumstances or changes that require additional work. The tradition of teamwork is that everyone pitches in, equitably, to get the job done. If you have an employee whom you know resists (or refuses) additional tasks, ask this employee to do things that are within the scope of the job description. Most job descriptions define tasks and responsibilities, not the amount of time they require. It's difficult for an employee to legitimately refuse a request to do more of something that is in his or her job description. Just be sure to make it clear whether this is an exception or if there are new expectations about how much work employees should handle. Many companies include the phrase "and other duties as assigned" in all job descriptions to avoid the technicality of this battle.

Chapter 12

Communication and Feedback

Communication is the ability to express yourself so that others understand both your words and your intentions. This is very important in all areas of life, especially the workplace. In order to work together effectively, members of a team must exercise clear communication, and a manager should oversee the various relationships between employees to make sure people can understand each other and get their work done in an efficient manner. What you'll learn in this chapter, though, is that some communication actually has little to do with words.

Translating Body Language

Your body is not always your friend when it comes to communication. It has a mind of its own, so to speak—or rather, escapes the influence of your mind, which is busy regulating the words that leave your mouth. Your body doesn't always tell the same story as your words. Maybe your eyes wander to the computer screen rather than remaining focused on the person in front of you. Your arms cross, and your foot starts to jiggle.

Your words say, "You did a great job with the presentation. I've had phone calls from several people saying how much they enjoyed it." But your body's sending very different signals: "Man, is she ever going to leave? There's that e-mail from Juanita I've been waiting for, I have a conference call in ten minutes, and Sal wants that preliminary budget from me by four. And now my stomach's growling!"

Meanwhile, there's poor Alice pouring her angst all over your desk, eager to hear that she's doing a great job—and while that's what you're saying, she's not buying it because your body language is sending such different signals. Which message would you heed if you were sitting in Alice's chair?

QUESTION?

What is body language?
Body language is the unspoken messages that a person's posture and gestures convey. Crossing your arms, twirling your hair, licking your lips, and slouching are examples of negative body language; shaking hands firmly, making eye contact, sitting up straight, and smiling are examples of positive body language. More importantly, body language reflects what we think of as subconscious messages, the content of communication that escapes the intellect's control and manipulation.

Most people can greatly improve the consistency between their words and their body language by paying more attention to what their bodies are doing when they're speaking. Here are a few tips:

- Maintain eye contact with the person to whom you're talking. It's okay to look away now and then; you don't want to create the impression that this is a stare-down.
- Open your posture. Let your arms rest on the arms of your chair if you're seated, and let them hang naturally at your sides when you're standing. Practice these postures in front of a mirror to become comfortable with them.
- Sitting directly across from someone can feel confrontational, especially if you are behind a desk or at a table. Unless there is a reason for you to maintain an image of power (and sometimes there is), sit beside the person instead.
- Don't sigh, play with your hair (including mustache and beard), jewelry, or pens and pencils. Don't practice your origami skills with pieces of paper you find on your desk, or craft paperclip sculptures. Such actions are distracting for the other person as well as for you. Any train of thought is likely to leave without you if you're concentrating on how to transform a memo into a swan.

The Importance of Listening

The communication cycle alternates between talking and listening. The exchanges are sometimes lengthy, sometimes rapid-fire. It's a back-and-forth process, with each participant playing both roles. Too many people view listening as a passive act when it's actually just as active as talking. The problem is that we tend to spend listening time thinking about what we're going to say next. Or about what to cook for dinner tonight, whether those concert tickets are still available, when the cat's due for her next set of shots—we think about anything but what the other person is saying.

Just as there is more to speaking than uttering a sequence of words, there is more to listening than processing the sounds that enter your ears. Sometimes the real message lies in what's *not* being said. It's important to listen between the lines to hear the unspoken messages. Pay attention to unspoken signals and nonverbal cues. When an employee says, "Yes, I'd be happy to research that information" in a high-pitched, tense voice, and she crosses her arms across her chest before she speaks, what is she really telling you? That she has enough work already without taking time-consuming assignments? That she's cold and wishes she'd brought her sweater to the meeting? That she can't stand the database librarian she'll have to contact to request the information? You can't know without asking further questions, but you should know there's more to the answer than the words she's spoken.

ALERT!

Words are only a small percentage of the typical communication process—just 7 percent, in fact. Body language and nonverbal cues account for 55 percent, while 38 percent is the tone of voice. Dialogue that takes place over the telephone is missing over half the content of typical communication!

Effective listening is an activity that requires your full and focused attention:

- **Engage your mind to slow down your brain.** Let it hear every word as if it were a delightful chocolate that you want to savor until it melts away, letting every molecule of flavor seep into your senses.
- **Beware the familiarity trap.** As soon as the words begin to sound familiar, the search for new information ends. "I've heard this before!" your mind says, and it turns its attention elsewhere. Bring it back! Most listening mistakes occur when you assume something that isn't so.
- **Don't cross the line from anticipation to assumption.** Anticipating someone's response or next question often helps you shape your end of the communication. But there's a fine line between anticipating and assuming, and assuming will almost always get you in trouble.
- **Maintain and keep eye contact, just as when you're speaking.** This shows that you're listening and demonstrates your sincerity. It also helps you pick up on nonverbal cues.

- **Don't formulate your response or mentally argue while the person is still speaking.** You can't be listening to someone else if you're busy listening to yourself.

Listening effectively doesn't mean you have to let conversations roam where they will. You can, and often should, shape the direction of dialogue (at least in a business context). Use natural pauses to ask questions or make comments that keep the conversation on track. Learn when you can interrupt smoothly and effectively. Ask structured, open-ended questions to frame the subject yet allow the person to respond freely: "What happened when you opened the box and discovered that all the templates were reversed?"

ESSENTIAL

Closed posture implies a closed mind. Folding your arms across your chest and crossing your legs is a classic defensive posture that delivers the message, "Don't mess with me." Rarely is this a message that's appropriate in the workplace. Your tendency to take this posture may be defensive, a subconscious effort to protect yourself from bad news or negative feedback.

Daily Interactions With Your Employees

It's amazing how many managers don't interact with their employees any more than they have to. This creates discomfort on both sides. Some of this stems from the way American businesses select managers: Those who excel in the skills of their jobs receive promotions to reward them for their abilities. The result is often managers who are not really people-people. They're skills-people. They're really great as accountants, programmers, sales representatives, or production workers who have done so well in their jobs that they've been promoted to management positions.

As satisfying as they find it to be moving up the corporate food chain, they're still uncomfortable—sometimes with being in authority and often with the social expectations that come with the turf. Coming into management on the wave of performance and productivity, many managers get caught up in their own day-to-day responsibilities. They remain focused on doing a good job, failing to recognize that now means helping everyone else do a good job, too. Bureaucracy, paperwork, and managing upward (office politics) also take their toll, consuming more time and effort than managers and employees feel is reasonable.

Employees need you to stop by every day to say hello. When you don't, they may assume something is wrong, or they may feel ignored. And when you don't interact with your employees, you begin to assume that they think and act in certain ways. From these assumptions, you draw conclusions that they are doing, or not doing, certain things. When we don't have information, we make it up. This is true for managers and employees alike.

Is small talk hard for you? That's okay. Communication is a craft each of us must learn. Although the ability to talk seems natural enough, circumstances that require structured dialogue can make otherwise competent adults sputter incoherently. So consider small talk just one of the new skills you must learn to excel at your job as a manager.

Each day, make it a point to stop by each employee's office, cubicle, desk, or work area. Greet the person with the name he or she uses when contacting you. If the employee's coworkers call him Mike, and his wife calls him Mitch, but he says, "this is Michael" when he calls you, then call him Michael. Or better yet, ask him what he prefers that you call him. Names often reflect a level of trust and equity; jumping to an informal variation (or using a formal variation when others don't) might make the person uncomfortable.

Ask each employee one question related to a personal interest. Yes, this might require you to do a little research. Careful listening can help you to build a mental "information file" about each employee. The general question, "How was your weekend?" can elicit an astonishing breadth and depth of information. Ask each employee one work-related question. If this is new behavior for you, employees might react with suspicion at first, thinking you're checking up on them (which you are, in a sense) or that something is wrong (which it probably isn't).

As employees realize these interactions are now part of your daily routine, they'll warm up. The first sign of progress is when they start telling you about things that are going wrong. But you know you're in your groove when they start telling you about things that are going right.

FACT

In most job settings today, people within one or two corporate levels of each other use first names when talking with or about each other. In some situations, protocol requires using professional or courtesy titles: Dr. Drake, Mr. Johnson, Ms. Hernandez, Sgt. Hamilton, Officer Michaels. Sometimes employees use these titles only in public or when customers are present; in other settings, they use them all the time.

The Open Door Policy

The open door is both literal and symbolic. If you tell employees they can come to talk with you any time but you work with your door closed, you are sending a mixed message. Most people see closed doors as stop signs. From childhood, we're trained not to enter without knocking, and we often hesitate to knock unless the need to talk to the person on the other side can't wait. Sometimes managers close doors out of habit or to block distractions. But are you blocking distractions for you or for others who might see or hear what you're doing? And what constitutes a distraction? Conversation? People walking past? The noises of a busy work group? Ringing telephones? An employee's question? It's difficult to define clear guidelines. Even if you truly want people to just open the door and come in, many will be reluctant to do so. Unless you're working on something that requires privacy, leave your door open. The only way people know you have an open door policy is if your door truly is open. Consider the following example.

When Mark became manager of the assembly group, he established what he believed was an effective open-door policy. He would see any employee about any matter—as long as the employee scheduled an appointment through his secretary and could provide evidence that he or she had tried to resolve the concern through what Mark called "first-level intervention." If the problem was about taking leave time, for example, the employee first needed to talk with the other employee who had already scheduled time off to see if the two of them could negotiate a compromise or with HR if the issue was policy or benefits related.

At first, employees welcomed Mark's approach. The group's previous manager only talked to people who were in some sort of trouble and kept group meetings focused on discussions of work tasks. In contrast, Mark seemed amazingly open. Within the first few months, every employee had scheduled an appointment to talk with Mark. While he was friendly enough in these one-on-one meetings, he kept them just as focused as the previous manager had kept group meetings. When an employee came to Mark's office for a scheduled appointment, Mark expected the employee to present a one- to three-minute summary of the problem and the steps the employee had taken to attempt to resolve it. He had little interest in casual conversation, and no interest in matters that weren't directly related to work processes or results.

Not surprisingly, appointments soon dropped off. Mark interpreted this as an indication that the group had finally come together as a smoothly functioning team capable of troubleshooting and problem solving on its own. But the employees grew increasingly dissatisfied. At least their previous manager had made it unmistakably clear that she had no interest in them and their problems. Mark gave all the appearances of being interested, but in the end was no more so than the previous manager. Requiring appointments to see Mark meant that his "open" door was shut tight to employees unless their needs fit into Mark's schedule. Although Mark believed he was available, his rules and procedures made him inaccessible.

The Feedback Loop

Feedback is a sort of buzzword that has different meanings in various contexts. In electronics, it is undesirable sound distortion. In the workplace, it is one person giving another person a reaction or response—which sometimes sounds like the annoying whines and screeches we associate with electronic feedback. In communication, feedback all too often becomes synonymous with criticism. When a manager says, "I have some feedback for you," employees often hear, "Let me tell you how you screwed up—again!"

Under ideal circumstances, feedback is a loop, a cycle of action and reaction. Neither component needs to be big or significant. In fact, when feedback becomes a communication loop, most people don't notice that it's even taking place. It's when feedback is absent, negative, or devastating that it garners any attention. Of course not all feedback is positive, and sometimes it is downright devastating. But on the feedback continuum, most should fall somewhere in the center.

The Manager's View

Employees always want to know how their managers view them and their work. It's human nature; we are creatures of response. We want to know what others think of us. It helps us to develop a sense of belonging (or not), accomplishment (or not), and confidence (or not). People constantly seek feedback from their managers. Some ask for it directly: "How did I do?" Others are less direct: "What did the client say?" Although conventional wisdom preaches that no news is good news, in the corporate world the reverse is more often the case. Or at least that's what employees think, as they fret and worry because they haven't heard anything from you.

Some feedback should take place in public, such as in a meeting. Take a few minutes to acknowledge an employee who has done an exceptional job. This makes the employee feel good; recognition in front of peers is the highest compliment. It also solidifies roles and responsibilities and shapes interaction within the group. People feel affirmed for their contributions.

Fairness and appropriateness are critical, of course; it's important that you avoid giving the impression of playing favorites. Public praise can backfire if it makes other employees feel less significant. Private feedback also has its place. Stop by an employee's workstation to offer congratulations on a report well written or a project completed ahead of schedule. This individual attention shows that you notice and care about individual effort.

To balance your limited time with an employee's high level of need for feedback, try breaking your comments into smaller bites. Instead of waiting until an assignment is completed to congratulate the employee on a job well done, offer compliments and suggestions along the way.

Feedback to Help Employees Grow

Feedback is a great way to regularly provide tips and suggestions to help employees improve and grow their skills. Given regularly and in small bits, such feedback quickly becomes a natural element of the work environment, and people come to expect it. Consistency and frequency of delivery removes any sense of discipline or heavy-handedness from the feedback process.

Comment on specific actions and behaviors. "Barb was very upset that you yelled at her about the delay at the print shop, and that you hung up on her" works better than "Johnson, you're an insensitive boor!" Whenever practical, give feedback that is specific yet offers choices. "In reading this report, I didn't get a sense of what the product actually is. Would you please restructure the introduction or add another section to part two?"

Look for ways to frame less-than-positive feedback in the context of realistic improvement. This is not about sugarcoating; most people resent attempts to cloak bad news in the trappings of compliments. "Customer complaints about delivery delays are up 35 percent this quarter. Let's take a look at the reasons for the delays and then brainstorm some solutions."

As much as possible, praise the entire work group for its collective efforts. This reinforces the team's value and reminds people that teamwork is about performance, not about personalities or stroking egos.

Some managers want to be good guys so they give only positive feedback, and this at the drop of a hat. It doesn't take long for employees to figure out that praise is always forthcoming, which diminishes its value. And when feedback that was initially positive is followed by a contradictory message, then the feedback becomes even less valuable. If the news is bad, just deliver it. These people are adults; they know, even if you attempt to hide it from them, that they make mistakes and that life is not all roses and chocolate. When less-than-positive feedback involves just one or two people, deliver it individually and in private. When the message is for the entire group, be direct but compassionate. Don't single out individuals in the group setting; if you have additional specific comments, deliver them in private.

Communication Through Writing

No discussion of communication is complete without mentioning the importance of effective writing skills. No matter what their position or level in the company, at some point all employees must put words on paper. You might need to write a memo, a report, or a performance appraisal. What you say matters; how you say it can matter more. Although writing is a life skill, not just a job skill, many people turn into babbling bureaucrats when they write. There's no reason for business writing to be any more convoluted than talking. In fact, it can be easier to write because you focus just on your presentation. In fact, it's as easy as three steps that you can view as your AIM:

- **Audience:** Who will read your message?
- **Intent:** Why are you writing?
- **Message:** What do you have to say?

Make separate lists to answer each of these three questions. Then use your lists as an outline and begin writing. Write as though your audience is sitting in front of you and you are talking to them. Hold the slang, but stay conversational. Write enough content (your message) to cover your intent—no more. Be sure the vocabulary you choose is appropriate for your audience; steer clear of jargon.

Don't let the process of writing intimidate you. It's just another form of communication. The best way to begin writing is to start with what's on your mind. Keep in mind that you don't have to start at the beginning. You can rearrange your blocks of words after you get them down on paper (or on screen). Word processing programs and computers make this very easy. Often one idea flows into the next once you get started, leading you through all of what you want to say. And remember, nobody gets it just right the first time. Writing is a process of editing and revision. If you don't like the way something sounds, change it.

Consider this advice from *The Elements of Style,* a staple on writers' bookshelves: "A sentence should contain no unnecessary words, a paragraph no unnecessary sentences . . . This requires not that the writer make all his sentences short, or that he avoid all detail and treat his subjects only in outline, but that every word tell."

Keep It Concise

To keep your focus clear and clean, make sure every sentence contributes to your intent and message in a way that is relevant to your audience. The myriad details of last month's focus group might fascinate you, but the employees receiving your report just need to know the problems and the suggestions for remedying them. The typical manager gives a written document, paper or electronic, about eight seconds to prove itself worthy of further interest and more time. Brevity counts!

E-mail Issues

Ironically, it's the proliferation of electronic communication that most graphically illustrates the need to address writing skills. The speed with which we can zip messages across the office or around the world makes us behave as though we must take every available shortcut to save even more time, circumventing the processes that effective writing requires. The instantaneous nature of e-mail makes us feel as though we have to read and write at the same speed. But we don't (and can't), and trying to is often a direct route to misunderstanding. The same guidelines for effective communication on paper apply in the paperless environment of cyberspace.

Because e-mail is instantaneous, it's easy to fire off responses and comments without thinking about potential ramifications. The fact that most of us delete e-mail messages once we've read or sent them gives the impression that they are temporal communications, existing only in time just like conversations in person or over the phone (and just as private). Wrong! This is a common and potentially hazardous belief. A growing number of companies capture and store electronic messages that travel through the company's networked computer systems. So far the courts have upheld the rights of companies to do this; what you do on company time with company resources belongs to the company and is the company's business.

If you wouldn't write something in a letter or a memo, don't write it in an e-mail message, either. With distribution lists and bulk forwarding, the message you send to your superior "for your eyes only" could end up on hundreds of other computers. E-mail messages have embarrassed presidents and secretaries alike, and they are an increasing source of evidence in legal proceedings involving everything from sexual harassment to wrongful termination. That offhand comment you fire off in response to a question about someone's performance could become an electronic ghost that returns to haunt you months or years from now.

Chapter 13
Productive Meetings

Most people will say emphatically that they are not meeting-people, yet the leading complaint in most organizations is that there are too many meetings. What gives? Meetings aren't really the inherently evil gatherings that suck the energy and ambition from even the most dedicated employees that they often seem to be. It's just that many meetings are unnecessary or that they include people who don't need to be there. This chapter covers information you need to know to make your meetings productive and meaningful.

Meeting Basics

Meetings don't have to be boring, time consuming, ineffective, or otherwise unpleasant events. In fact, they are meant to be just the opposite. The problem often is that everyone gets bogged down with details and peripheral matters instead of focusing on clear objectives. All it takes is some planning and organization to make a meeting go smoothly.

Before scheduling a meeting, determine why you need a meeting and who should be there. Here are some suggestions:

- Write down what you expect the meeting to accomplish. Focus on specific, tangible outcomes: to determine who will handle what stage of a project; to present new guidelines for using the company's Internet access; to solicit suggestions about how to accommodate an anticipated supply shortage.
- Make a list of the people who need to be at the meeting, and write down the contribution you expect each person to make. If you can't identify a specific contribution, scratch the person from your list. The only people who should be at a meeting are those who have a specific reason for being there. For those who only need to know the meeting's outcome, use a follow-up telephone call, memo, or e-mail.
- Ask yourself if you could accomplish your desired outcomes without a meeting. Is it important for each employee the topic affects to participate in discussions that relate to the other's involvement? Could you talk with one or two employees in your office or theirs, or convey information by memo or e-mail?

Meetings can be interesting, useful, and productive. Making them so is not only possible, it's your responsibility. A good number of meetings are nothing more than time-wasters because they have no reason to exist. If there is no clear reason for a meeting, don't schedule one. Here's an example of what you want to avoid.

At Acme Industries, there were so many meetings that departments seemed to do nothing else; many employees went from one meeting to another without ever making it to their desks. When someone in marketing wanted to talk with someone in purchasing, odds were that all of purchasing was in a meeting. When the purchasing clerk called back, the marketing department was having a meeting. And so it went, through the day and from day to day.

The purchasing department met daily at 10 A.M., ostensibly to address back orders and other product delivery issues before they became major problems. Everyone except the receptionist was required to attend these standing meetings, which generally lasted two hours or more. Often, the topics under discussion applied to only two or three employees, yet the entire department had to sit there and listen. Everyone hated it.

The marketing department met every day at 1 P.M. to brainstorm new ideas and update progress on existing projects. Marketing staff felt they were a great team, and they looked forward to their standing meetings as a demonstration of just how much of a team they were. There was a lot of conversation and camaraderie, and no dimension of any idea or project escaped examination—and re-examination and cross-examination and further examination. What didn't get enough coverage in the regular meeting went to one of the many committees, subcommittees, and study teams. People often showed up late because their committee, subcommittee, or study team meetings ran over. So the group paused to bring latecomers up to speed. The daily team meeting was scheduled to run two hours, but usually ended only when people ran out of things to talk about. Marketing employees frequently stayed in the office until late at night and came to work even before the cafeteria's coffee counter opened.

Not surprisingly, turnover in both departments was high. People grew bored and frustrated. People in marketing burned out. So the managers scheduled more meetings to try to get a handle on what was making people so unhappy. Too many meetings both annoy and spoil employees. Meetings eat time and give employees the impression that they have a voice in everything. If your employees really do, then provide structured, efficient ways for them to share their opinions and suggestions. If they really don't have much voice in department or company decisions, then giving them the illusion that they do will become clear and there will be a lot of negative reverberation.

So what's the solution? Obviously this depends on the nature of the business and the structure of the company, but here's an example. The administrative department at a large corporation resolved the problem of having daily staff meetings drag on and on by holding true "standing meetings," in which participants actually stood up for the duration of the meeting. Meetings were scheduled for fifteen minutes. If you showed up late you could only listen, you couldn't speak or otherwise participate. Discussions were brief, and decisions were prompt.

Who Should Attend?

Deciding who should attend a meeting should be as simple as determining who needs to participate or be informed and who doesn't. This decision is based on job tasks and responsibilities. Often, however, other factors come into play. Call it politics, call it personalities, call it whatever you like—but all managers sometimes feel compelled to include employees who really don't need to be there.

Sometimes this is a worthwhile means of preserving the peace and encouraging a sense of teamwork. If all of a department's employees routinely attend meetings with the same one or two employees excepted, there are bound to be hurt feelings. Those employees will feel left out not only of meetings but also of the team and its work. Depending on the personalities involved, you can talk with those people to explain the reasons and get a sense of how they feel about it. Or you might just decide to include them so they don't feel left out. Sometimes arbitrary factors determine who attends a meeting and who doesn't. These factors might include the meeting's location or time, the size of the meeting room, and other logistical issues.

ESSENTIAL

Consider having a different team member chair each department meeting. The chairperson can prepare the meeting's agenda and then lead the meeting. This provides good experience for team members, and it bolsters the team's collaborative spirit by strengthening each member's knowledge of other employees' projects and assignments.

If so many meetings are unnecessary, why even have them? If two or more people need to know the same information, it makes sense to get them together so you need to present the information just once. If people need to know different pieces of information about the same topic, it might make sense to bring them together—or it might be more effective to speak to each one separately. And if two or more people need to know different information about different topics, it's seldom efficient or effective to bring them together. They'll certainly tune out on topics that don't pertain to them, diminishing the likelihood that they'll pay attention to the information that *does* relate to them.

It's All about the Agenda

Every meeting should have an agenda. Start with the meeting's location, start time, and finish time. Cover no more than five topics. If you have more to discuss, schedule another meeting. Express each agenda item briefly, in no more than two sentences. If there is more to say, attach a separate discussion page or backgrounder that provides the detail you want people to know coming into the meeting. Keep the agenda items tangible and goal-oriented. Identify the amount of time you intend to spend on each agenda item. Put the agenda in writing. Distribute copies of the agenda to the employees who will be attending, and ask them to arrive at the meeting prepared to participate. Include the names of all participants, so everyone attending knows who else will be there.

Most of the time, the meeting will be one you're running. Just make sure you know what this means and how you're going to utilize your position. When the person running a meeting becomes too controlling—even with the best of intentions—things can go awry, as they did for Paul.

Paul was a nice-guy manager who liked for all of his employees to feel that their contributions mattered—in meetings, to the department, and to the company. At one meeting, the discussion turned to the new comp time guidelines. Paul knew this was a done deal that upper management would simply implement once the finishing touches were in place. Believing it was better to let his group feel they had a role in shaping the guidelines (though they in fact did not), he let them follow a path he knew was a dead-end.

Two months later, when the company implemented the guidelines, Paul's employees were angry that the new policy incorporated none of their suggestions. Paul could have averted problems had he handled the meeting differently. He could have said the policy was in its final development stages and any discussion would be more appropriate when it was finished. Or he could have said that although he didn't have any authority to offer suggestions, he was interested in knowing what his employees thought.

When you are leading the meeting, it's your role to establish clear boundaries and expectations. If you have decision-making authority, let employees know what they might influence and what is set in stone. Let employees know what kinds of information and feedback you want to hear. Don't set expectations that you can't meet; it damages your credibility. Some managers don't like to give any appearance that their power has any limits. Don't delude yourself. Your employees know exactly where the boundaries of your authority are, even if you're not sure yourself. Meetings give you an opportunity to establish your leadership role, and following the rules for leading an effective meeting can help establish your leadership image.

FACT

Companies devote considerable resources to meetings. The typical manager spends at least eight hours a week in meetings—one full workday. Studies suggest companies may spend 10 percent or more of their budgets on meetings. With all these resources on the line, it only makes sense to ensure your meetings are effective and worthwhile.

It's equally important to start the meeting on time. This sounds so simple. Yet in many organizations, starting meetings late is so much the norm that no one even shows up at the scheduled time. Sometimes this practice becomes a part of the corporate culture to the degree that it spills over into other functions. Employees arrive late for meetings with other departments, vendors, and even customers. The resulting hard feelings generate indifference and eventually lost business. No matter what your agenda, you diminish its value when you fail to start the meeting at the scheduled time.

A meeting is a showcase for a manager's behavior and leadership skills—and employees watch the performance very closely. Seeing is believing, and perception is reality. When you act like a manager and leader, your employees perceive you as a manager and a leader.

In addition to starting the meeting promptly at the scheduled time, keep it on track with its agenda, and end it at the scheduled time. If the discussion strays during the meeting, as it inevitably will, firmly but politely redirect it to the topics on the agenda. This is sometimes easier said than done, and there are many techniques to handle the task smoothly and professionally. (There are numerous workshops and books about conducting effective meetings that present these techniques; Appendix B provides more information.)

Finally, always show respect for the opinions of the employees in attendance even if the meeting is not the appropriate forum for expressing them. Sometimes you can offer to set up another meeting or to meet with smaller groups of employees to discuss their concerns. Sometimes further discussion would be fruitless, as it was with Paul and the comp time guidelines, in which case you need to just say so.

Shaping Interactions

The way you conduct meetings provides your employees with insight into you as a manager and into your company's values and operations. Companies in which meetings run rampant and structure is lacking have little sense of direction. Companies with strong strategic plans also have strong strategies for running meetings as well as other operational functions. When it comes to meetings, two dimensions of interaction are important for you to manage: yourself and others.

Presenting Yourself

You might be the most interesting person in one-on-one situations and still somehow transmogrify into a bumbling mumbler in meetings. In casual situations, the attention shifts back and forth among those participating in the conversation. Usually no one person's comments are more important than any other's. This dynamic shifts in group settings, such as meetings. When it's your meeting, all eyes and ears focus on you. It's natural to find this at least a little intimidating. Relax, and just be yourself!

When you speak, talk at a moderate pace—not too fast, not too slow—and enunciate. Form your words clearly and cleanly. Vary the tone and pitch of your voice. Some people drone on in a monotone when speaking formally, either to a group or to an individual, even though their conversational voices are friendly and full of personality. It's as though a little switch flips and their vocal cords can suddenly emit sound on only a single frequency. Unless you're passing out pillows at your meetings, monotone is no good.

One way to practice modulating your voice is to change the outgoing message on your voice mail every day. Strive for a different tone each day and to sound interested in the caller even though you're not there to take the call.

Gestures are often space-fillers. Are you waving your hands around to try to paint an air picture of something, or are you having trouble finding the right words? It's usually more effective to use a pencil and paper to sketch out your picture, or to simply pause for a moment to let the right words come to you. If you don't usually use gestures, consider adding a little movement to your speech. It's hard to listen to a talking head, no matter how interested you are in the message.

If you speak frequently in front of groups (including meetings), consider joining a group such as Toastmasters to hone your public speaking skills. (See Appendix B for information on this and other organizations.) If you've never had any formal public speaking training, it doesn't hurt to take a workshop or a class. And if these ideas don't appeal to you, try videotaping yourself (be sure anyone else in the room who might also be captured on film has no objections) or talking in front of a mirror.

Guiding Others

Offer everyone a chance to speak about agenda items. If a few employees begin to dominate the meeting, intercede to call on silent employees. Pull out your parent hat for a few minutes and let the group know that all members have something to contribute and all ideas are valid and worth expressing. If an individual or small faction manages to monopolize discussion of an item, there is probably no more to talk about, and you can bring discussion of the item to a close. "Okay, let's wrap this up. Any final questions or comments? Thirty seconds, then on to our next topic."

FACT

Researchers at the University of North Carolina who studied workplace meetings concluded that the value people ascribe to meetings has little to do with length or content. Rather, people feel meetings are valuable when they can leave with information useful to them in their jobs. Meetings become valueless when conversation digresses or when one person monopolizes the dialogue.

If an employee is being barraged with questions or criticism, step in to put an end to it. This is a meeting, not an inquisition. If employees see that those who stick out their necks end up getting their heads chopped off, they're not likely to be willing to speak up themselves, even when the topic concerns them. There is a balance between open dialogue and abuse, and it's your role to maintain it and to protect employees who present unpopular perspectives or information. Likewise, if the group keeps circling for another round of discussion or commentary on a particular topic, pronounce it dead and move on.

Bringing Meetings to a Close

Ten minutes or so before the meeting's scheduled end, it's time to begin drawing the meeting to a close. ("Closure" should be the last topic on every agenda.) If it was an educational meeting, recap the key learning points. If the meeting was to disseminate information, review the essential messages. If further action needs to happen, decide who will be responsible for what tasks. Make assignments, if necessary, and establish timelines and a process for following up.

If bringing events to conclusion will require another meeting with the same group, schedule it before breaking up, or at least let people know that a follow-up meeting will be scheduled. End on time. Doing so is as important as starting on time. Some people may want to linger after the meeting to talk with each other or ask questions. Invite further dialogue in your office, if appropriate. But leave the meeting location to emphasize the message that the meeting is over.

Productive Disagreement

Meetings present forums for the expression of ideas and concerns. Inevitably, different opinions collide. Each person feels strongly about his or her perspective, and the situation lands in your lap. It's time to pull out your mediator hat and put your communication skills to work negotiating a solution for all parties to accept and respect. Effective negotiation requires both sides to come to the table with the following:

- **A common allegiance:** Working toward common goals establishes a connection defined by similarities, not differences. If nothing else, both sides work for the same company and should support the company's goals, which gives them a common mission. When both sides want to achieve the same outcomes, they're often more willing to search for common ground.
- **Mutual respect:** Despite their differences, do the parties respect each other? If so, they will be able to focus on process-oriented solutions and to separate themselves from their disagreement. Respect

is the foundation for trust; people must respect each other before they can trust one another to fulfill the agreements they reach.

- **Open minds:** Each party must be willing to both talk and listen so that together they can explore possible solutions.
- **Willingness to change:** Obviously each party comes to the meeting believing its perspective is valid and correct. After listening to each other and discussing the problems, all parties must be willing to change their positions to accommodate suggested solutions.

Reaching an agreement to resolve a conflict doesn't necessarily mean that each side gets what it wants. Sometimes solutions are collaborative (all parties gain) and sometimes they involve compromise (all parties give something up). Each party must feel satisfied with the solution, or the conflict remains.

Flaring Tempers

People lose it sometimes. Little things add up, tensions and frustrations build. People feel powerless to control or change situations that they believe should be different but that persist because you (or someone else or another department or the company) intentionally created the circumstances. Whether there is truth to this perception doesn't matter; perceptions are reality as viewed through the ever-changing hues of emotions. And the forum of the meeting becomes the place to express dissatisfaction.

ALERT!

Emotions and anger, especially when pent up, may entirely derail a meeting's agenda. When it appears things are going in this direction, you have two options. You can channel the expressed frustration as constructively as possible and reschedule the intended agenda for another meeting, or you can interrupt the dialogue, acknowledge the emotions, commit to a separate meeting to specifically address the erupting concerns, and return to the scheduled agenda. The option you choose isn't as important as maintaining control.

Anger is an unmistakable sign that a person has exceeded his or her tolerance for a situation or behavior. It is an intense and powerful blend of emotion and action that often frightens even the person who is angry. Anger tends to feed on itself. The longer the shouting continues, the more volatile the anger becomes. Meetings can quickly become shouting matches, so it's crucial to defuse anger quickly. These steps can help you regain control:

- **Intercede immediately.** Don't wait for things to become truly explosive. Often, just the fact that you become involved is enough interrupt the cycle and start turning things around.
- **Remove the audience.** If an employee is yelling and otherwise going off in front of other employees, get him or her into an office or conference room, or ask the other employees to leave for a few minutes. Someone who loses control in front of others feels compelled to maintain or escalate angry behaviors. Removing the audience gives the angry person the freedom to back down without losing face and to regain composure.
- **Separate the behavior from the person, and request that the behavior change immediately.** Look away from the person to give him or her a few moments to pull it together, but stay in the room (unless you fear for your safety). By staying in the room, you make it clear that you're willing to do what you can to work things out and also cut short any approach to use anger as a manipulative behavior.
- **Be an active listener.** Let the person fully explain his or her position and frustration, even if you think you already know the problem or have heard it before. Until the full story is out, ask questions only to clarify details.
- **Ask what solutions the employee would like to see.** If one or more of the employee's suggestions make sense, discuss with the employee how best to implement changes. If the suggestions don't make sense, provide a brief and factual explanation and offer an alternative.
- **Reiterate any agreements, and establish a plan to follow up.** This formalizes the discussion so the employee knows the discussion was more than just blowing off steam.

Meetings are one way in which managers can model the behavior they want to see in their department. Employees watch the way managers treat them and others. The notice whom you acknowledge and how you acknowledge them. They watch how new ideas are accepted or cut off, and whether the established feedback loop is functional or merely lip service.

The Silent Treatment

Sometimes people come to meetings and simply sit. Even when you question them directly, they offer only perfunctory responses. What lies behind such behavior? Often, it's the perception that this is yet another useless meeting in which input and opinions don't really matter. Is it? This is a good opportunity to evaluate the reasons for meetings in your work group, the structure of the agendas, and the conduct of the meetings. Perhaps the meetings are important only to you, or it's your higher-ups who mandate the meetings. Are there more efficient ways for you to convey or collect information? Employees who have heavy workloads (and who doesn't) may resent meetings that take them from their assigned tasks, especially when there are no mechanisms for them to make up the lost time.

Keep a Sense of Humor

Humor is a great way to defuse situations before they become volatile or frustrating. However, it's important to know the difference between finding humor, which is appropriate and often useful, and cracking jokes, which is nearly always inappropriate. Humor arises from situations and carries the unspoken message of shared perspectives; it allows people to have fun. Jokes often poke fun at situations or people.

Follow Up and Follow Through

Most meetings end with the need for further attention to key agenda items. Even when you've assigned these responsibilities during the meeting, you need to follow up to make sure employees have the resources and information they need. Do you need to pave the way for interaction with another department? Do employees need your help to access information or data? Your follow-through is essential.

Follow-through after a meeting tends to be more effective when a summary of its intentions appears in writing. In other words, send a memo! If the meeting involved a large number of people or an entire department, post a printed copy of the follow-through memo where people will see it—above the copy machine, in the break room, by the doorway. Enterprising managers even post important information in the restrooms. The memo should clearly but briefly state the following:

- The problem
- The agreed-upon or determined solution
- The tasks involved in implementing the solution
- Who is responsible for each task
- The timeline for completing the tasks
- The method for measuring the solution's success

Often there is no reason for a follow-up meeting unless the solution failed to perform as expected. Even so, people like to know what happened as a result of their discussion and input. Make sure to communicate the outcomes of implemented changes and solutions, either as cursory agenda items on subsequent meetings or through memos or e-mails. Solicit employee feedback no matter what your formal assessment method; sometimes an apparent success resurfaces as another issue. Most importantly, thank people for their suggestions and participation.

Chapter 14

Performance Standards and Evaluation

With the Industrial Revolution, companies came up with performance measurements. Bosses with stopwatches came in and counted how many times one worker could do the same thing over and over. They did the math and came up with a definition of a day's work. Today, more than a hundred years later, this mentality underlies the concepts of productivity and performance measurement. But today's business environments are a far cry from the fields and factories of their predecessors. The jobs and tasks that comprise them are often difficult to quantify.

The Relationship Between Performance and Evaluation

It seems that there should be a clear and definable relationship between performance and evaluation. You should be able to measure, precisely and objectively, whether the employee does the right things in the right ways. The problem is, performance is not precise and objective. Human interactions are subjective; they involve factors of judgment and perception that exceed the capability of precise, objective measures.

Say, for example, that an employee's job is to make six widgets in an hour. Counting to six is easy enough, but there's more to measuring performance than counting. It's also necessary to determine if the widgets are made correctly. Is there a standard of deviation that's acceptable? If so, is it a precise measurement (each widget can be no more than 0.0032 of an inch larger or smaller than the template) or is it a judgment (each widget feels smooth to the touch)? Must the employee complete one widget every ten minutes, or is it okay for the employee to make all six in the last fifteen minutes of each hour? Can the employee make twelve widgets in one hour, then none in the next hour?

Now suppose it's another employee's job to sell six widgets an hour. Is the standard simply sales, or does it factor in returns? What if there are problems with the phone lines, or the employee calls forty prospective customers but can't convince any of them to actually buy a widget? These are variables beyond the employee's control, yet they directly affect the employee's ability to perform.

ESSENTIAL

Performance evaluation structures range from the nearly nonexistent—a few comments scribbled on the back of a telephone message note—to the compulsive—the minutiae of a job's tasks itemized and delineated on multiple-page documents. Some take their forms because they must (such as reviews mandated by government or licensing entities), and others because managers and employees alike inherently dislike evaluating performance.

In reality, objectivity is difficult. It would be so much easier for everyone if it were possible to devise a universal set of standards. But it's not, and that's a good thing. Many jobs require variability and flexibility. People are different in their needs as well. If there's one lesson you should know by this time in your life, it's that "one size fits all" really doesn't fit anyone.

Company Size Matters

On one end of the continuum are small or family-owned companies that might never formally evaluate anyone's performance. When there are just a few employees, it's pretty obvious when someone's not pulling a full load. There's no place to hide, no way to blend anonymously into a department or work group. Each individual has unique and important responsibilities; failing to meet them puts the company at grave (and usually imminent) risk. People who work in such settings tend to have strong motivations for being there and equally strong commitments to the company and its success. Many of them are likely to be family members. Performance evaluation might mean a pat on the back for an extraordinary success or a dressing down for screwing up—if either extreme ever arises in an environment where one is the expectation and the other could mean the company's demise.

Large corporations reside at the other end of the continuum. New employees typically receive a written manual that defines the company's expectations on everything from job tasks and responsibilities to shift hours and break periods. The performance evaluation structure is often rigid, commonly a numeric scale of some sort. However, within this apparently confining structure there is room for wide variation in performance. An employee can function at a substandard or mediocre level for a defined period of time without direct consequence to the company.

Most companies are somewhere in the middle of these two extremes. As small companies grow, they often add bits and pieces of formality to address specific needs that arise—to deal with the first new employee who doesn't work out, or determine how and when to give someone a raise. Despite the need for their existence, performance evaluations can be a major annoyance for managers and employees alike. Even when there are stringent guidelines, not all employees and circumstances fit within them. And when there are minimal or no guidelines, it's difficult to say to an employee, "Your performance needs improvement."

Performance and Pay

Many performance evaluation systems tie an employee's evaluation to his or her salary. Get a good evaluation, get a raise. Get an average or a poor evaluation, and the money stays the same. This establishes incentives (or disincentives) for managers to slant evaluations to meet needs other than performance issues. A manager might give a mediocre employee a better-than-deserved evaluation because the employee needs the raise—often with the hope that the employee will know this and be motivated to do better as a show of gratitude. Such motivation is likely to be short-lived, if it surfaces at all.

ALERT!

Union contracts often define performance standards, measures, and evaluation procedures. In most situations, you cannot change any of these (and often other) elements of the job without a written amendment to the contract. Whether the employee wants or agrees to the change is irrelevant; actions that violate contracts can have serious and far-reaching consequences.

An employee whose performance is substandard might not know this and believe the inflated evaluation to be accurate. Since the evaluation is the perception of performance that becomes part of the employee's records, it becomes difficult, if not impossible, to go back later to coach the employee about performance that really hasn't changed. Conversely, a manager facing a tight budget might decide that no one will receive higher than an average performance evaluation to avoid having to give raises that could push the budget to the brink of layoffs. While the manager might believe this action is justified because it will save everybody's jobs, employees are likely to feel cheated—they've been giving their best, yet the company views their performance as not good enough.

Performance Evaluation Structures

Regardless of its form, a formal evaluation structure benefits managers, employees, and companies. Say your star employee makes a huge mistake that costs the company big money and has your superiors all over your case. It's a major screwup, and everyone in the department knows about it. Will you remember it in six months, when it's time to do that employee's formal performance evaluation? If so, to what level of detail? The reality is that memories quickly fade, even (or perhaps especially) bad ones. You might swear at the time that you'll never forget, but you will.

And if that's not problematic enough, other employees will remember—but not necessarily the whole or true story. Employees talk, and as they do the details change. (Remember the childhood game of telephone?) It's not that people intentionally misrepresent the facts. They might have had limited knowledge in the first place, just a piece of the whole picture. So they fill it in, because everybody likes stories with details and endings. And memories fade—even theirs. What people can't quite remember, they create. It's human nature.

Many Shapes and Styles

There are any number of approaches, methods, and systems for evaluating job performance. If your company doesn't have one yet, Appendix B lists some resources for learning more about various performance evaluation systems. The particular structure your company uses isn't nearly as important as the fact that it has a structure of some sort in place.

Regular communication—daily or at least weekly—is the most effective way to both monitor and shape employee performance. It remains your most effective tool as a manager. Don't save things, good or bad, for a formal evaluation meeting. Nothing you or the employee says in a formal meeting should come as a surprise to either one of you.

A well-designed performance evaluation system includes processes to document extraordinary experiences at the time that they happen (and ideally to address them with involved employees at the time they occur). The most traditional structure features an annual review, usually on the anniversary of the employee's hire date, with supplemental quarterly meetings. Some companies review salary and performance at the same time, while others separate them. Be sure you know your company's policies; your mistakes could cost employees money.

Structure Means Consistency

Most of the time, you're better off following the structure your company uses, consistently and without deviation. This prevents, or at least minimizes, the likelihood that the evaluation will return to haunt you. And most managers don't like playing the bad guy. A performance evaluation system provides the documented support that you need to present your perspective or defend your position. From morale to legalities, a formal performance evaluation structure truly does benefit and protect everyone.

Some managers hate paperwork, but this doesn't make it okay to avoid structured procedures, like performance reviews, for that reason. Consider Beverly's situation.

It didn't matter why the paperwork was necessary; Beverly just hated it and avoided dealing with it at just about all costs. Her employees generally admired this attitude; it positioned her as somewhat of a rebel, making her seem to belong more to them than to upper administration. Clarence was one of those employees. In the two years he reported to Beverly, he hadn't had a single performance evaluation. He didn't work any less hard as a result; in fact, he put a lot of time and effort into his work because it felt less bureaucratic than the typical corporate environment. Of course, Clarence didn't get a raise during this time, either, since the company linked raises to performance. But he didn't really mind; he was well-paid already, and he believed all it would take was a good word from Beverly and he could circumvent that part of the process, too.

Before he got around to asking Beverly to do that, the company adopted new policies and procedures that forced Beverly to do formal performance evaluations for all of her employees. To his surprise, Clarence discovered that Beverly wasn't entirely happy with his performance. She perceived issues in several key areas of his job responsibilities and asked him to propose an improvement plan. Because of his relatively low measures on the formal evaluation, Clarence received a mediocre raise. He felt betrayed and stabbed in the back. Yes, he could see that he had tripped himself up in certain things, but that wasn't really his fault since no one (such as Beverly) had told him he was on the wrong track. Clarence filed a grievance.

Present the Performance Evaluation

For many managers, evaluating an employee's performance is not nearly as difficult as sharing that evaluation with the person. No matter how objective you are, there are emotions attached. People like to hear good things about themselves, and sometimes hearing about the need to improve sounds like criticism. The way you present your comments goes a long way toward shaping the employee's perceptions of his or her performance as well as feelings about what you say.

Schedule your performance evaluation meeting so you have plenty of time to address questions and concerns that arise. Establish ground rules at the start of the meeting. "I will tell you my assessment of your performance for each measure, then give you an opportunity to share your perspectives and comments. I ask that you not interrupt me, and I promise I won't interrupt you."

Stay focused on the topics at hand and keep digressions to a minimum. Give examples of observable behavior to support your comments. If issues surface that need further discussion, schedule another appointment to address them. Take notes, and encourage the employee to do the same. Offer the employee the opportunity to add his or her comments (on a separate page) to the evaluation packet that becomes part of the employee's file.

Present improvements from a positive perspective as much as possible. "You've done a great job developing a system for monitoring report status. Let's take a look at some ways that you can streamline your workflow to be more efficient." If there is bad news, it shouldn't be news to the employee. He or she should know, or at least suspect, that there is a problem. Be direct in presenting the problem, and have a sense of what action you intend to take in response. Conclude the meeting with a plan for improvement, whether this means correcting performance deficiencies or helping the person take steps toward his or her career goals.

Identify Performance Issues

A performance appraisal should incorporate the employee's areas of accomplishment as well as identify areas for improvement. Again, nothing you say in a performance appraisal meeting should come as a surprise to the employee—good or not so good. As manager, you should have ongoing interactions with employees that keep you and them aware of any performance deficiencies.

While you want to keep things friendly, this is not a casual chat. It could be the first step to the end of a job for this employee, although you hope it's the beginning of the turnaround you need to see. Meet someplace that assures privacy. Your office is fine if it has floor-to-ceiling walls and a door that closes. Otherwise, meet in a conference room or arrange to use someone else's office.

ESSENTIAL

The tendency in performance evaluations is for managers to focus on what improvements an employee needs to make. This is of course essential. But it is also important to give equal weight to the employee's talents and contributions and to recognize growth and development that has already taken place.

Come to a performance evaluation with a clear written agenda of what you want to cover. Have documentation of the problems you want to discuss—notes, memos, copies of e-mails, work that had to be redone, or whatever other evidence is relevant. Be discreet, of course—have the items in a file folder, not spread out on the desk when the employee arrives. Lastly, know, at least in general, what you want the employee to do to remedy the situation.

Focus on Specific and Observable Behaviors

If you or someone else didn't observe it, it didn't happen and you can't really talk about it. This is not a meeting about feelings or suspicions. It is about tangible actions and behaviors—work that didn't get done, assignments done incorrectly, inappropriate e-mail messages, and so on—that are creating performance problems for this employee. Have actual examples, like so:

- "Here is the memo you sent to accounts receivable about the Robinson account. It has the wrong balances, and you erroneously flagged the account as past due."
- "I've gotten complaints from other departments about the number of jokes you forward by e-mail. Here are copies of messages that people have given me."
- "When we established the timeline for the widgets, you agreed that it was reasonable and would accommodate the kinds of delays that might arise. I've checked with you every week, and you've said you had everything under control. The widget prototype still isn't to manufacturing, though the timeline says it should have been in full production six weeks ago."

What do you do when the problem is vague, such as a bad attitude? You might see the crux of the problem as attitude, and that could indeed be the case. But you still need tangible evidence—and usually there's an abundance of it, such as yelling at coworkers, badmouthing others, showing up late, and leaving early. Again, be specific and provide examples.

Unless you've asked other employees if you can use their names when talking to the problem employee, don't name them. Keep the conversation focused on the employee who is in the room with you and on behaviors rather than personalities. Explain why the behaviors are problems, just to be sure you and the employee have the same understanding (which is not to imply that you must agree).

Listen to the Employee's Perspective

Many employees are surprised when their managers confront them about their performance. Even when you've maintained clear and open communication, the employee might not perceive the situation as serious or as a problem. Before you dismiss the employee's explanations as worthless excuses, you owe it to the person to hear his or her perspective. Listen to the employee's side without interrupting. If you take notes, do so unobtrusively. Listen without judgment and without challenging the employee's perceptions. If you have questions, ask them after the employee has finished speaking.

If an employee is worth keeping, it's worth your time and energy to find solutions that will work for both of you. Consider additional training through classes or workshops, one-on-one tutoring with a more experienced employee, online or video training, job-shadowing—whatever looks to be effective, efficient, and even a little fun.

Sometimes there are issues within the work group or department that at least partially impede the employee's ability to perform necessary job tasks. Antiquated computer equipment, understaffing, inefficient procedures such as multiple signoffs, and many other factors can be legitimate barriers. Sometimes the employee doesn't know how to do a particular task or step in a procedure and doesn't know who to ask, or is afraid to ask, for help. If such factors are present, it's your responsibility to do what is possible to remedy the situation. If there are barriers you can't remove or minimize, it's not really fair or reasonable to hold the employee accountable. It might be necessary for you to modify your expectations or the employee's job responsibilities.

Job Performance Coaching

When we speak of coaching in the context of the work environment, we're addressing the process of formally meeting with an employee to discuss performance issues—and documenting that discussion through a letter or memo that goes to the employee and perhaps to his or her personnel file. In many companies, this is a step in the progressive discipline process. This is not counseling in the sense of "let's uncover what's really bothering you so we can make it better." You are not a therapist; you are a manager. You cannot address psychological problems, even if you know enough to see that they are present. Your role is to say to this employee, "There are problems with your performance that we need to discuss." The bottom line is that you want to improve the employee's work-related problems. If that also fixes his or her personal problems, great. But that's not your primary goal.

Often this approach feels cold-hearted and harsh. You are a compassionate human being who genuinely cares about this employee as a person, not just as a productive work unit. And while you can try to focus on the behaviors that you want the employee to change (as you should), you might believe that permanent change will come only when you uncover and somehow address the underlying issues. But that's not your role. Playing therapist (or even friend) can land you and your company in legal hot water. It's a delicate balance indeed, and one that can tip out of control before you know it.

ALERT!

If an employee is having problems at home—with a partner, children, elderly parents, or health—you can lend a sympathetic ear, but you can't intrude into these areas. Recommend that the employee seek outside help. If your company offers an EAP, refer the employee for assistance. If the problem is related to substance abuse, most state employment laws require companies to follow certain procedures for testing, mandatory counseling, and return-to-work agreements. Be sure to follow your company's policies and procedures.

If the employee identifies factors within the workplace that interfere with completing job tasks, establish a plan for you to address those concerns and a time by which you'll get back to the employee with answers or solutions. Every employee has unique needs when it comes to improving job performance, just as each has a unique work style. It's important to establish that this is a serious matter and that you are establishing the framework for remedying the situation yet also allow the employee to participate at a comfortable level. When the coaching meeting ends, you both should be able to leave with your dignity and self-confidence intact. After all, the employee really has more of a vested interest in improving than anyone else.

Documentation Is Your Friend

It's fine for you to take notes during your meeting—invite the employee to do so as well. Whether you do or not, take another ten or fifteen minutes immediately following the meeting (after the employee leaves) to write down a brief accounting of what transpired. Be sure to do the following:

- Note what specific examples you used, and how the employee responded.
- Write down the details of the improvement plan you agreed upon, as well as the steps that will be necessary to monitor progress.
- Record any contributing factors from the work environment that the employee feels interfere with productivity, as well as your intentions for addressing issues that involve the employee.

Before you commit your thoughts to writing, consider how your words might sound a few months or years from now, coming from a lawyer's mouth. Be sure your comments are factual and maintain the same tangible focus as your meeting. Laws vary among states, but in many the courts can subpoena any written materials you keep—including notes intended only for your use. If you have any doubts or concerns about what constitutes appropriate documentation, check with your company's HR or legal department.

Documentation is a good habit to develop. A good paper trail can demonstrate your and your company's consistency in addressing performance issues and can provide irrefutable evidence of your efforts to help the employee change and improve. More often than not, solid documentation deters rather than encourages lawsuits—especially when both manager and employee sign dated copies. This helps protect you and your company against accusations of wrongdoing down the road, when memories have become selective and faded (on all sides). Depending on your company, this could be more than sage advice—it could be corporate policy. Most companies have written guidelines and procedures for managers to follow.

FACT

Many managers are leery of committing adverse performance reports to writing, for fear that what they say will come back to bite them in court. However, attorneys who specialize in employment law generally believe documentation is a company's best safeguard against frivolous lawsuits. Written job descriptions and performance appraisals establish procedural consistency. The paper trail that is likely to cause trouble is the one built solely for the purpose of carrying out a particular action. Documentation should support decisions, not create them.

Agree to an Improvement Plan

After you've shared your concerns and listened to the employee's perspective, it's time to move into action mode. Identifying the problems is the first half of your task; identifying solutions is the second. Although you want the employee to participate in developing an improvement plan, you also want to be sure that plan achieves the goals that are important to you and to the company. Every improvement plan should include three core elements:

- Specific goals for, and descriptions of, the improvements you want to see. "Memos that leave this department must be free from grammatical and spelling mistakes."
- Specific steps for achieving the described improvements. "I want you to run the spellchecker just before you save or print any document. For the next two weeks, I want to sit down with you at 11 A.M. and 3 P.M. to review all outgoing memos. We will proof them together."

- Specific methods for measuring performance and assessing improvement. "I ran the spellchecker on these memos that I showed you, and each had at least seven errors. By the end of one week, I want the memos we review together to have fewer than three errors each. At the end of two weeks, I want every memo we review together to have no errors that the spellchecker is capable of detecting. We'll meet again at the end of two weeks to discuss your improvement."

Depending on the kinds of problems that exist and how complex the employee's job duties are, your improvement plan might consist of a few bulleted items or several pages of expectations and directives. Most improvement plans work best when they include an agreement to meet at determined intervals to review progress and make appropriate revisions. If an employee's problems involve numerous job functions, you might want to develop an incremental plan that attacks one problem at a time. Whatever form the plan takes, put it in writing. At the end, put a sentence that says, "I understand the requested improvements and agree to follow this plan to make them happen" (or words to this effect). Then sign your name and write the date, and have the employee sign. Each of you gets a copy.

Timely Follow-Up

In concept, performance is ever-evolving as the employee's skills and knowledge grow and expand. Every employee's performance has room for improvement. Although your company might have formal evaluation meetings just once or twice a year, change (whether to correct a problem or foster growth) requires regular follow-up and monitoring. You should establish the shape and form of this follow-up during the evaluation meeting or at a subsequent meeting if that's how you set things up. What are the employee's obligations and commitments? What are yours? Is the employee going to work with you to establish priorities, present you with realigned priorities, or rely on you to present priorities? Be sure the improvement plan establishes the following:

- A schedule of regular meetings to assess the employee's progress toward improvement
- Suggested improvement actions (expressed in terms of observable behaviors)
- Clear expectations for what each follow-up meeting will cover, and what the employee needs to bring or provide
- Exactly what improvements you expect to see (expressed in terms of observable behaviors), and when you will be satisfied that the desired improvements have taken place
- Consequences for failing to improve

If the employee raised concerns during the evaluation meeting that require your action, give the employee a timeline and sense of structure for expecting responses from you. As the manager, you are responsible for making sure that follow-up occurs, both in terms of the desired behavior changes as well as the meetings or discussions to monitor or confirm the changes. If you don't care enough to follow up, why should the employee care enough to follow through?

Chapter 15

Diversity, Fairness, and Equal Opportunity

You only need look around your company and at your customers to see how diverse the world of business is today. The global economy includes your company, no matter what your line of business. The people who work for your company create a broad spectrum of talents, interests, cultures, ages, and other qualities, making for an interesting and dynamic environment. It's very important for you to know the rules regarding fairness and equal opportunity in the workplace, as well as how to handle conflicts that may arise from any differences among employees.

Respect Differences

Respect sounds like such a basic, simple concept. You give others space to practice their beliefs and values, and they do the same for you. Kids today learn this concept as preschoolers, when differences don't matter. But people change as they grow up and gain experience in the world. They develop biases, intolerances, and prejudices—a sad reality of the adult world.

ESSENTIAL

Encourage employees to refrain from using their native language when other employees who do not speak the language are present. Regardless of what's being said, the practice excludes others from the conversation and is often perceived as rude and divisive.

Everybody is different somehow. Funny thing, though, is that people don't often see themselves as the ones who are different! They instead complain about the appearances and behaviors of other people as though they are somehow wrong. Or, as they're more likely to view it, as though they're somehow more right.

Nonmerit Factors

The laws that protect workplace diversity identify certain core characteristics as nonmerit factors, that is, factors that must be excluded from consideration when deciding whether an applicant merits employment. These include the following:

- Age
- Race
- Disability
- Gender
- Ethnicity
- Sexual orientation
- Religion

It violates federal and often state laws to treat employees differently on the basis of any nonmerit factor. State laws sometimes add to this list; as a manager, you must know the laws in your state. Additionally, your company may have policies that further define expected and prohibited behaviors in the workplace. Your company, and sometimes you personally, can face legal action and civil liability for violating these laws.

Later chapters in this book address the legal perspectives of equal opportunity, discrimination, and harassment. See Chapters 18, 19, and 20 to read about the laws and regulations that affect behavior in the workplace.

Celebrate Individuality

Getting along in the workplace doesn't mean that everyone should strive to be the same. From the narrow perspective of productivity in the workplace, each person's unique qualities are what make effective teams. They broaden perspectives, offering insights that can open new avenues of market share. From the wider perspective of human interaction, the sharing of unique qualities makes life interesting and fosters new bonds in the global community. These extended dimensions are especially essential for companies that have operations in other countries.

Generations Apart

The workplace has always had its mix of young and old. What's different about today's workplace is that roles and responsibilities are seldom linked to age. In former generations, "kids" were hired on and "old-timers" took them under wing, teaching them both job skills and social roles within the hierarchy of the company. Younger workers respected the wisdom of older workers, knowing that someday it would be their turn to receive such deference.

Now it *is* someday, but it's not quite what everyone expected. The American population is aging, and so, not surprisingly, is its workforce. We're living longer; it makes sense that we're working longer, too. What else are we going to do with ourselves? How else will we support our longer lives?

The Changing Status Quo

Technology, typically the glory field for the young, has upended the workplace status quo. Many younger workers enter the workforce at higher levels, stepping into management positions because of their technical knowledge and experience. Though there has always been a mix of young and old in the workforce, today older workers are just as likely to be learning the ropes from younger employees. And with the end of mandatory retirement, the age gap in the workplace may span two or three generations—fifty or sixty years may separate the youngest and the oldest employees.

FACT

The U.S. Bureau of the Census reports that the number of twenty- to thirty-four-year-olds declined by 6 million in the 1990s, while the number of people over age fifty increased by 12 million. By the year 2010, there will be more people age fifty or older holding jobs than people under age fifty. By the year 2020, 20 percent of the American population—62 million people—will be age sixty-five or older.

As new technologies such as personal computers and the Internet began booming in the 1990s, companies hired techno-whiz kids—young people with brilliant skills in narrowly focused technology areas—like crazy. Competition was hot, growth was fast, and the stakes were high. Web-based upstarts and established companies alike vied to lead the pack into a technology-driven future. In such an environment, the young hotshots flashed to the top. Once there, they hired people like themselves—smart risk-takers who supported, but didn't challenge, each other's ideas. People who didn't fit the new mold suddenly didn't fit in at all.

Older employees and even managers who had been in the workforce long enough to understand its dynamics grew frustrated. Corporate structure forced them to take advice and direction from superiors who knew little beyond the scope of their technology world. They didn't know about business models, and they didn't know the market. What could have been a "dynamic duo" level of collaboration instead became a standoff. As older employees tried to get comfortable with the new technology, the whiz kids resented their "interference" and continued to dictate solutions or use technology to retain their superiority in the workplace.

Meanwhile, older employees continuously tried to take a new technology and mold it to their own outdated ways of doing business. The result was often a disaster. Each age group resisted the other's knowledge. In many companies, the rocky start ended in disaster, with the company falling apart or returning to its previous business models. Ultimately, both sides—and companies—lost more than they gained.

Finding Balance

Such a clash of cultures presents unique challenges for managers. Younger and older employees tend to have different attitudes and approaches toward work. Younger people often want to be left alone to complete assigned projects without interference. They expect managers to trust them to do this. If they fail to come through, there's always an external reason. This is not, in the young employee's mind, an effort to escape accountability, but simply the way things turned out. Game over, push restart. Move on.

Older employees are generally accustomed to, and comfortable with, more structure. Their work and life experiences have taught them that progress is a series of steps, and moving through them is a matter of taking them one at a time, not all in a single leap. They expect their managers to show interest in these steps and to appreciate their steady progress toward completion. Today's manager must be able to work with both extremes, taking the time to understand the issues each generation's culture brings to the workplace.

Gender Neutrality

People begin to think in high school or even earlier about what they want to do and be as adults. While once sons followed fathers into their work worlds, now sons and fathers often inhabit very different environments. Today, fathers and mothers might well follow their sons or daughters into business. For the first time in America's history, there are more women than men in the workforce. Some work because they have no other option; long gone are the days when it was a young woman's role to marry a man who could take care of the family while she raised the children. Both stay-at-home dads and career moms have redefined today's workplace.

Today's younger employees (under age forty) inhabit a work world very different from the one that existed when they were born, when men were bosses and women were secretaries. Younger women today have no trouble being leaders, and younger men have no trouble recognizing and accepting women in leadership roles. People who entered or were already in the workforce twenty years ago—men and women alike—aren't always comfortable with the equality of roles in today's business environment.

Men in their forties and older (and some women as well) may be uncomfortable with women in management positions, either as their equals or their superiors. Younger women who are managers sometimes misinterpret this discomfort or are unable to adapt their behaviors to help bridge the gap. They might feel older men are disrespectful of their authority and knowledge. And sometimes these perceptions are accurate. Gender equity in the workplace is still an ideal despite the advances of recent years.

Women in the Workforce

A 2000 Gallup poll reveals that while women have greatly extended their presence within the ranks of management, Americans still prefer male to female bosses. Of those polled, 48 percent said they prefer to report to a man, while 22 percent said they prefer to report to a woman and 28 percent said it didn't matter. Women are more likely than men to prefer a female boss (26 percent to 19 percent), but men are more likely to have no preference (35 percent of men, 23 percent of women). In 1975, 63 percent of Americans preferred their managers to be male, compared to 7 percent who preferred women at the reins.

FACT

In 2004, women made up 59 percent of the American workforce. Women also fill half of all professional and management positions. However, women hold only 15 percent of upper-level executive positions in major corporations.

Like employees, managers have biases when it comes to gender in the workplace. It's important to realize this, and to recognize yours—they aren't always what you expect.

ALERT!

There's nothing wrong with employees having a good time together, of course. But it is important to draw a clear line between recreation and work. Discuss business matters at meetings when everyone can be present, not during activities that some cannot or choose not to attend.

Arthur was unaware of his biases until angry employees pointed them out to him in a staff meeting. It turned out that Arthur had a clear pattern of promoting only women. The women he promoted were deserving; that wasn't the issue. The issue was that equally competent men didn't get the same opportunities for advancement because of Arthur's bias toward women. This resulted in resentment among the male employees and created considerable divisiveness within the work group. The men's concerns arose during a meeting to address the inability of the group to work as a team.

Once his employees confronted him with the evidence, Arthur saw the pattern as well. He realized that he was more comfortable with women, more trusting of women, and less threatened by women. Though Arthur did not perceive his actions to be discriminatory, his pattern of behavior certainly was. It could have resulted in legal action being brought against him and the company by the men who were denied promotion opportunities.

An environment of openness is critical. A manager needs to encourage teamwork and collaboration and to identify roles and responsibilities to reduce the influence of biases in the group. Sometimes this forces people to work together even when they're not necessarily comfortable. But sometimes this is necessary so they learn to understand, and hopefully respect and appreciate, each other. An environment where ideas are encouraged and respected, even if not acted upon, helps to build a sense of equality.

Actions Speak Louder Than Intentions

If desire to foster equality in the workplace isn't enough to motivate some managers, a plethora of laws and regulations is at the ready to nudge them. Like other nonmerit factors, sex discrimination is illegal. Managers must understand what kinds of behaviors and promotional actions can be interpreted as biased, even when there is no intent to discriminate. Uninformed and insensitive behaviors can lead to serious legal and professional problems.

Sexual harassment remains a significant issue in today's workplace. One in six employees, the vast majority of whom are women, report that they experience sexual harassment in the workplace. Whether you believe incidents of harassment are real or perceived, you must make it clear that you're serious about enforcing the workplace rules to prevent it. Comments made in jest can come back to haunt you.

What Is Fairness?

Fairness is an underlying theme in many laws, regulations, standards, and policies that apply to the workplace. Of course everyone likes to be treated fairly. Does this mean that all people should expect the same treatment as all others? Well, not really. As much as people want to be treated the same, they also want to be treated as individuals. Fairness is a tough standard because of its subjective nature. What you like and dislike often become significant factors in defining what you consider to be fair. Some fairness standards make sense in discussion but become convoluted and complex when put into practice. Most people agree that everyone should have the same opportunities to pursue their interests and aptitudes. The water gets deep and murky, however, when it comes to figuring out just that means.

Then and Now

In kindergarten, the concept of fair is pretty simple. Everyone gets a turn, everyone tries the same tasks, and everyone gets attention from the teacher. Some kids excel and the teacher praises them. With equal enthusiasm, the teacher also praises the efforts of the kids who don't excel. In kindergarten, effort counts just as much as achievement. By college, however, the scales have tipped. You might study harder than you've ever studied before and still fail the geology test and get a bad grade. Fair? It's the same test everyone else took—some passed, some didn't. Maybe geology isn't your thing, but you can do calculus in your sleep. How fair is this? After all, everyone else is better than you in one, and you're better than everyone else in the other. But your perception is likely to be that geology class is unfairly difficult, and you could find it hard to believe that others feel that way about calculus class.

The same goes for the work world. Some people simply have more aptitude than others. You might want to be a novelist or an astrophysicist, but unless you clearly have abilities and aptitude, these doors aren't open to you. Is this fair? If you have the abilities and aptitude, you probably think so. If not, you likely don't. What makes it fair overall is that you have the opportunity to compete, even if you're eliminated in an early round. This is pretty much the concept of fairness that applies in the workplace. Just as in college there are tests and grades, in the workplace there are performance standards. The clearer the guidelines in either setting, the fairer the outcomes feel.

Competition for promotions is often intense. Sometimes there are hard feelings after the decision is made, and it's natural to want those who didn't get the promotion to feel better. Helping is fine, as long as you can do so without violating the privacy of the promoted employee. Keep discussions focused on the unhappy employee and the issues with his or her performance compared to the job's performance standards rather than other employees.

In every work group, each employee brings certain strengths. Such diversification is essential, even when job functions are similar. Some are always going to shine behind the scenes, or in a supporting role, while others will always be more visible. Unfortunately, the one in the visible role gets a lot of attention, not only from the manager but also from clients. This often leads to more opportunity, responsibility, and money.

Handling Conflicts

In the workplace as well as in life, those who are more visible continue to be perceived as more deserving. But lose a few of the background players and see how quickly your productivity takes a dive. What happens when the bookkeeper gives notice—on her way out the door? Or the office manager quits, or the technical writer? Watch how quickly the so-called stars start to flounder—usually with you right along beside them. Managers need to constantly reinforce with employees that they are all working together and that each person is contributing.

When trying to explain a situation of apparent inequity or favoritism, focus on the employee who is complaining, not the one (or ones) whom he or she is complaining about. It's not your responsibility or your place to defend your actions regarding other employees; those are between you and them, and revealing too much information can result in complaints (often justified) about breaching confidentiality. When an employee does come to you with an accusation of unfairness, address it completely and thoroughly.

If you don't know the details, schedule a meeting to discuss them after you've had a chance to do some research. Collect as much information from as many sources as possible. Going into a discussion about why someone else got promoted without knowing the circumstances is like scuba diving without checking the air gauge on the tank. It won't be long before you're in serious trouble.

Be kind, yet direct and factual. Speak in terms of observable behaviors and measurable results. Refer to the specific performance standards or company policies that apply to the situation. Focus on the person's strengths and how he or she can improve them. Even when the issue is a deficiency or weakness, identify it in such a way as to support whatever strengths lie within it. "You did a great job with the Robinson account, bringing it in on time and under budget. This shows that you have the ability to manage multiple job functions concurrently. However, the client felt you focused too intensely on the budget and not enough on their needs. Let's talk about how we can improve your communication skills."

Finally, ask the employee about his or her goals—with your department, with the company, with his or her career. Where would this person like to be in three, five, and ten years? How does he or she see the current job as leading to the fulfillment of long-term goals? Structure a formal improvement plan, with the employee's full and equitable participation, that supports those goals to the extent possible.

Recognizing and Nurturing Potential

As a manager, you have the obligation to help employees identify their potential (put on your coach or your mentor hat). The first step is to ask the employee what he or she wants to achieve, and what route appears likely to travel in that direction. What obstacles exist? How can the employee overcome them? Are the employee's perceptions of ability and potential the same as yours? If not, why?

ESSENTIAL

Cultivate the talents and abilities of people who already work for your company whenever possible. Your company already has a considerable investment in its employees, and statistics show that employees promoted from within are more likely to succeed than are new hires brought into management positions.

Opportunity is a significant element of equity. This means opportunity for growth as well as recognition. How can this person best contribute, now and in the future, as an individual? Opportunities come alive for people when you, as a manager, take the time and interest to assess their interests and work with them to realize them. Such opportunities are not always obvious or what they seem. To help cultivate an employee's potential, you could do the following:

- Send the employee to several work-related seminars and conferences each year.
- Invite the employee to accompany you to a meeting or event that he or she otherwise wouldn't be able to attend.
- Incorporate a discussion of future goals and objectives into every formal performance evaluation, including follow-up from the previous evaluation.
- Ask each employee several times a year what you can do to support his or her career aspirations. Pay attention to goals that change; goals *should* change if the employee is making any progress toward meeting them.

Ongoing training or continuing education is often required for many technical and professional staff, though could be easy to overlook when it comes to support staff. While a course in computer code might hold little appeal for an administrative assistant, a class in creating PowerPoint presentations might. Every now and then, if your budget allows, let employees attend workshops that aren't directly related to their jobs but that interest them for some reason. A technician might enjoy a class in graphic design, or a sales representative might like to go to a seminar on construction methods. Some choices might seem a bit far afield, but most people will choose options that appeal to their longer-term goals.

Take time to thank the person in the mailroom, your secretary, or the department coordinator. It's easy to praise the people who do the most obvious tasks, but don't forget about all the others who work to make those tasks possible.

The Risks of Playing Favorites

Favoritism is generally a personal matter. A manager likes someone, so he or she gives that person breaks. Sometimes favoritism is obvious; other times it's subtle. In every case, however, favoritism divides. It pits employees against each other (not always consciously), forcing them to compete for your attention. No one likes to feel left out or passed over. Experiencing these feelings as adults often recalls memories of unpleasant situations from childhood. It's one thing to compete for something and lose because the winner is truly better. It's quite another to lose because you didn't have a chance in the first place. Sometimes favoritism arises from a genuine desire to do something good for an employee that then evolves into a mentor-turned-monster scenario. Often favoritism exists as a form of office politics, with employees jockeying for position in the kiss-my-shoes line.

A Favoritism Example

Beware! Favoritism can come back to bite you before you know what happened. Here's an example.

Phillip came to work one day and dropped a bombshell on his manager's desk: his letter of resignation. He'd had it, he said; what had once been a very pleasant work environment was now a nightmare. He was tired of the complaining and the backstabbing and the lack of cooperation from certain others in the office. And now he'd been passed over for a project he'd proposed in last month's staff meeting. The project went instead to one of those others.

"Those others" were a small clique everyone called by the name of "Jean's disciples." They had coffee every morning with Jean, the department manager. Throughout the day, Jean called on one or more of these employees to run errands and handle special assignments. Because the work team continued to produce results, Jean was oblivious to the dynamics of the workplace. Other team members could see that she was out of touch, but Jean didn't respond to their hints. By the time Jean realized there was trouble, she was holding a valued employee's resignation letter.

In many ways, Jean was lucky the only cost to her and to the company was the loss of Phillip's employment. Though that cost continued because Phillip took a position with a competitor, things could've been much worse. Often, circumstances of favoritism end up as harassment claims, when the favoritism fades, or as discrimination claims from employees denied opportunities.

Star Players

When an employee truly does bring a special and highly valued talent or ability to your department, of course you must recognize that in some way. High performers need constant challenge to keep them interested and motivated. They need new responsibilities, recognition and praise, and higher salaries. At the same time, it's important—and essential—for you to make it clear that you are committed to providing opportunities for all employees who report to you. As valuable as one person might be, your department cannot succeed in meeting its goals without the full cooperation and collaboration of all its members.

Nowhere is this delicate balancing act more obvious than in professional sports. The news media overflow with stories about the astronomical salaries of talented young stars, many of whom have little experience going into the professional arena but who appear to have potential the team simply can't live without. Talent, of course, isn't everything. Yet talent leads many young athletes, even unproven in the professional arena, to believe they are entitled to such riches and rewards. In sports that have salary caps limiting the amount of money a team can spend overall for players, such high-cost players can prevent the team from keeping or acquiring other valuable players.

The business world is no different. When "star players" come into the company at inflated salaries or with other benefits that other employees don't get, it's difficult to maintain any sense of fairness. And when entire companies build around such inflation, it doesn't take a crystal ball to see that eventually the balloon will pop.

Chapter 16

Promoting and Hiring

Hiring and promoting people are essential functions within any company. Both offer great potential for mutual benefit—when you handle them properly. Mishandled, however, employment and promotion choices can cost your company far more than money. Studies suggest that hiring and promoting from within is more successful than bringing in outsider candidates. But companies are twice as likely to look beyond their current employee population when new jobs become available. Sometimes, of course, going outside is the only way to acquire new talent that your company needs. So how do you find the best people for the job?

The Right Start

The hiring process varies widely. Small companies, particularly family businesses in small towns, may still do business on the basis of a promise and a handshake. Other companies have extensive procedures and paperwork. Though prospective employees often believe there are laws and regulations that govern the hiring process, legal guidelines are broad, and they target big issues like discrimination and equal opportunity. There are no laws that say you must hire the most qualified candidate for the job. Most employment laws attempt to define the ways in which a private sector company or manager can do the following:

- Establish job requirements (but not what they are)
- Interview applicants
- Make employment opportunities available
- Treat the employee on the job with respect to work hours and conditions, workplace safety, and certain other factors
- Terminate employment (in some states)

Laws also require companies to treat employees in certain ways, and they may regulate such factors as benefits packages and work hours. (Chapter 18 provides information about laws and regulations that apply to the workplace.) Depending on the industry, the company's size, and the amount of bureaucracy, these requirements may be more or less flexible.

In an ideal world, a written job description defines the basic expectations that you and your company have for employee performance. This message runs consistently through advertising, interviews, and performance evaluations. How closely reality matches the ideal varies widely; many small companies do not even have job descriptions because employees perform so many tasks essential to keeping the business running.

Beyond laws are corporate policies—the internal guidelines that tell managers what they can and cannot do when it comes to hiring, evaluating, promoting, and firing employees. It is always important to start with your HR department to make sure you are acting in a responsible manner from the perspective of the law as well as complying with internal policies. Key questions to address include these:

- Must you interview and consider internal applicants before seeking external applicants?
- If internal applicants meet the job's basic requirements, must you hire them?
- Do union contracts include stipulations and procedures for considering potential employees?
- Do requirements differ for employees hired to fill vacated versus newly created positions?
- Do requirements differ according to the job's classification (hourly, salaried, exempt, nonexempt, permanent, temporary)?
- How can (or must) factors such as race and gender affect your selection process?
- Can you decide to hire someone with less experience or fewer qualifications because that person shows an eagerness and aptitude for learning, or must you accept the candidate whose actual skills are the strongest?
- Can you go through the entire interviewing process and decide that rather than hiring any of the candidates you want to post the job again?

The rules are different for public sector (government) jobs, union contracts and collective bargaining agreements, and certain other settings. In these settings, stringent details may regulate the entire process of hiring or promoting, placing any influence beyond your control.

The Job Description

Managers discuss the elements of the job description when they interview job applicants, so employees coming into the company know these actions are among their responsibilities. A job's specifications should be reasonable and realistic, yet they should also allow for expansion and growth as circumstances change within your company and the industry. Advances in technology might ratchet up expectations; it's important to communicate even in the job interview the need to stay ahead of the curve. When written correctly, the job description is the platform for the job's measurable standards. The more effectively you establish this in the job interview, the greater clarity new employees will have about your (and the company's) expectations.

Clarity and specific details should characterize all job descriptions, even if performance is difficult to quantify. Sometimes you need to take a step back to look beyond the apparent tasks of the job to assess what factors are within the employee's control. It's neither fair nor wise to hold people accountable for actions and results beyond their influence. Within the factors employees can control, identify and describe specific behaviors. Rather than expressing the concept of "follow-up," identify the task: "Send thank-you notes to clients after projects are finished." This distinction makes clear the precise action you expect an employee to take and that you will measure.

Many managers overlook the most highly qualified candidates: current employees. Even when companies routinely post jobs internally before conducting outside recruiting, managers may perceive the need to look outside the company. Taking an employee from another job leaves that department's manager looking for a replacement. But current employees have knowledge of the company and often have surprising skills and interests they don't use in their present jobs.

Ironically, many managers have little or nothing to do with writing descriptions for jobs in their departments. In many companies, the writing of job descriptions, and even the interviewing and hiring processes, are the venue of HR or personnel. This is often the case in companies that operate under collective bargaining agreements. It doesn't hurt, however, to offer your suggestions.

Applications, Resumes, and References

Job applications and resumes have a single purpose: to get the candidate an interview. It's asking for trouble to make an employment offer solely on the basis of written qualifications. You want to meet the person and have the opportunity to ask questions about his or her qualifications. Many people, particularly those who apply for technical or organizational jobs, have backgrounds and experiences that make for interesting conversation. There also is nothing like the "eyeball factor" to help you gauge how well someone might fit into the work group you supervise.

FACT

According to the *Wall Street Journal*, one-third of job candidates lie about their experience, education, or employment history on their applications or resumes. With alarming frequency, the news media report stories of people caught in the lies of their resumes, from upper-level executives to college professors to research scientists.

But intuition is sometimes a faulty barometer. The sad truth is that more people than not lie on their resumes and on job applications. They may inflate their experience and qualifications or leave out less favorable details. Sometimes the misrepresentations have honorable intentions, such as the person who claims a college degree while still completing the last few credits. People may fudge employment dates to cover extended periods of unemployment, even when those periods occurred for reasons that would not harm their chances at future jobs.

Employment experts urge prospective employers to consistently check references to make sure at least the facts are correct. Many companies—and yours might be among them—are reluctant to do more than confirm of dates of employment and job titles, but most will at least do that as such information is purely factual. Mismatches tell you that the person has either made a significant error or outright lied. Such actions are cause for immediate termination should the person make it past the hiring stage. When the lie is significant, it is difficult for it to escape detection for very long as the person's inability to perform the tasks becomes apparent.

Interview Basics

The job interview is a two-way street. As you're trying to determine whether this person is a good fit for the job, department, and company, the person you're interviewing is also evaluating those same factors. Though the pendulum swings along the job availability continuum, an applicant is no more likely to take your job, no questions asked, than you are to offer it.

The most effective approach is to structure the interview as a dialogue in which you ask a few questions about the candidate's experience or education, then let the candidate ask a few questions about the job and the work environment. Prospective employees want to know how you envision applying their skills and abilities; they will also be curious about the other employees in the department and what kinds of working relationships they might expect.

ALERT!

Is the perfect candidate for your job someone in another job in the company whose shoes would be hard to fill? Discuss transitional measures with the other manager. Sometimes passing over someone for a new position because the person is exceptionally good at his or her current job is enough to cause the person to leave for opportunities elsewhere. Better at least to keep this talent within your company.

Some people may be most concerned with factors such as whether they can put family photos on their desks, while others want to know how you as the manager can separate the contributions multiple employees make to the same project. By the time the candidate reaches you for an interview, he or she has likely already made it through a preliminary interview with human resources. You may choose to offer a tour of the department or work area or to introduce some of your key employees.

Finding the Right Match

Most jobs actually have two sets of requirements: those related to expertise and experience, and those related to personality and work style. Requirements related to skill sets appear to be fairly clear-cut and easy to establish. This is probably true for jobs in which the tasks are highly structured or even rote. If you need to hire someone to operate a punch press in the production department, it's easy enough to determine whether an applicant has the knowledge and skill to do this. Because the job itself is highly structured, the person's personality and work style are less relevant to performance. If you're hiring to fill a position in the sales department, the situation is far more subjective. Because the job involves forming relationships (however short-lived they might be), work style and personality are significant factors.

An Interview Example

There is more than one way to conduct an effective interview. Like Michael, you may employ a multilevel approach.

Michael was the manager of a software company's marketing department. His work group spent a lot of time together, and its productivity depended on how well employees could work collaboratively. It was crucial that new employees had both the appropriate job skills and the right "mesh" with the rest of the group. There was little room for frail egos or high-and-mighty attitudes, and Michael could sniff out either all the way from the lobby. His department needed people who were talented yet genuinely humble. They spent much of their time in meetings or on the phone with clients and prospective clients. They had to be people-people, and they had to be good listeners.

The company's HR department confirmed resumes and conducted preliminary interviews, then forwarded the applicants who met the job's technical qualifications and the company's basic requirements. One "test" Michael incorporated into job interviews was to drone on and on about a particular subject to see how the applicant responded. This gave him a sense of how the person might respond to a client who did the same thing. An applicant who maintained eye contact, nodded and smiled, and appeared to remain interested even when Michael began to bore himself earned an invitation to tour the department and meet with the group. An applicant who checked his watch, fidgeted in his chair, interrupted, or whose eyes glazed over was not likely to make it to the next round.

It was also important to Michael that the people he hired have diverse interests. His department supported a wide range of clients and projects. So he also engaged applicants in dialogue about events in the news. He broached topics of interest to the local community, to see whether an applicant could pick up the threads and weave them into a conversation. And he asked both work-related and more general-interest questions, just to see how he felt as he and the applicant talked. At this point, intuition guided many of Michael's reactions. Was this a person he wanted to spend time around? Was this someone he wanted to mentor or nurture? Was this someone who would get along well with the department's current employees and clients?

The final step in Michael's hiring process was to have the applicant meet with a number of his employees. He usually scheduled a formal meeting in which three to five employees sat down with the applicant to describe their work and ask the applicant questions. Michael also tried to have several informal connections take place, to get "first impression" feedback from employees as well.

Before making a final decision, he reviewed all the factors and responses, and compared them to what he knew were his personal biases. One of those biases was about attitude. Michael felt it was nearly always a better decision to hire someone who was eager and cooperative but a little short on practical experience than someone whose experience was astounding but who had an arrogant attitude. When Michael was satisfied that he had a balanced and quantifiable perspective, he consulted with HR one last time and then made a decision.

There are aspects of Michael's approach that appear arbitrary. It encompasses intangibles on Michael's end, such as his ability to select employees that his experience tells him are good choices for the work and the department. These are inherent dimensions of subjective judgment. But if you look closely, you'll see that Michael's approach incorporates a great deal of consistency as well, following the same pattern of questioning in each interview.

The Interview from Start to Finish

Interviewing is a craft. You won't excel at it right away, but you can become quite skilled as your experience grows. There are many books and workshops that focus specifically on interviewing; if your job involves more than one or two interviews a year, invest in some training. At the very least, take an HR specialist or manager to lunch and ask for tips and suggestions. In general, in your interview you should do the following:

- Describe the actual job activities. Explain what a typical day in your department is like and what kinds of successes and challenges employees encounter.
- Describe the work environment. Is it collaborative or independent? Do people get individual recognition, or does the group sink or swim as one? Is there a lot of overtime, and what compensation is there, if any, for putting in extra hours?
- Ask a few questions that require simple, factual responses about information on the resume or job application. Watch for hesitancy in responding or for answers that don't match what's on paper.
- Ask the applicant for examples that demonstrate his or her abilities and skills in particular areas. If building relationships with prospective clients, ask the applicant to describe two or three similar experiences that relate to your circumstances.
- Press for specifics. If an applicant says "I like that kind of environment," ask how it is similar to or differs from work environments the employee has experienced in the past. If the employee says he or she has done "something like that," get details. Just how, exactly, was the applicant's previous experience "like" the requirements of the job?

- Listen for grandiose claims or statements that don't make sense. If in doubt, question. Again, press for specifics and ask for examples. Back-pedaling and convoluted explanations should raise the red flag about the candidate.

Keep your comments neutral and your thoughts to yourself. Unless you know without a doubt that this is the person you intend to hire, don't give the impression that this is the case. Likewise, don't imply that you're not hiring this person, either. No deal is a done deal until the hired candidate shows up for work. It's worth your while to remain open and positive with candidates who come in second or third. You may be able to go back to them when other jobs become available or if your first choice washes out for any reason. Some human resources experts estimate that as many as a third of new hires do not stay in their new jobs.

Maintaining Balance

The challenge for all managers is to balance the book and the story. The book—laws, regulations, policies—follows a strict structure. The story—personalities, work styles, potential—exists within and at the same time extends beyond the book. While it's crucial for you to go by the book as far as laws and company policies go, it's also essential for you to make decisions that are consistent with the story of your department (its needs). There has to be a happy medium between finding the best person to advance the interests of the company and to be a positive fit in the group.

This isn't to say that you should only hire people you like or that your employees must approve of new members to the team. Not all jobs require close interaction among employees. Use sound and rational judgment. It's more important for a computer programmer to know your company's network and applications inside and out than to be able to discuss the political environment in the Middle East. It might even be acceptable for this person to be a bit on the antisocial side—computers don't engage in dialogue—as long as he or she has the right skills and isn't toxic to others. You might not want to go for coffee with this employee, but he or she will make a positive contribution to your department or company.

Play It Safe

There are a lot of topics you cannot ask about in an interview. Among the obvious should be age and religion. Also high on the taboo list are birthplace, marital status, children, sexual orientation, or anything that might allow you (intentionally or unintentionally) to make a judgment based on class, background, lifestyle, or other factors not related to the job's requirements. Be sure you discuss all of these factors with your HR representative and understand, fully and completely, your legal obligations. Failing to do so can have serious consequences for you personally as well as for your company.

If the employment process truly were as simple as following all the laws and rules, there would be no need for employment attorneys. But employment law is a growing field, which tells us that laws and policies aren't enough. Jobs are about more than skill sets. Jobs are about the people who fill them, no matter how much companies might want to diminish that factor.

Concluding the Interview

When it's time to conclude the job interview, let the candidate know what to expect—when he or she might next hear from you, your timeline for filling the position, and whether to anticipate another round of interviews. Some managers like to ask the person for any final thoughts or questions. A few are ready to extend a job offer or decline the candidate at the conclusion of the interview, though most prefer to assess all the candidates a final time before making any decisions. It is especially difficult to say, "Thanks, but no" in person to someone who hopes to get the job.

Reference Checks

No matter how good a candidate appears on paper and in an interview, an important final step in the hiring process is to check references. Many companies have waiver forms for prospective employees to sign that grant permission to contact references. Most references, especially former employers, will not even confirm employment without such a form. When contacting references, focus on verifying the facts the candidate put on the job application. Ask the reference source to provide details: "When did Stacy work for you, and what positions did she hold?"

Question discrepancies with care; this is often a road worth traveling only when the candidate is at the top of your list. Listen for carefully worded responses. Sometimes you learn more from what people *don't* tell you. As during your interview with the applicant, refrain from asking personal or lifestyle questions such as those about marital status, health concerns, or children. Not only is this information none of your business; it's also against the law to consider such factors when making job or promotion decisions.

The Offer: Let's Make a Deal!

You've made your choice, and now it's time to close the deal. Most managers first telephone the person to extend the job offer, and then follow up with a written letter to confirm. You're enthusiastic and excited to welcome this person aboard, so let it show! Though in some situations the job offer is a process of negotiation, most often the candidate knows the terms of employment. Nonetheless, you should review them in your phone conversation.

Some people, especially those who work in technical or competitive fields, have applied for multiple jobs and may be considering several offers. Other people want to take some time to think about working for you and your company. Extend a time period for the person to consider your offer—forty-eight hours is reasonable. Call back after that time. If the person accepts, send the confirmation letter by mail (return receipt requested or certified mail is a good idea).

What if your chosen candidate declines your offer? Hang up the phone and move on to your second choice. People change their minds or are not interested after an interview for any number of reasons. Some will contact you to take themselves out of contention, though most will wait to see whether you offer a job. When the person was someone who seemed very enthusiastic during the interview, you might ask the reason for the change of heart. Sometimes there are factors you didn't consider or circumstances about the job that the candidate misinterpreted. You may have a chance to encourage your top choice to reconsider if you feel he or she is highly qualified and desirable for the job.

Chapter 17

Downsizing, Layoffs, and Firing

Things change: company leadership or ownership, market share, technology, regulations affecting particular industries, people. As a result, departments and sometimes even entire companies consolidate, combining resources in attempts to get more with less. Such changes often affect people across the company through no actions of their own. In other circumstances, people instigate change themselves through poor job performance or disciplinary issues the company can resolve only by severing ties. Sometimes hiring or promoting a person was a mistake. In nearly any scenario of change, managers shoulder the burden of swinging the axe and cleaning up afterward.

When You're the Bearer of Bad News

Although it's difficult to be the bearer of bad news, laying off employees doesn't have to be a nightmare you relive over and over. There will be challenges, and there may be reverberating effects of layoffs and downsizing, but you'll only prove your strengths as a manager if you handle the situation gracefully, as Rosalyn did.

Rosalyn learned in September that her company would reduce its workforce by 30 percent in February. As a manager, Rosalyn had to assess her staff to determine how the skills and strengths of each employee would fit within the new structure. These assessments would determine who would stay and who would be let go. Knowing so far in advance also gave Rosalyn time to think through her decisions and frame the decidedly negative situation in the most supportive way possible.

When the day finally arrived for Rosalyn to issue pink slips, people were understandably upset—even those who didn't lose their jobs. Rosalyn talked individually with each employee being laid off, explaining that it was purely economics and had nothing to do with performance. Even so, the employees, both surviving and laid off, felt the company and Rosalyn, their manager, had betrayed them.

After the laid-off employees left, Rosalyn called a meeting with the survivors. She explained that she understood and accepted their perceptions of the situation but wanted the opportunity to explain her actions. She told each remaining employee that she was very sorry to see each laid-off employee leave, but there had been no choice about cutbacks if the company itself was going to survive.

Then Rosalyn pulled out some charts and reports and started talking about the company's economic status. She showed employees what the company had to produce in terms of billable days just to cover operating costs and make a minimal profit. Everyone was surprised at what it took to keep the company running. The meeting gave them a greater understanding of the challenges the company faced and also an appreciation for the careful way in which the company had approached the downsizing.

Another dimension of the downsizing was restructuring. Several other departments that had also laid off employees were consolidating, which meant Rosalyn's department was gaining employees and functions from other parts of the company. Rosalyn discussed how these employees would fit into the department and allowed her employees to help decide how to reorganize the department to accommodate them. Rosalyn concluded the meeting by thanking the employees for the good work they'd done and expressing her confidence that their strong performance would continue.

Rosalyn handled a bad situation with grace and honesty. Everyone could see that though the situation was beyond individual control, Rosalyn made informed decisions that matched the company's changing needs with the abilities of the employees in her department. Though everyone was angry about the situation, they could not fault Rosalyn for the way she handled it. As a manager, you will undoubtedly face such unpleasant challenges yourself. No one likes shattering another person's world. But everyone has the capacity to handle such a task with professionalism and compassion, as Rosalyn did.

As a manager, you have to be ready to meet the demands of restructuring and downsizing in two ways. First, you need to prepare your employees and support the company by making the changes work. Second, you have to protect your own career.

Big Picture: Restructuring and Downsizing

Companies restructure or downsize to conserve resources and cut expenses, generally because the marketplace has become viciously competitive and there's no longer any way to stay profitable without significant changes. (Restructuring nearly always means downsizing in some way.) Sometimes these are desperation measures made in an attempt to pull the company back from the brink of bankruptcy or closure. While an acquisition or a merger generally has benefits for both companies, individuals pay the price. Some jobs *will* disappear when your company or even only your department merges with another.

Restructuring and downsizing have become more the rule than the exception in today's business world. Industries change rapidly, technology changes rapidly, and companies across industries have learned that survival means being nimble. Companies must meet opportunities and demands, and employees must be ready to be shaken up along the way. Even stodgy industries like insurance are changing seemingly overnight. New consumer trends mean new expectations for all kinds of products and services, from computers to life insurance.

Open the Channels of Communication

Communication is critical in times of challenge. As much as possible (and only when the company is making the information available to employees), managers should try to let people know what actions the company is considering and how these actions might affect individuals. As a downsized or restructured department moves forward, it's important for the manager to be sensitive to workflow, personality conflicts, confusion over who does what, and potential problems.

The restructured group might perceive its manager as somewhat of a stepparent, with partiality toward his or her original employees. If you are this manager, you might feel damned if you do, damned if you don't. Employees are likely to accuse you (or, less personally, the company) of overworking them to increase profits. Sometimes there is a grain of truth in this perception; the company wouldn't have downsized in the first place if it could support all of its resources. Doing more with less, whether equipment or people, is both a challenge and a goal.

Protect Yourself

Major changes in your company will undoubtedly lead you to reconsider your own career. Although you must be cheerleader, mediator, parent, and coach for your employees, you might not believe in the company's new direction. When departments are restructured, managers are sometimes among the first to go as the company attempts to shave costs by retaining the people who actually do the work. You need to be ready to move within the company or to another company. This is the reality of the marketplace.

Companies want loyalty, but at the same they expect us all to accept change and be ready to move. They are not there to provide us security for life. You need to keep your professional skills current. Stay abreast of current thinking and technology, both in your field and in general. These are the factors that will help you make a move when you need to. There is nothing sadder than a person with twenty years in at the Big Corporation who knows nothing beyond how to survive at the Big Corporation.

Small Picture: Individual Failings

There's little satisfaction in watching someone fail. Even the most cynical managers don't want to see that happen to their employees, if only because it implies that they, too, have failed in some way. This is when your parent hat can obscure your vision. Parents don't like to see their children struggle, and often they will do what they can to reduce or eliminate their suffering. Never mind that mistakes are part of learning; they just don't want the lessons to be so harsh. To an extent, this is a good thing. Care and compassion are important ingredients for growing employees and cultivating loyalty. But there comes a point when the parent hat slips too far down on your manager's brow, and caring goes too far.

Where is that point? Well, it can be hard to see until you cross it. Take the following quiz. How often do you find yourself...

Taking time out of your day to redo what an employee has done?
- ❏ Never
- ❏ Once or twice a week
- ❏ Daily

Redoing the same tasks for the same employee over and over again?
- ❏ Never
- ❏ Once or twice a week
- ❏ Daily

Missing opportunities to encourage employees to grow by indicating your expectations and how you'll measure progress?

❑ Never
❑ Once or twice a week
❑ Daily

Spending time after hours on work tasks that aren't really yours, when you have other responsibilities or you could be having a life?

❑ Never
❑ Once or twice a week
❑ Daily

Waking up at night worried about how an employee is performing or whether the employee will complete a project correctly and on time?

❑ Never
❑ Once or twice a week
❑ Daily

Defending an employee's incomplete or incorrect work to other team members, your superiors, or clients?

❑ Never
❑ Once or twice a week
❑ Daily

Asking other employees to pick up extra work to cover for an employee who isn't pulling his or her load?

❑ Never
❑ Once or twice a week
❑ Daily

If you never do any of these things, you might not be paying enough attention to what's going on in your department or work group. It's normal for managers to have to step in every now and then; even exceptionally proficient employees occasionally stumble. But if you're doing three or more of these things once or twice a week, you have an employee who is flailing—and failing.

The Difference Between a Mentor and an Enabler

Troubled employees need guidance on what is acceptable or unacceptable behavior. The correct way to handle a situation in which an employee has gotten off track is to address the problem promptly and directly. This might be all it takes to turn a difficult situation around. Taking another approach, such as covering or making excuses for the person, may seem generous and helpful on your part, but in reality, you may just be enabling the employee to continue making errors. A mentor helps an employee become better at both his abilities and his job. An enabler intends to do that but instead encourages dependent behavior by making excuses and redoing work. This is not a favor to the employee or to the organization. Consider the following scenario.

Randall was a brilliant but inexperienced writer, fresh from the journalism program of a prestigious university. His press releases captivated readers, and the news media often ran his stories just as he had written them. He had very tight deadlines, and he met them. Unfortunately, Randall just couldn't seem to get the facts straight. He transposed numbers, misquoted executives, and made things up when he couldn't contact the people who could give him the details he needed. Marjorie, Randall's manager, spent a lot of her time undoing the damage Randall did. Her superiors suggested that she reassign Randall to other tasks in the public relations office until he was more seasoned, but she resisted.

After all, everyone makes mistakes—that's how she learned, and that's how most people learn. So Marjorie had the department's administrative assistant intercept all of Randall's press releases before they were sent out, and she corrected them. It was a process doomed to fail, and it did. Marjorie had emergency surgery and was out of the office for two months. Randall wrote a press release erroneously suggesting the company would post a loss in its third-quarter report and stock prices plummeted. Marjorie's boss fired Roger and came very close to firing Marjorie as well.

Randall reminded Marjorie of herself when she was an enthusiastic neophyte in the corporate world. That world eventually stomped the enthusiasm out of her, though, with all of its rules and procedures, and she always wondered what would have happened if she'd been more resistant. She viewed her intercessions with Randall as protecting him from also being stomped into compliance, as safe-guarding his ability to express his creativity and earn recognition for his talents. She saw herself as Randall's mentor, the guide who would lead him through the entanglements of the corporate jungle. Marjorie failed to see that Randall made different, and more serious, mistakes than she had made when she was a novice publicist. And she failed to see that Randall was not a good fit for the company, and perhaps not for PR writing at all. He had talent, certainly, but he wasn't apply-ing it in ways that would help his abilities broaden and grow.

However noble Marjorie's intentions, in truth she wasn't so much "sav-ing" Randall as she was salvaging her own ego. Ultimately, her actions were about herself, not about him. And in the end, she was the one who still had a job, although the situation reflected poorly on her as a manager.

Employees are adults, and they need you to treat them as such. They need you to offer guidance on how to do things correctly, efficiently, and in keeping with company policies. They don't really benefit when you do things for them. This teaches them that there are no consequences associ-ated with responsibility.

The Right Way to Help Out

There's nothing wrong with wanting to save an employee who is flounder-ing. In fact, that is part of your role as a manager. But make sure your actions are truly helping. Involve HR, and perhaps coworkers or your superiors, depending on the circumstances. Take a step back, push your parent hat up, and evaluate the nature and scope of the employee's problems. Other employees are watching, too, despite any efforts to handle matters confiden-tially. They can't help but be interested—the situation involves them as well, as members of the work group and also in terms of how they perceive the fairness of events.

When working with a struggling employee, it's important to establish a few basics:

- Whether the employee wants your help and is willing to comply with efforts to improve his or her performance
- Clear goals and priorities for the employee, making sure the employee understands how those goals and priorities affect the work group or department and the company
- Clear and unequivocal procedures and steps for the employee to follow to meet goals and priorities, with the employee fully aware that it is his or her responsibility to follow them
- Ongoing communication to address any problems that might arise or difficulties that the employee encounters in completing the assigned tasks and steps
- A process for monitoring compliance and progress, with positive and negative consequences at each step
- An endpoint beyond which the employee will move to the level of independence the job requires
- An understanding of what happens if the employee is unable to make the necessary adjustments

Writing up an employee for poor performance or other problems on the job is a more serious step than counseling, and in most cases it should take place only after counseling has failed to achieve the desired improvements. It is not the same thing as documenting behavior or counseling meetings. In counseling an employee, your objective is to present the elements of job performance that are unsatisfactory and create a plan for improvement; these are corrective actions that demonstrate you're giving the employee a fair chance to change. Disciplinary action is formal notice that the employee's job is on the line.

In most situations, if you have not counseled the employee, you will find yourself in hot water by moving directly to disciplinary action. There are exceptions, of course—serious mistakes or actions that jeopardize someone's health or well-being could be grounds for jumping to discipline or even immediate termination. (Hopefully your company has policies and procedures that define these actions; if not, work closely with your HR or legal department to respond appropriately.) There could come a point at which you need to ask for a voluntary resignation, suggesting that the employee find work elsewhere, or to fire the employee.

Firing an Employee

No manager enjoys the prospect of firing an employee. Firing someone is the most serious consequence for failing to improve. Before you come to the decision that you need to end a person's employment, you must be sure in your heart of hearts that this is the right thing to do. Then you must make certain that you have complied with any and all relevant laws, regulations, and company policies and that all of the paperwork is completely in order. Laws may regulate employee actions such as firing in your state. Most companies further establish strict policies that require extensive documentation affirming that you have followed those policies. Work closely with your HR department, if your company has one, to be sure you do things right—for your sake as well as the employee's. This is a decision from which there is no turning back.

FACT

Most private sector (nongovernment) jobs are "work at will" positions in which the employee works at the will (and sometimes whimsy) of the employer. Though most mid-size to large companies have specific "fire for cause" policies and terms of employment, these protections are not as yet required by law. In "work at will" states, companies do not need reasons to fire employees, though federal discrimination laws may apply in some circumstances.

The decisions you make regarding an employee's job status—to promote or not, to give a raise or not, to fire or keep on—are not decisions to make without careful deliberation. Plan the meeting to fire the employee according to your company's policies and procedures. Some managers prefer to conduct a firing at the end of the workday, so the employee can collect his or her things and leave without everyone else watching. Will a security guard have to escort the fired employee back to the office to gather his or her possessions and then out of the building? Do you or an HR representative need to supervise the packing?

As humiliating as such requirements might seem, they are often necessary safeguards for the company to prevent theft or sabotage. If the employee has valued work saved on the company's computer network or on a company computer, back up all the files the night before you intend to fire the employee as an added protection. Before the meeting, rehearse what you intend to say. Practice speaking clearly and unemotionally. When you do meet with the employee, take the following steps:

- Have an HR representative or your boss present as well. This bolsters your authority and lessens the likelihood of emotional pleas or outbursts.
- If your company policies or employment agreements allow the employee to have a representative present, make sure the scheduled meeting accommodates this.
- Keep the conversation short, to the point, and unemotional.
- Review the conversations and documentation that support the decision to fire the employee.

In this meeting, it is not necessary or advisable to invite the employee's comments or perspective. The time for that is long past. If you've done your job as a manager, the firing shouldn't come as a total shock to the employee (although the finality of it might be temporarily stunning). You've counseled the employee about his or her performance issues or whatever problems have led to this point, and you've given the employee plenty of opportunities to fix the problems. Keep your cool and stick with the script you've rehearsed. If it is necessary for someone to escort the fired employee from the premises, be sure that person is ready and waiting.

E ALERT!

Union contracts, collective bargaining agreements, and other binding pacts may stipulate the conditions and procedures for firing an employee. It is essential to follow such stipulations to protect yourself and your company from legal action down the road.

As soon as possible after the terminated employee has gone, assemble the other members of the team to give them the news. Keep the reasons for the employee's termination to yourself; such information is confidential. It's important to treat people with respect after they've been fired, regardless of the reasons for firing them. Chances are, the other team members knew this was coming and they know better than you do why this was the only option. Sometimes, however, you need to reassure other employees that this was a matter specific to the fired employee; it's natural for them to feel some fear and apprehension about the security of their own jobs.

Other employees may want to talk about how they feel, but it's generally better to focus on how duties will be reassigned, what the plans are for hiring a replacement, and other such work-related details. The key is to move on. Those who remain will watch how you handle things, and their perceptions will affect their attitudes, performance, and loyalty.

Handling the Fallout With Other Employees

The problems and performance issues of a coworker often affect other employees, sometimes deeply and often well before the decision to fire the employee. No matter how swiftly you might have moved to intervene, they probably think it took too long. And if it did take you a while to catch on to the reality of the situation, other employees are likely frustrated and resentful. They may retaliate by deliberately dragging out timelines, refusing to do anything beyond the minimum required of them, or quitting. Leaving problems to fester poisons the entire work group and can permanently damage the team's cohesiveness and collaborative spirit. Ultimately the situation reflects poorly on you as well; managers stand or fall based on the effectiveness and productivity of their employees.

If this is a big deal—the company lost a major account or other departments became involved—consider a team meeting. One employee's troubles have likely created performance issues for other employees who perhaps couldn't complete their assignments or had to watch their efforts go to waste.

As when you met with the employee, plan your direction and comments. Meet in a location where you and the work group can speak candidly and without being overheard. Establish parameters and limits from the start: no bashing, no gossip, nothing leaves the room. Explain that you know about the problems, met with the involved employee, and established an improvement plan that includes measures for follow-up. Then invite the other employees to share their concerns. Keep the conversation focused on processes and outcomes—don't let the focus stray to people and personalities. A certain amount of venting is inevitable, in most situations—just strive to keep the tone from turning belligerent or derogatory.

It is inappropriate and often illegal for you to discuss another employee's difficulties with the group. Given that performance problems affect the entire team, it's probable that the work group has become a part of those difficulties, but you must still keep the employee's difficulties in strict confidence.

It's important for other employees to understand that you know and care about how the problems have affected them and their work. As much as they might be concerned for their coworker, they also need reassurance that their performance is fine and their jobs are safe. Most people are compassionate and forgiving; if they see that you have responded thoroughly and fairly, the work group will support your efforts. Crisis has the ability to cause groups to pull together or fall apart; if this is a cohesive and well-functioning group, it will rally. If trust and confidence within the work group is severely damaged, however, it might take considerable time for the wounds to heal and the group to return to full function.

Chapter 18
Following the Rules

Laws, regulations, and policies affecting the workplace typically cover issues of safety, health and welfare, and fairness. Employment laws are numerous and complex, existing at the federal, state, and industry levels. Some apply to organizations that employ more than a certain number of employees, while others affect everyone who works. Federal and state regulations that derive from them—along with the workplace policies and practices that result—change as legislatures pass new laws and agencies develop new rules. It is your responsibility as a manager to be familiar with the laws and regulations that apply in your state and industry.

Why Workplace Policies Are Important

Workplace policies define a company's responsibilities and obligations to its employees and customers and vice versa. They also define company expectations and standards. Policies are written for both legal and practical purposes. Some policies explain how the company complies with certain laws and regulations. Some policies delineate procedures and expectations. In most situations, you inherit the policies you must comply with and enforce.

Company policies cover a broad spectrum of topics, but their bottom line is simple. Policies tell employees how to behave. Most company policies are in place to ensure safety in the workplace as well as fair treatment for employees. Most company policies evolve from efforts to interpret and apply laws and regulations, and they thus have a component of compliance that has legal undertones. You might appear to be in compliance when in fact you're not—a situation that can create problems for you as the responsible manager as well as for your company.

FACT

The Equal Employment Opportunity Commission, or EEOC, is the federal agency charged with overseeing compliance with federal laws and regulations aimed at supporting fairness and preventing discrimination in the workplace. These include Title VII of the Civil Rights Act, the Americans with Disabilities Act, the Age Discrimination in Employment Act, and the Equal Pay Act. The EEOC receives about 80,000 charges, or complaints alleging discrimination, a year. Roughly 10 percent of those are charges of sexual harassment and 14 percent are harassment of other kinds.

Other company policies stipulate actions and behaviors important to the company. Your company may have policies that spell out what kinds of jewelry you can wear to work, for example, or which employees must sign noncompete agreements as a condition of employment. Most companies have policies that define the company's attendance expectations, promotion procedures, and scheduled work hours. Departments may further have policies that define their procedures and expectations.

Employment Laws and Regulations

When you look around your company today, hopefully you see a diverse, relatively happy group of people working in a safe environment. However, the workplace has a long and ugly history of unfair and unsafe practices. Depending on how long you've been employed and in what field or industry, you may have experienced some of this history firsthand.

Laws came into effect first to protect employees from hazardous working conditions, particularly in occupations with high risk for injury or death, such as factory work, logging, shipping, railroading, and mining. Over the decades, such legislation expanded to establish protections for employees in all industries. In the 1960s, Congress began tackling issues of discrimination, passing laws such as the Civil Rights Act of 1967 and the Age Discrimination Act of 1967. These laws initiated sweeping and far-reaching changes across all areas of daily life, including the workplace.

Periodically, Congress updates these and other laws that affect employment practices. Fairness and equity legislation outlaws unfair (targeting a single person) or discriminatory (targeting a particular group of people that have in common a characteristic such as race or gender) employment practices, although they have by no means eliminated them.

What Laws and Regulations Mean for Managers

Managers sometimes look on employment laws and regulations as intrusions into the workplace that keep them from doing their jobs. Yes, employment laws do sometimes protect employees who shouldn't receive protection. There are people who will take advantage of every little loophole to avoid doing the work they were hired to do. Every manager (and probably every employee) knows such a person. Yes, it's also true that all these laws and regulations mean there is often a lot of paperwork involved in what used to be simple, even word-of-mouth processes—hiring, raises and promotions, and firing. It used to be, a generation or two ago, that a handshake sealed employment offers and a boss's good mood meant a raise. No more—there are letters of intent and contracts and fair labor standards and—well, you get the picture.

ALERT!

If you don't know your state's employment laws and regulations, look into one of the many professional organizations that sponsors workshops and seminars about employment laws and related issues. Educate yourself about these laws and stay up to date on any changes. Not knowing does not excuse noncompliance.

It's a different world—and one that is by and large much better off than a generation ago. The unpleasant truth is that we have all these fairness laws and regulations because there is such an extensive history of egregious wrongs. People once worked in dangerous conditions for next to no money, with no help from the company if they became injured or even killed on the job. Jobs were available—or not—purely on the basis of race or gender. The laws and regulations that structure the modern workplace became necessary to create a workplace that is equitable to all.

Regulatory Influences

Depending on the state and the industry, as well as the level of employee, various laws, regulations, and rules govern the workplace environment. These regulations might be general, or they might be detailed enough to specify when employees must take rest and meal breaks as well as when overtime can and cannot be required. While as a manager you like to feel that you have some flexibility in terms of how your work group functions, it's essential to remember that there are laws that could supersede your desires. You must stay abreast of these laws! Regulatory influences that affect your workplace might come from any of these sources:

- U.S. Department of Labor, the federal agency (and its dozens of agencies and offices) responsible for administering and enforcing the nearly 200 federal laws that apply to employment and the workplace
- OSHA, the federal government's Occupational Safety and Health Administration, which regulates and enforces a broad spectrum of workplace well-being issues
- NIOSH, the U.S. National Institute of Occupational Safety and Health, an agency of the U.S. Centers for Disease Control and Prevention (CDC) that focuses on research and education to prevent workplace injuries and deaths
- State labor agencies, responsible for administering and enforcing state labor and employment laws
- City and county agencies

Your company is also likely to have policies and procedures to safeguard employee safety and health. You may have a risk management department that oversees employee education and training in safety matters, or you may yourself have such responsibility. Regardless, you have some level of accountability in assuring that employees, as well as the workplace, comply. Be sure you know what that level is.

A Safe Workplace

Every employee is entitled to a safe place to work. As straightforward as this sounds, it is a floating target. There are innumerable laws and regulations that define what "safe" means for specific industries and kinds of workplaces. Each manager is responsible for knowing these requirements and assuring that they are met. In general, managers need to be on guard for environmental hazards as well as aspects of the environment that interfere with productivity. This runs the gamut from tripping hazards (boxes, chairs out of place, wires) to safety railings, adequate lighting, and appropriate protective equipment. Many companies have formal safety committees that regularly review safety issues and investigate workplace injuries to better understand how to prevent them.

When employees complain about their work environments, check out the complaints. Improvements can be as simple as rearranging office furniture and equipment to reduce ergonomic stress or installing brighter light bulbs. Many changes employees want are inexpensive yet can result in vast improvements in productivity and efficiency. Involve employees in finding solutions for bigger concerns. Collaborative efforts often produce creative answers, especially when budget constraints or other factors might keep you from implementing the ideal solutions. This also helps all those involved to understand the problems, the possible options for resolving them, and the pros and cons of each. People also tend to be more accepting of remedies that they help to design and implement.

People who feel that the company doesn't care about their safety and comfort are not likely to be productive. They may take shortcuts that further jeopardize their health and well-being. And companies that don't pay attention to minor concerns are likely to find themselves paying for major problems.

Equity and Fairness

We all have biases. Most are harmless and have little effect on other people. Maybe you don't like blue, prefer to have your telephone on the right side of your desk, or drink only organic coffee. Some biases may consciously or subconsciously affect choices and decisions you make. Perhaps you feel a connection to others who have tattoos and piercings, or maybe you find such adornments repulsive. Your feelings may influence your choices when it comes to hiring, job assignments, or promotions. However, they are biases that could cost you a potentially good employee.

Preserving Equal Opportunity

It's important for managers to recognize that while people are not equal, every employee is entitled to equal opportunity. It's equally important to recognize the role your personal biases, however subtle, play in influencing the perceptions others form about your actions and behaviors. When you're making decisions about an employee's performance, capabilities, and potential, ask yourself these questions:

- How much of this is about the employee and how much about me?
- Does this employee deserve the benefit of the doubt? An extra push?
- Under what circumstances am I making this decision? Is this decision based totally on merit?
- Whom else have I considered? What made me decide in favor of one employee versus another?
- Why am I deciding this way? What are the observable behaviors and quantifiable factors?
- Do I like or not like this employee?
- How are my biases affecting my decision?

This is not to suggest that you list your biases and send them in a memo to HR, of course. That would be of little benefit to you or the company. Your biases are your own. But by acknowledging them to yourself, you can take a step back and think when you are in uncomfortable situations. Your biases are a natural part of you. You don't need to like all of them and probably don't. They're most likely to sneak in on you when you're reacting on autopilot. When you're aware that this can happen, you're more likely to take the extra time to separate your biases from the situation and the action you need to take. The outcome might be quite different.

Crossing the Line: Discrimination and Harassment

There is a point at which biases become discrimination and even harassment. The line of demarcation is often hazy and hard to find—until you cross it. Generally, you've done so when any of the following are true:

- You draw automatic assumptions about individuals based on generalized, collective factors: "She's upset because she's a woman and women are always emotional."

- You hire or promote certain employees for reasons that have nothing to do with their qualifications for the job, notably race, ethnicity, gender, sexual orientation, religion, or physical attractiveness.
- You fail to hire or promote certain employees for factors not related to job abilities or performance, such as race, ethnicity, gender, sexual orientation, religion, or physical attractiveness.
- People are uncomfortable around you, or they complain to others about your actions because of the way you talk about or treat people who are different from you.

Federal laws that protect employees from discrimination in the workplace have spawned volumes and volumes of regulations and procedures. The Fair Labor Standards Act (FLSA), passed in 1938, was the first of these. It established the forty-hour workweek, set a minimum wage, and placed restrictions on child labor. Its numerous revisions established equal pay for equal work and procedures for calculating compensatory time given in lieu of wages. Modified through the years, the FLSA remains the foundational legislation regulating employment practices in the United States.

QUESTION?

What does "exempt" mean?
Exempt means you're not protected under federal law from practices otherwise regulated by the FLSA, such as work hours, paid overtime, and equal pay for equal work. Many companies use the designation "exempt" interchangeably with "salaried" to denote an employee's FLSA status.

Though the FLSA most likely protects the employees that report to you, ironically it may not cover you as a manager. You are exempt from (not protected by) the provisions of the FLSA when you meet the following guidelines:

- You are salaried (you receive a constant paycheck without overtime pay for extra hours worked or docked pay for missed days).

- You have "hire and fire" authority.
- You direct the daily activities of two or more employees.
- You make your own decisions about how and when to do the tasks of your job.
- You spend 80 percent of your time engaged in management activities.

Nearly 200 federal laws regulate the actions of today's employers and the environment of the workplace. Among the most significant are these:

- The Equal Pay Act, passed in 1963 to further clarify the concepts of equal pay for equal work, specifically prohibited companies from paying women less than men for performing the same job tasks.
- The Civil Rights Act was passed into law in 1964. Title VII of this federal legislation makes it illegal for companies that have fifteen or more employees to discriminate in hiring, pay, promotion, and firing on the basis of race, color, religion, gender, or national origin.
- The Age Discrimination in Employment Act, passed in 1967, makes it illegal for companies with fifteen or more employees to discriminate against people who are age forty or older.
- The Americans with Disabilities Act, passed in 1990, established requirements for companies that employ fifteen or more employees to provide "reasonable accommodations" for individuals with disabilities.

Each state has its own further set of laws and regulations, many of which are more restrictive or explicit than federal legislation. Sexual harassment laws, relative newcomers to the discrimination scene, evolved as a result of U.S. Supreme Court rulings that found sexual harassment in the workplace to be a variation of gender discrimination and thus covered under Title VII of the Civil Rights Act. For more about sexual harassment and related issues, see Chapter 19.

Antidiscrimination Policies and Practices

Increasingly, discrimination is subtle and circumstantial. What looks like discrimination in one situation might not be in another. What you need to know as a manager is that behaviors that imply or reflect bias lead to perceptions of discriminatory actions. It's your responsibility to understand what constitutes discrimination from a legal perspective. There are dozens of books that deal specifically with issues related to discrimination in the workplace; Appendix B lists some titles you might find helpful.

FACT

Between 1990 and 1998, the most recent reporting period at the time of this publication, the U.S. Justice Department reported that job discrimination lawsuits tripled, from just under 7,000 to just over 21,500. Furthermore, 65 percent of the more than 43,500 civil rights lawsuits involved employment matters such as discrimination in hiring, promotion, pay, and firing. And 9 percent accused the federal government itself of discriminatory actions.

The most important strategy your company can employ to fight workplace discrimination, as well as to keep it on the right side of the legal fence, is to have strong and stridently enforced policies that define discriminatory actions. These policies should also outline the procedures for employees to take when they feel they've been the victims of discrimination.

As a manager, it's your first responsibility to be sure you do not behave in ways that are or could be interpreted as discriminatory. Be aware of things you say and do that others could perceive as discrimination. Your intentions do not matter nearly as much as the interpretations. Second, be on the alert for discriminatory and/or harassing situations around you. Your failure to take action can make you just as liable as the person committing the actions.

Just Kidding Around or Harassment?

Unwanted social or sexual advances that create an unpleasant work environment or place pressure on an employee are illegal, a violation of Title VII of the Civil Rights Act. Monetary penalties for those found in violation—individuals as well as companies—can be stiff. Career consequences can be severe. Sexual harassment takes many forms, and it involves women pressuring men as well as men pressuring women.

Sexual harassment is a complex area of law, policy, and behavior. Companies can define it in different ways, which doesn't necessarily mean they'll find the courts on their side if an employee files a lawsuit. It's important to realize that much depends on how the person who complains perceives the behaviors. The most insidious sexual harassment is often the least obvious—the male manager who stands just a little too close to female employees, makes comments that can be interpreted as suggestive, compliments female employees on their clothing or perfume. Also in the wrong is the woman manager who does the same with male employees—men are victims of sexual harassment, too, although not as often as women.

ALERT!

All too many harassment defenses start with "But it was just a joke!" What you find funny, someone else might find offensive. When it comes to telling jokes in the workplace, the real punch line could end up knocking you right out of your job. Keep the jokes to yourself.

Unfortunately, what constitutes harassment is not always clear cut. Which of these incidents do you think constitutes harassment?

- A key executive asks his department coordinator to meet him at a restaurant for dinner and to talk with her about how things are going. He presents the invitation as a reward and a way to talk uninterrupted by the chaos and frenzy of the workplace. He just happens to make their reservation at a hotel restaurant. During dinner he casually mentions that he has reserved a hotel room for the night and asks if she would like to join him.

- A new director, a single man brought in from outside who is also new in town, wants to get to know the employees in his department and the town. So he asks a couple of the single women if they would like to have dinner with him and help him get acquainted with the area.

- A female manager and a male subordinate are traveling together on business. She picks him up at his apartment to go to the airport. It is summer and very hot, so he is wearing shorts. Twice in the car she tells him that he has great legs.

If you pegged each of these incidents as sexual harassment, give yourself a pat on the back. Harassment is generally in the perspective of the victim, regardless of the intention of the overture. The new director in the second scenario, for example, was dumbfounded when he learned that the women he invited to dinner complained to the human resources manager. He viewed his actions as cordial and gentlemanly. It made sense to him to ask single women to join him because he felt they would have the freedom to do so. Bad judgment all the way around! Even as he was defending himself, he could hear that he sounded just like a scenario in a sexual harassment training workshop—which is exactly what he became.

Family Matters

There are still a lot of workaholics out there who take on whatever work they have to do and more, but there as many others who insist that work strike a balance with family. This is not only mothers, but also fathers, middle-aged people with aging parents, and even young couples without children who want to balance their careers with their time together. Much is made of the changing characteristics of the American family. Both parents work in 60 percent of two-parent families, and the number of single-parent families has reached an all-time high.

While the influx of women into the workforce over the past two decades spurred many of the changes around company expectations and practices, it's important for managers to recognize that it's not only women who have child-care responsibilities. Many men share parenting activities. Their wives might also have full-time careers; they could be divorced dads sharing custody; or they might be single dads with sole parenting responsibility. Fathers need the same opportunities to take time off for sick kids and school activities as mothers do.

It's not uncommon for dads to choose to stay at home with the kids. Shirley, a vice president at a large corporation, and her husband Paul made this decision when their children became teenagers. They realized their kids needed a parent at home and available for the many school and after-school activities they participated in. Shirley had made sacrifices for Paul's career, including moving to their current location. Then she had a great job opportunity. So they decided that it was his turn to stay at home and her turn to be the breadwinner.

Legislation to Protect Families

When Bill Clinton became the forty-second president of the United States, his first official act was to sign the Family and Medical Leave Act (FMLA) of 1993. The FMLA allows people to take unpaid time off from work—up to twelve weeks if necessary—to care for a newborn or newly adopted child, a seriously ill family member, or because of their own medical conditions, without losing their jobs. The FMLA does not apply to everyone who works, however. To find out if it covers you, talk with your company's HR department or contact the U.S. Department of Labor (see Appendix B for contact information).

Family-Friendly Workplace Policies

Changes in our society, changes in the workplace, and changes in the laws regulating workplace behavior have combined to create work situations for many Americans that are more family-friendly than ever. Companies offer various benefits to support working parents, from child-care referral services to on-site day care, day-care subsidies, and emergency child-care arrangements.

Companies realize that the stress of caring for family members affects employee productivity. They also recognize that they can't pretend these problems don't exist in the lives of all employees, from top executives on down. As employers expect more from employees, they understand that they have to give more in return as well.

ESSENTIAL

It's easy for family issues to spill over into the workplace. Many companies offer the benefits of an employee assistance program (EAP), which can provide guidance and resources for working parents and adult children dealing with aging parents.

Many companies have opened "Bring Your Daughter to Work Day"—originally an effort to encourage mothers to share their professions with their daughters—to include all parents and children. Many organizations, public and private, provide some sort of open house or similar opportunity for employees to share their jobs with their families.

Another area of growing involvement for companies is in addressing the needs of employees who are caring for aging and ailing parents. Companies that offer EAP benefits often include counseling and assistance with decisions about health care and long-term care for elder parents, as well as time off from work to handle these decisions. An increasing number of companies are also offering employees the opportunity to purchase long-term care insurance as an employment benefit, just as they might buy life or disability income insurance.

Personal Accountability

Managers are accountable on several fronts for their performance in the workplace: their bosses, their employees, the company, and the various laws and regulations that apply. In some situations such accountability can take a very personal turn, such as when someone names you as party to a legal action or your conduct violates the law. Regulations hold companies accountable for compliance; companies similarly hold their managers accountable. Your company certainly expects your actions to remain within its policies; step outside the boundaries, and you could find yourself standing in the unemployment line.

Consistency and realistic latitude should coexist in company policies. There are times when following the rules to the letter is counterproductive. Granting exceptions demonstrates an understanding that individuals sometimes have differing needs. Establish a process for considering exceptions that looks at the specific circumstances, the benefits for the employee, and the benefits for the company. If you decide to deviate from policy, explain your reasons for making the decision and emphasize that this is an exception, not a new way of interpreting the policy.

As a manager, you have your own accountability to consider as well as the accountability of the employees that report to you. It is part of your role to make sure everyone understands the laws, regulations, policies, and practices that apply to them and the conduct of their jobs. You may have formal responsibility for arranging or conducting in-service training and other educational processes to familiarize the employees who report to you with relevant health and safety regulations and practices. When you encounter questionable practices or circumstances, question them. This encourages employees to do the same. And when employees bring concerns to you, take prompt action to investigate them.

Chapter 19
Socializing at Work

One benefit of having a job is that you get to spend time with other people. As much as these people might frustrate, annoy, and even anger you, they also provide a venue for social interaction. This is necessary; this is good; this is how it should be. Humans are, after all, social creatures. Most jobs require a certain amount of socializing—at the very least, talking among coworkers to collaborate or talking to customers. But at what point does socializing become dysfunctional? It's another one of those issues where the line can be hard to see until you cross it.

Workplace Personalities and Office Politics

No matter how focused you might want the workplace to be on job skills and performance, many aspects of going to work have more to do with personalities than abilities. Relationships form the foundation for effective teams—people working with other people. The resulting relationships bond people by commonalities. When positive, this synergy establishes a unique and dynamic blending of individuals and personalities that makes the team as a whole more than just the sum of its parts. The negative flip side is competitive divisions, and sometimes "enemy camps," that polarize and often immobilize the work group.

A sort of "relationship language" evolves after a time. People learn to get what they want from each other through indirect methods. These tactics have a give-and-take nature that causes us to view them as "playing games." In the workplace, we call them office politics. The motivations they reflect are personal—a desire for individual gain, a need for individual attention, a longing for recognition and reward. Because satisfying the motivation often comes at the expense of someone else, we tend to perceive these behaviors as manipulative and self-serving.

Office politics—those intersections between whom you know, how much you support the ideas and pet projects of others, what relationships you cultivate and which ones you discourage—often play into promotion decisions, at least minimally. A leadership personality is important for a manager, and that encompasses the ability to schmooze. Job skills matter too, of course. But it's important to make sure the right people know your thoughts and see you shine. Although we all profess to abhor office politics, everyone who works with other people becomes engaged in them to some extent.

Drive, Desire, and Manipulation

At work, everybody wants something—money, status, power. Most people want to come to work and do a good job. They expect recognition, reward, and responsibility. Seems straightforward enough—so why is this such a problem? Because people are human. They are naturally competitive. They may do a good job, but they worry that someone else is doing better or receiving misplaced credit. This gives rise to that little bit of manipulation that will maybe assure that others notice their contributions.

The various faces of such manipulation are familiar to all managers. An employee might drop in on the manager, alone, and casually mention a specific achievement or ask for advice on some work in progress. This self-gratification doesn't usually hurt anyone else unless the person is taking credit for work someone else did. A more damaging variation on this theme is the employee who uses the forum of a meeting to ask another employee an embarrassing question, putting the person on the spot. More insidious still is the employee who requests a confidential meeting with the manager to, out of sincere dedication and as much as he hates to have to do this (not!), alert the manager to certain people who are not pulling their share of the workload or are incompetent or are overqualified or who need remedial help, or, or, or. And then there's the employee who consistently ignores assignments her manager gives her, but gushes, "Gosh, I wish someone had suggested this to me earlier!" when her manager's boss assigns the same project or asks why no one is doing the work.

ALERT!

Managers need to be constantly on guard for office politics. Communicate regularly with all of your employees. Don't jump to conclusions about who is doing what—get all sides of the story. And beware of your own need for strokes. Office politics proliferate in part because managers themselves have hungry egos.

Technology gives people new ways to polish the apples they want others to notice. An employee can send out a grandstanding e-mail—one that gives the impression she is managing the project instead of the team member who really is—and copy everyone in the department or (oops!) the entire company. E-mail has become the latest weapon in political agendas, replacing drinks after work and standing outside in the rain to grab a smoke as the ideal venue for pitching an idea or shining shoes. Who gets copied in and who is left off the list is the ultimate political move—checkmate!

Squelch the Rumor Mill

Few employee behaviors are as frustrating to managers as the perpetuation of rumors. Rumors can undermine morale and productivity far faster than any genuine bad news. To shut down the rumor mill that exists in most companies, some managers use a system similar to a suggestion box. Employees can deposit their questionable information, and the manager then investigates and posts responses on a bulletin board or e-mail them to employees. Other managers appoint an employee committee to handle these activities. If you're worried that this could lead to breaching confidentiality or leaking proprietary information, consider that some form of information is already out there. The truth is seldom as damaging as the rumors.

Where to Draw the Line

It is possible, and desirable, to set reasonable standards for socializing in the workplace. Work should be fun—just not so much so that no work gets done. Here are some ways you can moderate workplace socialization:

- Encourage socializing that is friendly and supportive. Use positive language in your dealings with employees to set the tone and example.
- Discourage gossip and rumors. Establish a "rumor central" where employees can bring rumors to find out whether they're true.
- Support collaborative efforts among employees on projects that warrant more than one participant.
- Encourage employees to consult one another to share knowledge and expertise.
- Provide opportunities for people to just talk, such as when the workday first begins or for a few minutes before meetings start.

If you don't draw the line somewhere, people will take advantage of your apparently laid-back demeanor. Here's an example of what can happen if things get out of hand.

Early in her career, Kathleen worked for a totalitarian boss who allowed no talking at all among employees unless to ask questions or share information that was strictly business related. Employees could talk about personal matters in the break room or at lunch. Kathleen swore that when she became a manager, she would have a "human" department. So now that she was, her department continually buzzed with conversation and laughter. Sometimes it got so loud that other managers came over to ask that employees settle down. Kathleen thought they were being a bit uptight; what was the big deal, as long as people were getting their work done?

But there was the problem: They weren't. Customers were complaining that no one was answering the phone; indeed, at times you couldn't even hear the phones ring for all the chatter and noise. Other departments started complaining, too—they weren't receiving reports and information on time or sometimes at all. Kathleen held a department meeting and told her employees, with obvious reluctance, that they needed to curtail their conversations and focus more on getting their work done. Everyone agreed to do so, but within a few days the noise was back to peak levels. Finally Kathleen's superior called her upstairs. The meeting was her last action as the department's manager.

Learn from Kathleen's mistakes, and always remember that while you aim to be a friendly manager, you aren't just a friend. Most people are willing to settle down to work after greeting each other in the morning. They will keep personal conversation to an acceptable level throughout the workday if this is the standard you establish by policy as well as by example.

Workplace Relationships

The more time people spend at work or involved in work activities, the more likely it is that the workplace will become the primary venue, or at least starting point, for social activities. After all, the workplace already provides something in common. Friendships and even romantic relationships start and thrive in the workplace. This is especially true in jobs that demand long hours, intense focus on complex projects, or frequent travel.

ESSENTIAL

The need to belong is basic to human beings. We need other people in order to survive as well as thrive. In primordial times, when survival consumed every waking minute, numbers meant safety (not to mention food). Exile from the group was life threatening. In a certain way, this need remains even in the modern workplace, where cooperation and collaboration are often essential for everyone to keep their jobs.

Most of the time, workplace friendships benefit the employees, the department, and the company as a whole. Workplace friendships can make work more fun, which often increases employee satisfaction as well as productivity. Having a strong system of support through workplace friendships can help employees weather the inevitable downs and hard times of work life, making such experiences more tolerable. Such a network of friends can even keep employees in jobs when they might otherwise feel inclined to leave.

When Friendships Turn Sour

Though workplace friendships are very often positive experiences, every now and then friendships turn sour. This can have far-reaching ramifications for the involved employees as well as other team members. Consider the following example.

It didn't take long for coworkers and peers Robin, Chris, Carol, and Brad to become friends. They had similar interests and tastes, and they often met for lunch and sometimes for drinks after work or for dinner. They became the bedrock of the department, a solid team their manager and their coworkers knew they could count on to shift effortlessly into high gear when challenge reared its ugly head. The four friends incorporated their work friendship into their lives outside work, introducing each other to friends outside of work to create an even wider circle.

One weekend Robin and Brad had a falling out. Unlike previous disagreements that they patched up after just a few days, this one festered into a feud. The dispute splintered the circle of friends, and the work team's productivity plummeted. Robin left the team and joined another, creating havoc in both. The discord between her and Brad intensified and became the source of much office gossip and speculation.

Brad grew increasingly dissatisfied with conditions in the department and surreptitiously contacted a headhunter to explore opportunities with some of the companies that had been interested in him before he took his current position. Still friends with Robin, Carol and Chris let slip a comment about Brad's actions. When Brad came to work the next morning, no one would talk to him. When he opened his e-mail, he discovered why. Copies of a half-dozen e-mail messages between him and the headhunter in which Brad had candidly and bluntly described his dissatisfactions with his coworkers, the department, and the company had been forwarded to just about everyone.

High School Redux: Cliques and Exclusion

It's not just friendships that turn sour that can divide and disrupt a department or work group. In high school, cliques frequently formed around star athletes or cheerleaders. They were the "in" crowd, and everyone knew who belonged. In the workplace, it's not always so easy to see the core of cliques. Workplace cliques may form around outside interests such as sports, hobbies, social activities, and even religious activities. Sometimes what starts as a friendship develops into a clique when members exclude rather than welcome others who might drift in and out of the circle.

When to Step In

Unfortunately, managers don't have all that much control over how work friendships form or whether cliques develop. As long as employees are doing their work, then there's no reason or right to interfere with employee interactions. But you do need to keep your eyes open. Don't hide in your office or pretend you don't know what's going on. Knowledge is power, regardless of whether you use it to take action. There are, of course, times when you must intervene. It's time to step in when you notice any of the following:

- Employees are spending more time socializing than working. They can't possibly be doing what they've been hired to do if they spend the entire workday in gossip-and-giggle mode or dissecting last night's ballgame.
- One group keeps others from being successful by undermining its efforts, or keeps information from other people and groups. This is a clique, and its actions are counterproductive.
- Office politics turn vicious, and rumors and gossip abound. A bit of chitchat is not a bad thing. People are curious and often legitimately concerned about each other when they talk about situations and the other people involved in them. When talk turns destructive, it's no longer conversation—it's sabotage.

QUESTION?

What are cliques?
Cliques are groups, usually small, that form around specific interests and then exclude those who do not share those interests. Cliques at work can be particularly damaging to other work groups and the department because they interfere with the usual social formations that are essential to effective teamwork.

If you do see that friendships and socializing are interfering with productivity or preventing some employees from doing their work, you might need to distance people from each other. You can split a work team into smaller groups and assign them different projects. You can also take steps to promote new, positive working relationships by realigning project partnerships. And you can model an appropriate balance between socializing and working in your own behavior. If your employees see you standing in the doorway chatting about the guy in accounting who's dating the senior vice president's daughter, they will believe it's okay for them to do the same thing. As trite as it sounds, actions speak infinitely louder than words.

Workplace Romance

Sometimes one thing leads to another, and before you know it there's a story that would make any manager blush. But we'll keep things publishable. (You don't need a book for these stories, anyway; just look around your office or company.) When people spend most of their waking hours together, it's natural for them to want to get to know each other better as people, not just as coworkers.

ALERT!

The odds of a work relationship blooming into something more increases with the level of commitment the job demands. High levels of intensity suspend reality and put personal lives on hold. It's an ideal medium for mutual attraction to germinate and grow.

High-tech wonder company or conservative corporation, it happens everywhere. Coworkers date. Two people see each other across a crowded room—even a room turned into a maze by the cubicles that cordon workspaces into territories—and something sparks intrigue and even passion in each of them.

Sometimes dating between coworkers appears to be a good thing. Two people in different departments meet in the company cafeteria and the rest, as they say, is history—they start dating, they fall in love, they announce their union to their respective work groups that then celebrate with a joint after-hours event. The happy twosome comes to work and leaves for home together, shares a parking space, and names the baby after the company president. It's a match made in—well, maybe not heaven, though it certainly appears magical enough.

As much as we believe in magic, reality can be harsh. Couples fight—it's part of life. When spouses work for the same company, the normal battles of relationships spill over into the workplace. What starts as an argument about breakfast cereal could end up costing a major account—or a job. Consider Rhonda and Patrick's situation.

Rhonda and Patrick met when each was running an errand to the copy store. She worked in advertising; he was an industrial engineer. Their departments never interacted, and the company had no policy prohibiting dating or marriage, so they felt safe in pursuing their relationship. They eventually married. Then the company went through a period of restructuring and downsizing. Both kept their jobs, though the advertising department had to cut half its staff. As a result, those who remained had to pick up the slack, which meant considerable overtime.

Patrick worked out at the health club with Carlos, Rhonda's manager. During a lunch workout one day, Patrick asked Carlos to excuse Rhonda from the mandatory overtime because it was creating problems in their relationship. Carlos refused and chastised Patrick for imposing on him in such a way. Rhonda's workload eventually stabilized and she returned to a regular workweek, as did everyone. But her relationship with Carlos remained strained, and Carlos and Patrick no longer spoke to one another. During the next round of consolidations, both Rhonda and Patrick lost their jobs.

FACT

Surveys suggest that as many as 40 percent of employees have dated coworkers at some point; many people view the office as an ideal opportunity to get to know someone with relative safety. If things work out, the explorations move to activities beyond work. If not, no harm done. Right? Not always. Failed relationships are a leading factor in sexual harassment claims and lawsuits.

When coworkers begin dating, it's important to be aware of potential conflicts and to watch for signs of favoritism or even competition. Nothing is more demoralizing for other employees than to look down the hall and see two coworkers prancing along with smirks on their faces—especially when the relationship somehow places other employees at a disadvantage. You might need to step in to review decisions that involve the happy couple, such as overtime and off-site assignments. Even if all is on the up-and-up, other employees might perceive the dating duo to be getting choice assignments or evading unpleasant ones.

Dating a Subordinate

Dating between a manager and a subordinate employee, even across department lines, is always a bad idea and often violates company policy. It's impossible to escape the scrutiny of other managers and employees, regardless of how discreet you think you are. It's equally impossible to avoid perceptions of favoritism while the relationship is hot—and discrimination or harassment if it fails.

Make sure you know your company's policies and corporate culture regarding interoffice dating and particularly managers dating subordinates. Some companies permit dating among coworkers of relatively equal status but discourage or prohibit dating between managers and subordinates.

The greatest risk is for managers who date employees who report to them; even if company policy doesn't prohibit this, it's poor judgment. How can you fairly and objectively evaluate the job performance of the person who shares your life and knows your deepest secrets? Certainly you can't control personal attractions, and many people are happy together because something drew them together. If you find yourself attracted to a subordinate, try taking these steps:

- Start by considering the end. Where could this relationship lead, and what are its possible consequences? Can both of you accept them?
- Remove yourself from a position of authority over the person whom you are dating. You might need to transfer to another job within your company or change employers. Sometimes such transfers are easier for the employee, though initiating the transfer yourself could lead to later accusations of harassment. It might not seem fair, but someone's career trajectory will need to change or both could easily fade to nothing.
- Conduct yourselves with discretion, but don't for a moment let yourself be deluded into believing that no one else knows about your relationship. Someone does, if not everyone.

Whatever you do, don't sneak around, especially at work. If anything, the onus is on you to go out of your way to avoid situations that make it look like you're sneaking around.

The Legalities of Workplace Romance

Dating between coworkers is not against the law, although it might violate company policies intended to minimize the potential for claims of favoritism and harassment. When such policies exist, every employee should know about them before accepting a job offer; violating the policy can have serious consequences.

FACT

Company policies prohibiting married employees from working in the same department or even anywhere within the company could run afoul of the law in states that make it illegal to consider marital status in employment and other decisions. The results of court cases involving these issues are mixed, making it difficult for companies to know whether their policies will help or hinder their efforts to maintain an equitable employment environment.

Policies prohibiting married employees from working in the same department or even in the company at the same time are more common than policies against dating. In legalese these are called antinepotism policies, and their proscriptions typically also apply to employees who are related to one another in any way. Some companies promptly fire one or even both employees if coworkers do marry in defiance of policies prohibiting it. Such policies should explicitly state what behaviors are not allowed, what is necessary to invoke the policy ("rules of evidence"), and what consequences the employees face. As with all policies, consistent monitoring and enforcement are crucial.

Because so many sexual harassment claims involve coworkers who once dated each other, it's important to view such a claim as a potential outcome of employee dating. Document, document, document!

Office Parties and After-Hours Events

The office party—it's a wonderful way to let employees relax and socialize together in a less stressful environment than the workplace. Right? Well, sometimes. The occasional office party does help people get to know one another in another context. Just as they might wear hiking boots and jeans in the woods or business suits in the office, people tend to adopt certain behaviors for specific environments and circumstances. Seeing each other outside the usual climate can break down barriers and encourage greater cooperation in the workplace.

A party can be a reward for a job well done, something the company gives to employees to show appreciation for their extra effort and hard work. This makes people feel special and also reinforces the value of teamwork. People get the chance to mingle and get comfortable with each other while someone else foots the bill. We all like to feel that we're getting something for nothing.

When Partying Goes Too Far

Parties lose their charm when they get out of control, however, and can serve to further divide, rather than unite, a work group or department. The hope and intent for an office party is to bring people together. If a work group consists of very diverse personalities, a party can magnify rather than minimize differences. Parties that cater to one group make others feel left out. People may feel obligated to attend parties and other company activities even though doing so interferes with other plans. This is especially the case when employees are expected to bring their spouses or families.

Parties are more relaxing when they are less frequent and held off-site. If it's been a rough day or week, the last place people want to be to unwind is at the workplace. People are creatures of habit who tend to follow the same patterns of behavior in their environments. A work group at a party at the workplace will sit together, likely in the same seats they take at meetings or lunch, depending on the party's location. It doesn't do much to break people from their routines if they end up sitting with their usual group at their usual table.

Not all after-hours events are purely social. Some companies sponsor community contribution days, on which employees donate their time and talents to service and charitable organizations. This might be a day spent serving lunch at a homeless shelter or building a house with a volunteer organization such as Habitat for Humanity. When community giving is involved, many employees feel a sense of satisfaction and contribution.

Hold the Booze

No matter how much people expect to find alcoholic beverages at parties, drinking is a problem. People often like to have a drink or two to unwind and loosen up. It's hard to feel comfortable in new settings, especially when the socializing appears contrived and your coworkers are not people with whom you'd ordinarily go out. Because the point is to relax, many companies hold parties at locations that serve alcohol. This gives the impression that it's not really the company that's supplying the drinks and makes people feel more comfortable about drinking. They relax and have fun, and that's what parties are all about—until someone gets out of control.

FACT

According to several studies, 70 percent of companies serve alcoholic beverages at office parties and 60 percent of employees drink enough to become intoxicated. Most office parties feature beer and wine, if not cocktails. Drinking is a social activity for many adults, and most people expect it at adult functions. Problems arise when people drink too much, and then say or do things they or others will regret.

Increasingly, there are consequences for such actions. Managers and employees alike may have a tough time returning to pre-party behaviors and relationships. Managers might lose the respect of their employees; employees might lose the trust their managers had in them. More frightening and severe consequences can arise if an employee leaves the party drunk and drives, getting into an accident on the way home.

It's certainly not your job to baby-sit employees at parties; after all, they're adults and can make their own judgments and decisions. But if you knowingly allow a drunken employee to drive away, you could end up holding the accountability bag. A court could find you and your company partially responsible for whatever damage the employee did—including taking someone's life—because you failed to intervene.

Chapter 20

Check Your Baggage at the Door

We all tend to carry "baggage" to work with us—emotions and reactions rooted in other dimensions of our lives. Much of the time, the behaviors and responses we carry from setting to setting and person to person are subtle enough that we might not even recognize what we're doing. Knowing that this is how the human mind functions helps you to break free from unproductive and sometimes inappropriate patterns. It's important to learn to recognize your own patterns of behavior, identify what triggers them, and use them appropriately in the setting of the workplace.

It's Not Me, It's You

Some managers seem to believe that it is not they, but everyone around them, who needs to adjust. People in positions of power often feel that they shouldn't have to be self-aware because those around them should be aware of them. But not knowing what pushes your own buttons ends up interfering with objectivity and fairness. Let's take a look at a few scenarios. In situations such as these, employees lose and so does the manager. Do any of these scenarios sound at all familiar?

William lands a dream internship his senior year in college. The dream quickly becomes a nightmare, however. His boss, Donna, is brilliant but aggressive and often abusive, especially toward the interns. Her tendency to launch into tirades at the slightest provocation causes people to scatter whenever there's word that she's coming down the corridor. Though Donna's outstanding reputation in the industry continues to draw intern applications from colleges and universities across the country, few interns last the full term.

No matter what time the workday or a meeting starts, Carmine is the first to arrive. Nine people report to him; his department troubleshoots customer orders. Though the situations Carmine's employees investigate are often complex and confusing, Carmine feels employees take advantage of this so he implements a tracking board. Everyone must sign in and sign out whenever they come and go from the department, no matter the reason. Upper management consistently holds out Carmine's actions as the desired attention to timeliness. However, employees consider Carmine so focused on the clock that he's willing to sacrifice their good work just to force them to toe the line—*his* line.

Russell is a very nurturing kind of guy, really sensitive to other people's feelings. His employees feel they can come to him with any problem and find a compassionate ear. Russell immediately wants to make it better and is quick to commiserate when talking to the distraught employee. Employees have voted Russell "manager of the year" for five years running, though Russell's boss placed Russell on probation last month because his department consistently fails to meet productivity targets.

In each of these situations, blind patterns direct behaviors that have both positive and negative consequences. It seems, however, that the inappropriate behavior receives the most reinforcement. Even Russell, who is now precariously close to losing his job, continues in the behaviors that cause him trouble. Each of these managers needs someone to help him or her step back and see a more balanced picture. The higher you go in the company's hierarchy, however, the fewer mentors you're likely to encounter. You must become your own mentor—not an easy hat to wear.

Angry Employees

Anger is common in the workplace. People get upset with other people, circumstances, and situations. We get angry when we feel afraid, sad, threatened, insecure, disappointed—when things are out of our control. Anger elicits a response when other efforts fail to do so, which can give a false sense of control. Anger is uncomfortable for others to experience, so they often do whatever it takes to put an end to their discomfort—which often means placating the angry person by giving what the person wants.

The Straw That Breaks the Camel's Back

Everyone gets angry, and everyone has gotten angry with the wrong people for the wrong reasons at the wrong times. For most people, the expression of anger represents the culmination of feelings they can no longer control. However, the actual event that sends them over the edge is often something minor that might not even be related to the reasons they're angry. The challenge for you as the manager is to identify and expose the underlying issues. Here's an example.

Carolyn, an administrative assistant in the accounting department, blew up when Stephen, an accounts payable clerk, stopped at her desk to tell her the break room was out of coffee. "I've had it! Get your own damn coffee!" she screamed at him. "I'm not the only one in this department who can walk two lousy blocks to the store to buy a package of fine grind! It doesn't take a college degree! Just go get it yourself!"

John, the department manager, heard Carolyn shouting and came out of his office to see what was going on. He asked her to take a walk with him. Once they were outside the building, he asked her what had happened. Still agitated, Carolyn repeated her exasperation that everyone in the department seemed to believe buying coffee was her responsibility and hers alone. "I don't even drink coffee!" she said. "Nowhere in my job description does it say that it's my job to buy the coffee! No one notices anything else I do, but when we run out of coffee, everyone comes running to me!"

John immediately agreed that it was not Carolyn's job to buy coffee. It wasn't even a job responsibility at all, for anyone. It was a pattern the department slipped into because she had once been willing to do it, he observed, but it certainly wasn't an aspect of her job. John assured Carolyn that he would post a memo asking the coffee drinkers to decide among themselves how to maintain the coffee supply.

As they walked and talked, it became clear to John that Carolyn was very frustrated because her job was not giving her the opportunities to advance that she had anticipated it would when she took the job three years ago. In her career plan, she was to have been an accounting clerk by this time—but here she was, still an admin assistant running to the store to buy coffee. "I know just as much as the other clerks, probably more, but no one notices that I'm the one who corrects their statements and records," Carolyn told John. "There have been three openings in receivables in the past six months, but you've selected someone else each time."

John explained that the department used educational requirements to screen applicants, and that Carolyn didn't have an undergraduate degree with a major in the any of the required fields. He agreed that she did have exemplary knowledge of the department and its functions, and said he would check with HR to see if there was a way to flex the education requirements to accommodate Carolyn's degree in communications. John also reminded Carolyn that he had an open-door policy because he wanted people to come to him with their concerns. If she had come to talk to him when the job openings were first posted, he could have talked to HR then. As it was, there weren't any vacancies now, and he didn't know when one would surface. John and Carolyn agreed to meet in one week to discuss what John was able to find out from HR.

Carolyn felt unappreciated and unfairly overlooked when it came to promotional opportunities. This aroused nagging doubts about whether she truly was qualified for the job she wanted to have; if no one noticed how good she was, maybe she wasn't really that good. So she tried even harder to get John and others in her department to notice her work and recognize her abilities—she left Post-It notes on people's desks whenever she corrected paperwork they submitted that was incomplete, and joined in on discussions about department procedures and accounting matters. That no one picked up on these attempts to gain recognition further fueled both her frustration and her self-doubt.

QUESTION?

When is anger more than blowing off steam?
Anger becomes dangerous when others feel threatened by the person's expression of it. Such expressions may include direct or indirect threats, yelling, actions such as slamming or throwing things, and physical gestures or contact.

Assuaging the Situation

As Carolyn's manager, John should have had a better understanding of Carolyn's career goals. Career planning was a key part of the company's performance standards and evaluation process. Each employee met with his or her manager every six months to review progress toward stated goals and objectives. If Carolyn was vague in these meetings, John should have pinned her down at least to be assured that he understood what she hoped to accomplish during her employment and in her career. When Carolyn hit crisis mode, however, John reacted swiftly and appropriately:

- **He removed Carolyn from the scene.** When someone bursts into a rage in front of other people, it's nearly impossible for him or her to back down without losing face. Since frustration and fear are among the core emotions that ignite anger, a person in outburst mode is not going to willingly validate them by surrendering. Removing an angry person from any audience removes the need for the person to continue raging. It also provides an opportunity for the person to regain composure and dignity.

- **He agreed with Carolyn that her feelings were valid.** This put them both on the same side, giving them common ground from which to work toward a mutually acceptable solution.

- **He stayed focused on the issues.** While John didn't support Carolyn's behavior, he didn't criticize it, either. He directed the discussion to tangibles—Carolyn's disappointment and frustration about not being promoted, and the company policies that impeded her efforts. This allowed John to present possible solutions.

- **He concluded the discussion with tangible actions and a follow-up plan.** Without making promises he might not be able to keep, John told Carolyn exactly what he would do to try to resolve her frustration and when they would meet for further discussions.

Carolyn's anger of course had nothing to do with poor Stephen, whose words simply happened to be the trigger that released Carolyn's frustrations.

Angry Managers

Although angry employees are a key concern for most managers, angry managers are just as often a key concern for employees. Employees are unfortunately convenient when a manager blows a gasket—again, often for reasons completely unrelated to the anger. Managers, like employees, sometimes carry problems from home or other dimensions of their lives into the workplace. A fight with your spouse or kids might start your day with a sour outlook. Because you know you have to go to work and deal with all the pressures there, you try to stay calm and collected at home so you can at least leave with the delusion of peace and harmony. But when you get to work, an employee says or does something that triggers those feelings you've swallowed, and back up they rush. Before you know it, you're dumping all over this employee whose only offense was to be in the wrong place at the wrong time saying the wrong thing.

There are many pressures in today's world, both at home and at work. Your company's employee assistance program (EAP) can be a good resource for employees and managers alike. Most EAPs provide short-term counseling to help people find solutions to their problems. Many EAPs extend consultation services to managers and supervisors, offering advice and recommendations about workplace issues. Such interventions help managers deal with stress and the factors that cause it, and they can head off problems before they become serious.

Managers can get away with a lot of abusive behavior toward employees, or at least they think they can. They can close the door and say what they want and get away with it—for the short term. But the toll in loss of morale and even legal issues at some point catches up. Employees learn quickly to read the moods of their managers. When managers have problems at home or are feeling pressure from other departments or their superiors, employees learn to anticipate venting and tirades. Some duck for cover behind work projects that take them out of the office, while others get angry themselves.

When a manager loses control, and particularly when the loss unleashes anger toward employees, the consequences can be severe and far-reaching. When you feel anger rising within you that you know is going to splash all over some employee, take a deep breath and ask yourself a few questions:

- Is this employee the source of my anger?
- If so, why?
- If not, who or what is?
- Am I really feeling angry, or am I disappointed?
- What, realistically, can the employee or I do to remedy the situation?
- Can I talk with the employee about this without losing my cool?
- What is the worst that can happen if I just walk away from this and address it later?

If you can't talk to the employee without losing your temper, do whatever you need to do to cool off before you say anything to anyone. Then, before you approach the employee, write some notes to yourself that explain the problem as you see it, what adverse consequences occurred as a result, and what solutions you propose. Stick to this "script" in your conversation (even if you need to refer to your notes while you're talking) to help keep yourself calm and focused.

FACT

Sometimes managers use anger as a way of turning employees against the company. A manager may not like the direction of the company, for example, so he incites anger in his employees, hoping that he can hurt the company by hurting them. This gets everybody angry and unites the work group in battle. Although employees are often unaware that this is what's going on, they are likely to suffer the consequences in terms of lost opportunities and bad reputations.

Managing Your Stress

There are a lot of reasons for stress in the workplace, and each individual has unique triggers. In general, workplace stress is the result of tiredness and competing demands, whether at work, at home, or both. We all lead busy lives that seldom make it easy for us to take time off from anything.

Most people feel the greatest amount of stress when they're working hard or long hours and feeling that they're not getting anything in return for their efforts and sacrifices. For some people this is money, though more often it is recognition that is lacking. Money loses much of its charm after a while, but praise for work well done lives in memory for a long, long time.

Life beyond the workplace further adds to stress. It seems that what makes the office pressure worse is that our home lives are not always what they should be. Either life at home is great but we can't really enjoy it, or it is not so great so there is no relief from work even when we leave the workplace.

Stress is really about balance. A certain level of stress is necessary in life, of course—without it, we don't feel motivated or interested. But when there is too much of it, we don't feel motivated or interested, either. If life is all work, fasten your seatbelt—a crash is inevitable. So what can managers do? In the first place, recognize the symptoms of your own stress, such as these:

- Anxiety and worrying about things you can't change
- Inability to sleep or lack of adequate sleep
- Fatigue and feelings of exhaustion
- Flying off the handle
- Depression and lack of interest in normally pleasant activities
- Feeling sorry for yourself
- Engaging in passive-aggressive behavior

Even if you don't see these indicators when you look in the mirror or listen to yourself when you're talking with employees, the people in your work group have learned to read your moods. They might not know what to do with their interpretations, but your employees become less effective because you are less effective.

Avoidance might be a good diversionary tactic, but it doesn't work over the long haul. An environment based on avoidance becomes confusing and frustrating for everyone. Eventually employees lose track of whether this is a stress day or the storm has blown over, and they're not sure how to behave. As the manager, you've already established the "stress protocol" for your department and your employees. Others do what you do. If it's not the one you want everyone to follow, change it. Managers need to set examples, and being open—even about stress—is one of them. Here are a few ideas:

- If you're feeling stressed, go into your office, close the door, and take a few slow, deep breaths. If you meditate or do yoga, take ten minutes to indulge in these great stress relievers.
- Tell your employees that you're feeling stressed, and offer a brief explanation. "I didn't get enough sleep last night, and I have to get this report finished by noon." This often makes you and your employees feel better.
- Try not to say things you'll regret or have to apologize for later. The "count to ten" rule comes in handy in times of stress. Ten seconds is not too long to pause before responding to a question or a comment, and the extra time to think can save all involved considerable embarrassment and frustration.
- Remind yourself that this is a temporary situation, and it too will pass.
- If a few days off would help, take them. Your department and the company will survive without you.

You also need to watch your lifestyle and encourage your employees to do the same. If your workload is overwhelming, what will make the situation better? Are you taking too much on? Not delegating? What should you do? What can you do? Stress starts with you, so set a positive example. (You're already setting an example of some sort; now's your opportunity to shape it into the one you *want* to set.) What do you need to do when you are stressed out? Do you need a vacation or a long rest? Is so, take the time and do it. And encourage your employees to do the same.

Identifying Stress in Your Work Group

Sometimes stress builds up in the department and the manager is not aware. There might be rumors circulating about layoffs and plant closings, causing people to fear for their jobs and their security. Actual layoffs or closures, or bad news about the company's products or stock values, also cause people to become concerned (sometimes overly) about their futures with the company. Sometimes employees become resentful when they perceive that one employee is doing less work than the others. And sometimes personality conflicts are severe enough to cause stress for those involved as well as those who catch the fallout. Here are some signs that the people in your department might be feeling too much stress:

- Rumors and excessive gossip
- Groups of employees congregating at one employee's workstation, in the break room, or in the restroom—behavior often closely related to rumors and gossip
- Discord and disharmony—people just not getting along with each other
- A noticeable and unexplainable drop in productivity or efficiency
- A general bad attitude—people badmouthing other employees, managers, upper-level executives, the company, or its products

When you see these signs, it's your responsibility as manager to get to the root of the problem. Talk to people and be a sounding board. Being able to talk about worries and fears is one of the most effective ways to put them in perspective, even when they are founded.

Things are seldom as bad as people imagine them to be, but the imagination's power knows no bounds. Problems won't disappear by themselves, no matter how desperately you wish they would or how hard you try to ignore them. Identifying or confronting the problem is often enough to act as a release for the stress it generates.

Clark was a very laid-back, easygoing guy. As a manager, he preferred to stay on the periphery, letting people and problems work themselves out. While this approach was fine for Clark, it didn't work well for most of the employees in his department. Several people were aggressive, domineering, and territorial. Clark's hands-off attitude gave them free rein and the impression that he approved of their behavior and tactics. Other employees were either less experienced or did not deal well with aggressive people. This created an imbalance of input. Mild-mannered employees with good ideas got squelched by their more belligerent colleagues, who bullied through their ideas and suggestions. There was much in-fighting and just plain bad feelings. It was a stressful environment to work in because either tempers flared or people just walked away and seethed.

Despite the impression Clark made of being calm and aloof, in truth the thought of becoming involved in any sort of confrontation or conflict sent him into stress overload. So rather than stepping in he stepped back, hoping that the reasons for the arguments and discord would go away as mysteriously as they had appeared. Of course, there was nothing mysterious about it. People had opposing views and didn't know how to express them without being adversarial. But these kinds of problems seldom fade away. In fact, the stress usually intensifies before it breaks, and the resulting explosion often leaves damage behind.

It's important for managers to get in the middle of things, to find out what's wrong, to talk with people about their concerns and fears. Put on your parent hat and have your coach hat ready—it's your job to set parameters and establish rules. Sure, some people are going to be unhappy. But they're unhappy now. At least when there are rules in place and it's clear that you intend to enforce them, you begin to re-establish a sense of fairness and equity.

One of the most common and significant stressors in the workplace is change. Change frightens and confuses many people. There is an inherent insecurity when the not-yet-familiar replaces the tried-and-true. It takes time for people to figure out their roles and places in the new scheme, even when they desire and embrace the change.

And yes, if you confront people some of them are likely to push back, just to see if they can and to test how far you'll bend before you snap. It really is a test, just as it's a test when your six-year-old decides bedtime is when he feels like hitting the sheets, not when you tell him goodnight. As a parent it's your duty to establish boundaries for your children that provide them with what they need, regardless of whether they know or agree that they have such needs. The same holds true in the workplace. You are the manager, and it's your duty to set the limits for behavior and performance.

Chapter 21

Guiding Your Own Career

When you're involved in guiding the careers of others, it's easy to overlook the need to monitor and direct the course of your own. This can be a costly oversight—for you as well as for your company. You made it to the head of your work team, and now you're caught up in the day-to-day functions of managing. But you have to remember how to get your hands dirty. That's what got you this far, and that's what is going to keep you valuable to the company. When you let your primary job skills erode, you limit your options and your opportunities.

Keep Your Skills Sharp

As a manager, you make decisions that affect people, projects, and productivity. While you are probably not an expert in every function or task that the employees in your department perform, you should have considerable expertise in key jobs—manufacturing processes, art direction and account management, lab techniques, whatever functions are your department's responsibilities. If your primary strength is your people skills, you're the manager most likely to get left behind when downsizing or a power struggle hits.

Sean and Christine were both managers at Artful Advertising. Sean had the rare ability to get along with almost everybody, which is how he ended up being promoted to manager of the customer service department. Even irate customers calmed down when Sean took their calls or came to the front counter to listen to their complaints. Sean had been in his position for five years and had allowed himself to become comfortable. Processes and procedures changed, but he didn't do much to find out how. As long as he knew enough to oversee the efforts of his employees to address customer service issues and handle the difficult situations himself, Sean didn't feel a need to keep up on the details of every aspect of the company's functions. After all, he was a manager, and his job was to manage the people who performed those functions.

Christine was the production manager. She had started as a film assistant in the printing department seven years ago, and worked in various positions including copy writer and account representative. One reason Christine was so effective was that she knew everyone's jobs well enough that she could do them herself, so she knew who to assign to which projects. Under Christine's direction, the production department operated smoothly and efficiently. The employees in her department respected Christine as a manager they could come to for anything.

Then Artful Advertising's CEO retired, and there was an intense internal struggle for power. One of the two vice presidents vying for the vacated top spot favored consolidating departments to streamline operations, while the other advocated acquiring a smaller competitor to expand the company's market presence. In the end the consolidator won out. The realignment trimmed six management positions and realigned others. Managers who wanted to stay with the company had to apply for the jobs they wanted.

The new executive management regime wanted managers with diverse capabilities. Although Sean had once known the company inside and out, he had let his knowledge and his skills slip. His interview went poorly, and he chose to resign before the final decisions came down. Christine was promoted to director of what became the production division, responsible for overseeing the art, copywriting, design, and printing departments.

Maintain Your Core Skills

There are many ways to keep your core skills sharp. If you are a working manager, you have daily exposure to the changes taking place in your profession. Pay attention to these changes, even if it seems they don't affect you directly. At a minimum, you should do the following:

- **Enroll in any workshops or classes your company offers.** Large companies often have training departments that develop and deliver classes to teach customer service skills, quality improvement methodologies, computer and technology skills, and other subjects relevant to the needs of the company's employees.
- **Maintain active membership in relevant professional organizations.** Don't just sign up and pay your dues; go to the meetings, conferences, and workshops. Network. Build relationships with people who work for other companies.
- **Maintain any licensure or certification essential to work in your core skill area.** If you are a licensed professional working in an area that doesn't count toward the hours your state requires to maintain licensure or certification, work some evenings and weekends in a job that will give you countable hours (sometimes volunteer hours count).
- **Take continuing education (CE) courses.** Some professions require continuing education, while in others it's optional. It's always to your advantage to stay abreast of current developments in your career field.

- **Continue your formal (college) education.** If you have a two-year associate degree, go back for a four-year bachelor's degree. If you already have an undergraduate education, consider a graduate program. Many degree programs have options targeted to working adults, including evening and weekend classes, Internet classes, and correspondence classes.

Many companies will pay, or reimburse, you for costs related to keeping your skills current or learning new skills that are relevant to your job. Even if you're not technically a working manager, it's a good idea to keep yourself involved in the functions of the jobs within your department or work group.

Stay Sharp As a Manager

Of course, it is possible for a manager's core skills to be in management. Some people who excel in directing and mentoring might not have core skills in the areas they supervise, though this is becoming increasingly uncommon as companies continue looking for ways to get the most from or for the least ("efficiency in resource management"). If you are such a manager, it's all the more important that you remain ahead of the curve when it comes to changes in trends and approaches. Make sure you know the latest management theories, principles, and practices.

FACT

A 2000 Gallup poll reports that 78 percent of Americans believe recent changes in technology that have changed the landscape of American business have been good for the country. The poll also reports that 89 percent of Americans use e-mail, 60 percent use e-mail in place of making telephone calls, and 95 percent use the Internet to find information.

It's still a good idea for you to develop some skill strengths in areas that will continue to be important across the board in business. Learn the basics about the key tasks of employees who report to you so you understand their contributions and how each piece fits into the whole. This also helps you to delegate more effectively and to monitor progress as well as outcomes using measures that are relevant and appropriate.

Stay Ahead of the Technology Curve

Some managers believe they are up on technology, yet it is their administrative assistants who do all the work. If you don't really understand the technologies that are part of your daily work life, read professional journals and enroll in classes to bring yourself up to speed. It's an investment that could save your career.

When the people who report to you improve their skills and expand their knowledge, it's almost impossible for yours to remain stagnant. When your employees grow, you grow. When people are growing, their loyalty—to their managers and to the company—also increases. They perform better. And you have more time to focus on strategic issues, including your own career objectives. In a sense, it's an upward domino effect.

Should you find yourself looking for other opportunities, your technical knowledge may well be what puts you across the line in the sand that separates applicants from contenders. Most job interviews include questions about technology specific to the job as well as in general. You will need to be able to speak intelligently, and with real-world knowledge, about technology that is relevant to your field and job interests.

Learn to Read the Writing on the Wall

Every day, companies lay off employees and managers. Could you read the writing on the wall telling you that your job was in jeopardy?

Harold, like many managers, missed the signals. The first warning came when upper management restructured manager responsibilities to give Harold fewer projects to oversee. With the projects went the employees assigned to them, leaving Harold with fewer direct reports. Harold's new projects had short, defined timelines. Oddly enough, Harold joked about his "good" fortune. Although he had seen upper management ease other managers out using these same tactics, it never occurred to Harold that the same thing now might be happening to him.

Sure, sales were slumping. But every company in the industry was going through a slow time. These cycles were normal, and sales would climb again in due time. The problem was, upper management wasn't interested in due time. Stockholders were getting anxious and wanted a better bottom line now. Finally Harold's boss, a senior vice president, took Harold to lunch. Harold interpreted the invitation as camaraderie and commiserated with his boss's concerns rather than offering proposals for improvement. When Harold received a layoff notice two days later, only he was surprised.

In the Middle: Insulation or Isolation?

Being in middle management might insulate you from the pressures at the top and the struggles at the bottom of the corporate ladder, but don't let it isolate you from reality. You are only as good as your last success, and only for as long as others remember it (which is never as long as you do). If your company begins laying off staff, don't let yourself get lulled into a sense of false security because you're a manager. Managers are not inherently immune to staff reductions. In many situations, in fact, managers might find themselves among the first to go.

If you suspect that your job is on the line or a layoff is imminent, is there anything you can do to save yourself? No, not usually, unless the issue is purely performance (and this should never be a surprise to you, just as it should never be a surprise to your employees when it comes time for their performance evaluations). Ask your direct superior; sometimes he or she will be able to give you a straight answer.

ALERT!

As a manager, you are judged not only by your own performance but also by the performance of your employees. If your department's productivity is down, it looks like your problem—regardless of the real reasons (which might have little to do with you personally). And when it looks like your problem, it is.

Always Be Prepared for the Worst

Recognize, however, that often upper management cannot give you advance notice that you are about to be laid off or your job is about to be eliminated. Sometimes a sympathetic manager might give you a heads-up, but this could be at great personal risk. Most companies have policies and procedures they must follow to avoid discrimination and wrongful termination claims. It's always a good idea to be prepared to find yourself on the seeking end of the job hunt. If your company is downsizing or reorganizing, it's critical. Here are some ways you can stay ready for whatever changes might come your way:

- **Keep your resume current.** Every time you attend a training program or workshop, take on new responsibilities in your job, complete a major project, or achieve a key success, update your resume. At the very least, pull out your resume every six months to review it.
- **Network.** Collect business cards from people you meet at professional gatherings and even social events. Once a week, make it a point to call, have coffee with, or go to lunch with someone you know who works for another company that has people who do what you do.
- **Determine how your skills and experience could translate into positions in other fields.** Could you teach, work in health care instead of the computer industry, or be a customer service manager in an auto dealer's service department rather than in a retail setting?
- **Consider volunteering in positions different from your job.** In addition to fulfilling needs within your community, this will help you to expand your skills and extend the network of people you know.

Finally, try to set aside enough financial resources to carry you through three to six months of unemployment. This is a challenge for most people, who tend to live from paycheck to paycheck. Just setting aside a small amount from each check—as small as 2 to 5 percent—can quickly add up to a tidy emergency fund.

Change Is the Only Certainty

The only thing that's certain in today's business environment is that nothing is certain. Although change has always been inevitable, it hasn't always happened at the speed of light as it seems to now. The days of migrating upward into a cushy middle management job in a "safe" industry are gone. Even monolithic companies are vulnerable to sudden change. Tides rise and fall—within industries, companies, and professions. Being in management doesn't protect you from those rises and falls. Rather, it offers opportunity and vulnerability in equal doses. You can't have one without the other.

ALERT!

Slipping information to employees about pending changes within the company can do more than just jeopardize your career. Having information get out before the company is ready to announce it could jeopardize the company's competitive position. Information that influences decisions to by or sell stock could violate federal securities regulations, putting you on the wrong side of a criminal investigation. If you know about coming changes, keep the knowledge to yourself unless it is your role to announce it to your department.

Two examples of abrupt change in the business world are mergers and acquisitions. A company doing well buys out a competitor that is not doing so well. Sometimes the buyer is bigger than the company it acquires; sometimes it's a small company that has a big appetite. Companies often do very little to get their employees ready for these mergers and acquisitions. Beyond rumors, employees hear little and know even less. A company's stock price is vulnerable to rumors, and quite frankly that becomes more important than the feelings and concerns of employees. Managers do sometimes get advance warning that a merger or acquisition is pending. They might even have a voice in determining who will stay and who will be let go in their departments.

If you find yourself in this situation, you'll quickly discover that it's a mixed blessing. On the one hand, the manager can help ensure that decisions are based more on merit rather than being utterly random. On the other, you must be fair and objective. You must also recognize and accept that you truly are in the middle. It is your role to carry out upper management's intentions and plans, even though you might feel your first loyalty is to the employees who report to you. As much as you would like to sneak in a few hints or even make a few midnight phone calls to certain employees to give them a heads-up, you can't.

No, it's not fair. But it is the only way to be equitable. No one enters into a job with the promise of perpetual employment (and few people really expect this to be the case). Companies exist for purposes beyond providing paychecks and benefits to employees, and in the end their objectives win out. Employees with the right skills and experience will stay; others will go. This is one of those times when it's nice to have performance evaluations and job descriptions handy. These bureaucratic annoyances become quite useful when it comes time to make objective decisions.

Mergers and acquisitions can be as difficult for the employees who stay as it is for those who are let go—managers as well as employees. If you are a manager who stays to become part of the new structure, you have your work cut out for you. Your cheerleader hat is going to get a lot of wear. Here are a few important tips:

- Always break the news to each employee individually, whether the person is staying or leaving. Although a group meeting might be easier for you, it could be very difficult for people who react emotionally to the news. There's nothing easy about hearing that the world you've become accustomed to has suddenly changed through no fault of yours—and that there's nothing you can do to change things now.

- Allow people who are losing their jobs to gather their belongings and leave with dignity. Some employees might want to say good-bye to their coworkers, but most people aren't very good with good-byes and prefer to leave without a lot of attention. People who are friends will arrange to meet if that's what they want to do.

- Meet with the surviving employees as soon as possible to explain what has happened and why. Hold this meeting in a location where it is safe for people to express their true feelings. They might feel angry that friends are now out of jobs and guilty that they still have regular paychecks.

- If your department is gaining new employees as a result of a merger, before they arrive, explain to the other employees why they are getting jobs when other people were let go. Sometimes all you can say is "That's just the way it is," but it's important for you to say even this to acknowledge that employees need to hear a reason.

- When new employees arrive, welcome them and do your best to make them feel comfortable, even if you must set aside personal feelings to do so. It's not their fault that they're in this situation, any more than it's your fault.

Mergers and acquisitions often mean that new people and potentially a new corporate culture have to be integrated.

When Grapevine Applications and SophistiWare merged, it was a match made in heaven for stockholders but a clash of cultures for employees. Grapevine was a small company located just outside San Francisco. Its hundred or so employees were California-casual, wearing cutoffs and sandals to work. SophistiWare was a larger company based in Chicago. Its several hundred employees dressed to the nines—men and women alike wore trendy suits to work every day. Though Grapevine purchased SophistiWare, SophistiWare's president was tapped to run the new company.

Grapevine's employees were unhappy about this. Grapevine's president was a hands-on leader who knew each employee by name. SophistiWare's president, by contrast, was as formal as his attire. He didn't want to know names; he only wanted to see results. Doug, the Grapevine HR manager, tried to ease the transition for his employees. He met with them as a group to point out some of the strengths of the merger. "We're in a very competitive environment, and quite frankly our opportunities are shrinking," he told them. "We need them, and they need us. It's about the bottom line and about survival, pure and simple."

Doug let his employees express their concerns, but he held a firm line. People had no choice but to conform if they wanted to keep working at the company, and that was just the way things were. They needed to work together to make the adjustment to the new company's structure, procedures, and place in the market. Doug made sure everyone always knew what was happening and why, and how the changes affected jobs and responsibilities. To let people know he understood their concerns, he made jokes about finding a shirt and tie to match his cutoffs. This helped everyone to maintain some sense of commitment to a company that all knew would never be the same again. Doug sent California employees to Chicago in small teams, to get to know their counterparts and better understand SophistiWare's processes. He also had small teams of Chicago employees come to the San Francisco office for the same reasons. When Chicago employees were visiting, Doug tapped into the department's petty cash fund to pay for a barbecue to let people socialize and get to know each other.

Although Grapevine's employees weren't happy about all the changes, they felt loyal to Doug and even to the new company because Doug rallied them into a support group for each other. They still had some bad feelings about the merger and the new company as a whole, but they formed positive feelings about the individuals they met. Although the road was sometimes bumpy, they continued to function as a very productive department.

You might feel fairly insignificant when others come in to restructure your department and the ways your employees work. But you're the only one, really, who can make it all work. Even if you feel you won't want to remain with the new company that results from an acquisition or a merger, it's in your best interests to do all you can to make the transition a success. It's always better to leave on a high note, with people at various levels of the

THE EVERYTHING MANAGING PEOPLE BOOK

organization singing your praises. You'll feel better about yourself, and you might open doors you didn't know existed. People notice your actions and their consequences; it's up to you to shape them to present the perspective you want others to see and remember.

Keep Looking Forward

No doubt being a manager represents achieving a key career goal for you. This is a good thing, of course, and an accomplishment of which you should feel proud. But don't rest on your laurels. Even if your little environment seems stable, the world around you is changing. Keep your eyes and ears open for new opportunities. It doesn't hurt to interview for a job or two each year, just to keep your interviewing skills honed. While your history forms the foundation for your future, what used to be won't necessarily prevail in the years to come—witness film cameras, videotape players, slide rules, typewriters, floppy disk drives, and parallel printer cables. These former staples of the work environment are now nothing more than memories. Keep your career in your hands, not at the mercy of factors you can't control.

Glossary

360-degree feedback
A performance review approach in which managers collect feedback about an employee's job performance from others who interact with the employee. Feedback typically includes comments from the employee as well.

acquisition
When one company buys another.

Age Discrimination in Employment Act of 1967
Federal legislation that makes it illegal for companies with fifteen or more employees to discriminate in hiring, pay, promotion, and firing practices against people who are age forty or older. The ADEA makes it illegal for companies to mandate retirement based on age.

Americans with Disabilities Act of 1990
Federal legislation that establishes requirements for employers with fifteen or more employees to provide reasonable accommodations for individuals with disabilities.

benchmark
A standard that provides a baseline of measurement or assessment.

blog
A personal Web site that presents comments and information in a dated, log-style format originally called a weblog.

body language
The unspoken messages a person's posture and gestures convey.

CDC
Acronym for "U.S. Centers for Disease Control and Prevention," the federal agency responsible for research, investigation, preventive efforts, and response to public health emergencies, including occupational injuries.

Civil Rights Act
A series of federal legislative acts that establish criteria for equity in employment and promotion opportunities and prohibits discrimination. The Civil Rights Act of 1991 updates and strengthens the Civil Rights Act of 1967. Title VII of the Civil Rights Act

of 1964 makes it illegal for companies with fifteen or more employees to discriminate on the basis of race, color, religion, gender, or national origin in hiring, pay, promotion, and firing.

cliques
Groups, usually small, that form around specific interests and then exclude those who do not share those interests.

contingent jobs
Temporary jobs that are expected to last nine months or less. *See also* Temporary employee.

corporate culture
The pattern of beliefs and behaviors that exists within an organization; a company's code of conduct. Also called company culture or organizational culture.

desk rage
Manifestation of workplace violence consisting of threatening or abusive language and behavior.

dot-coms
Companies that sell their wares (products or services) via the Internet; term derives from Web addresses that end in ".com".

downsizing
Reductions in a company's workforce and sometimes production, usually to accommodate a downturn in the economy.

downturn
Situation within the economy when sales and earnings drop, causing companies to tighten the budget belt. Often marked by consolidations and restructuring.

EAP
Acronym for "Employee Assistance Program." A collection of services, usually for basic counseling and related needs for employees and their family members, available as an employer-paid benefit.

e-commerce
An Internet-based platform for conducting business. Amazon.com and eBay are among the most recognizable e-commerce businesses. Many retail companies have both conventional ("brick and mortar") and e-commerce operations.

EEOC
Acronym for "Equal Employment Opportunity Commission." Federal agency that oversees compliance with federal legislation to support fairness and prevent discrimination in the workplace.

Equal Pay Act of 1963
Federal legislation that mandates equal pay for equal work to specifically prohibit employers from paying women less than men for performing the same jobs.

essential functions
The core or primary tasks and responsibilities of a job that the employee holding the job must be able to perform.

ethics
The philosophies and beliefs that shape and guide a company's business practices; a company's moral code of conduct.

exempt
Job classification that signifies an employee is not protected under the Fair Labor Standards Act, which mandates worker protection in categories such as work hours, paid overtime, and equal pay for equal work. Exempt employees are usually salaried.

FLSA
Acronym for "Fair Labor Standards Act." Federal legislation originally passed in 1938 and modified through the years. Defines many aspects of employment compensation, including the standard of a forty-hour workweek, minimum wage, child labor limitations, equal pay for equal work, and compensatory time calculations.

Family Medical Leave Act of 1993
Often referred to by its acronym, FMLA. Federal legislation enacted to require employers to provide unpaid time off from work for an employee to care for a new child (newborn or adopted), a seriously ill family member, or because of their own medical conditions, without losing their jobs. The FMLA generally applies to companies that employ twenty or more people.

FTE
Acronym for "full-time equivalent." Method to quantify staffing based on full-time employment of forty hours per week. Two people sharing a full-time position are each .5 FTE; someone working thirty-two hours a week is .75 FTE.

harassment
Language or actions that create an intimidating or hostile work environment. Harassment is a violation of federal and state laws.

Internet
Worldwide network of computers that serves as the infrastructure for electronic information and commerce.

ISO 9000
Widely accepted quality measurement standards developed by the International Standards Organization (ISO). Many companies strive for ISO certification for their products and processes.

job sharing
A single position shared by two people, who divide responsibility for its tasks and responsibilities, salary, workspace, and other elements. Usually the division is equal, though sometimes one person might have a larger share than the other.

mediation
The process of finding common ground, of seeking win-win solutions to differences and disagreements that will be acceptable to both parties.

mentor
An accomplished professional who takes a novice under wing to guide him or her in making appropriate career choices.

merger
The joining of two or more companies, combining staff and functions to create a single company.

NIOSH
Acronym for "National Institute for Occupational Safety and Health." The federal agency that monitors and reports on workplace health and safety issues. Unlike OSHA, NIOSH does not conduct inspections or enforcement activities; as a division of the CDC, NIOSH's primary functions are data collection and reporting.

OSHA
Acronym for "Occupational Health and Safety Administration." The federal agency responsible for enforcing federal workplace safety laws, rules, and regulations.

outsourcing
The practice of contracting with an outside provider for specific services and functions. A company may outsource its payroll tasks, for example, or the typesetting and printing of documentation and materials for products the company manufactures.

paradigm
A clear and unmistakable pattern of behavior that is widespread in its acceptance.

policies
Written guidelines an employer creates that establish procedures for complying with laws and regulations, operational functions, and behavior expectations.

productivity
Ratio between effort and costs expended and results.

restructure
A company's reorganization of its operations to function more efficiently and competitively.

shadowing
Allowing employees to observe actions and behaviors without participating in them, as a learning experience.

telework
Working from home or another location different than the regular workplace; also called telecommuting or distance working.

temporary employee
Person whose job is expected to last nine months or less; sometimes called a contingency worker or, more casually, a temp. Temporary employees often fill in for regular employees who are out for an extended time (such as for maternity or sick leave), or to bolster staffing during peak seasons.

Uniformed Services Employment and Reemployment Rights Act of 1994 (USERRA)
Federal legislation that establishes reemployment rights and benefits for people called to active duty in the U.S. armed forces.

WIIFM
Acronym for "What's in it for me?" Refers to the interest people have in knowing how they benefit from situations and decisions.

work style
Combination of skills, knowledge, and personality that determines how an individual approaches job functions.

workaholic
Person who works excessively, to the extent that work activities interfere with or prevent a life beyond the job.

World Wide Web
Also known as www; the prefix for most Internet addresses. The interfaces and structures that make it possible to post and locate information on the Internet.

Resources

Books

Blanchard, Ken, and Sheldon Bowles. *Gung Ho! Turn on the People in Any Organization.* William Morrow & Co. (NY), 1997.

Blanchard, Ken, and Spencer Johnson, MD. *The One Minute Manager.* Berkeley Publishing Group (CA), 1993.

Buckingham, Marcus, and Curt Coffman. *First, Break All the Rules: What the World's Greatest Managers Do Differently.* Simon & Schuster (NY), 1999.

Byham, William C., Ph.D., with Jeff Cox. *Zapp! The Lightning of Empowerment: How to Improve Quality, Productivity, and Employee Satisfaction.* Fawcett Books (NY), 1998.

Covey, Stephen R. *The 7 Habits of Highly Effective People: Powerful Lessons in Personal Change,* Fifteenth Anniversary Edition. Simon & Schuster (NY), 2004.

Esty, Katharine, Richard Griffin, and Marcie Schorr Hirsch. *Workplace Diversity: A Manager's Guide to Solving Problems and Turning Diversity into a Competitive Advantage.* Adams Media Corporation (Holbrook MA), 1995.

Fiorito, Barbara D., editor. *Directory of American Firms Operating in Foreign Countries,* 18th edition. Uniworld Business Publications, Inc. (Millis, MA), 2005.

Johnson, Spencer M.D., and Kenneth Blanchard, Ph.D., *Who Moved My Cheese? An Amazing Way to Deal with Change in Your Work and in Your Life.* Putnam (NY), 1998.

Katzenbach, Jon, and Douglas Smith. *The Wisdom of Teams.* Harper Business (NY), 1994.

Lencioni, Patrick M. *The Five Dysfunctions of a Team: A Leadership Fable.* Jossey-Bass/John Wiley & Sons (SF), 2002.

Lundin, Stephen C., Ph.D., Harry Paul, and John Christensen. *Fish! A Remarkable Way to Boost Morale and Improve Results.* Hyperion (NY), 2000.

Miller, Marlane. *Brainstyles: Change Your Life Without Changing Who You Are.* Simon & Schuster (NY), 1997.

Morgenstern, Julie. *Time Management from the Inside Out.* Henry Holt & Company (NY), 2000.

von Oech, Roger, Ph.D., *A Whack on the Side of the Head: How to Unlock Your Mind for Innovation,* Revised Edition, Warner Books (NY), 1998.

Tannen, Deborah, Ph.D. *Talking from 9 to 5: How Women's and Men's Conversational Styles Affect Who Gets Heard, Who Gets Credit, and What Gets Done at Work.* Harper Paperbacks (NY), 1995.

Tieger, Paul D. and Barbara Barron-Tieger. *The Art of Speed-Reading People: Harness the Power of Personality Type and Create What You Want in Business and in Life.* Little, Brown and Company (NY), 1998.

Magazines

Fast Company
The online version of this publication features limited free content and extended subscriber content. A print version, twelve issues per year, is available by subscription.
🖱 *www.fastcompany.com*

The Industry Standard
This publication covers the Internet economy including news, analysis, and new products
🖱 *www.thestandard.com*

Red Herring
This monthly magazine, established in 1993, covers the business of technology.
🖱 *www.redherring.com*

Web Sites

Center for Research in Electronic Commerce
This site provides information, reports, and advice for Internet-based commerce. Numerous private and public organizations cosponsor the CREC.
🖱 *http://cism.mccombs.utexas.edu*

The Gallup Organization
This site reports Gallup poll findings. It also has a section about management, with articles and information as well as poll analyses.
🖱 *www.gallup.com*

MaturityWorks
Sponsored by the National Council on Aging (NCOA), this site provides information for and about older workers.
🖱 *www.maturityworks.org*

Monster.com
This commercial job placement Web site provides articles and information about business and career topics for both managers and employees.
🖱 *www.monster.com*

Nolo Self-Help Law

This site features legal information, software, and forms for both personal and business matters.

www.nolo.com

U.S. Bureau of Labor Statistics

This site provides extensive data and analysis of employment trends in the United States.

www.stats.bls.gov

U.S. Department of Labor

This site provides extensive information about employment laws and issues, as well as links to numerous federal Web sites for more detailed materials.

www.dol.gov

U.S. Equal Employment Opportunity Commission

This site provides information about fair labor practices, antidiscrimination laws and regulations, and the process filing discrimination complaints, as well as about pending or completed discrimination actions and lawsuits.

www.eeoc.gov

U.S. Occupational Health and Safety Administration

This site provides information about workplace safety and health, including injury prevention suggestions, OSHA requirements and inspections, and compliance.

www.osha.gov

U.S. Small Business Administration

This site provides much useful information for small and family businesses.

www.sbaonline.sba.gov

Workplace Doctors

Communication consultants Dan West, William Gorden, and Tina Lewis Rowe host this site, featuring a free forum of questions and answers about communication in the workplace.

www.west2k.com/wego.htm

Organizations

American Management Association

This membership-based management development and training organization provides seminars, conferences, and special events for the more than 700,000 managers and executives who are members worldwide.

www.amanet.org

American Marketing Association

The American Marketing Association is the professional organization for marketing practitioners, managers, and executives. Founded in 1937, the association today has 45,000 members in 100 countries. The Web site provides free information and also features extensive resources for members only, including a reference library and job posting center.

www.marketingpower.com

American Society for Training and Development

The American Society for Training and Development (ASTD) is a membership association representing professionals in workplace learning and performance fields. ASTD conducts and reports on research, provides education, and serves as an information clearinghouse for its members.

www.astd.org

Toastmasters International

The goal of Toastmasters is to help people build their communication and leadership skills through public speaking and by organizing and conducting meetings. Toastmasters International has clubs in cities throughout the United States (and the world). Look in your local phone book to find one near you.

🖰 *www.toastmasters.org*

Society for Human Resource Management

The Society for Human Resource Management (SHRM) is a membership organization for human resource professionals. Its Web site offers articles, news stories, research reports, and other information about issues and concerns in human resource management. Some services are available only to SHRM members.

🖰 *www.shrm.org*

Forms

Business and Legal Reports (BLR)

Though the services of this Web site are available only to paid subscribers, BLR offers a free fourteen-day trial subscription. BLR's vast library of documents and reports includes state-specific forms to accommodate unique laws and regulations that may vary among states.

🖰 *http://hr.blr.com*

HR.com

This Web-based company offers services and information for human resource management, training, and jobs. It features extensive free content as well as downloadable forms and reports.

🖰 *www.hr.com*

HRTools.com

This online resource offers extensive information about all aspects of human resources, including staffing, legal compliance, training and development, benefits and compensation, and workplace safety. The site offers a wide variety of standard forms (downloadable) and HR toolkits.

🖰 *www.hrtools.com*

Index

A

accountability
of employees, 63
of managers, 41–42, 230–231
advocate, for employees, 9–10
Age Discrimination in Employment Act, 225
agenda, for meeting, 151–153
alcoholic beverages, at office events, 246–247
Americans with Disabilities Act, 225
anger
of employees, 251–254
of former coworkers, 18
of manager, 255–256
manipulation and, 128
at meetings, 157–159
violent behavior and, 81–84, 253
applications for employment, 195
attire, 77–79, 80–81, 122

B

"bad" manager, tips for replacing, 4, 19–22
behavior
creativity and, 100–101
inappropriate, 45–46, 80–81
manipulative, 127–129, 234–235
body language, 134–135, 136, 137
bullies, 5
business coaches, 29

C

career path, managing own, 263–274
keeping up with technology, 267
layoff possibilities and, 267–270
maintaining skills, 264–267
preparing for change, 270–274
carpal tunnel syndrome, 87
certification, importance of, 265

change
   handling of, 25, 261
   preparing for, 270–274
cheerleader, manager as,
   35–36
Civil Rights Act, 225
cliques, in workplace,
   237–241
coaching
   coaching services, 29
   to improve job
      performance, 170–174
   manager as coach, 28
communication, 133–145
   about downsizing, 204–
      206
   body language and, 134–
      135, 136, 137
   daily, with employees,
      7–9, 137–139
   effective teams and,
      115–116
   employees' expectations
      about, 56
   feedback and, 44–45,
      141–143
   keeping comments
      positive, 8–9
   listening and, 135–137
   open door policy and,
      139–140
   in writing, 143–145

company size, performance
   evaluations and, 163–164
computer viruses, 93
conflicts
   between personalities,
      116–118
   resolution of, 119–120,
      186–187
consistency, employees'
   expectations about,
   54–56
counterproductive
   behavior, handling, 45–46
coworkers, managing
   former, 16–19
creativity, 98–102

D
dating
   between coworkers,
      241–243
   of subordinates, 243–244
dead-end promotions, 68
decorations, in offices,
   79–80
delegation, effective, 6–7
Department of Labor, 221
discipline, enforcing of, 19
diversity, 177–190
   avoiding favoritism, 189–
      190

fairness standards and,
   184–186, 222–228
gender issues, 181–184
generational issues,
   179–181
handling conflicts, 186–
   187
recognizing potential,
   187–188
respecting differences,
   178–179
documentation,
   performance evaluations
   and, 165–166, 172–173
downsizing, 202–212
   explaining of, 204–205
   individual failings and,
      207–212
   managers' positions and,
      267–270
   mergers and acquisitions
      and, 270–273
   restructuring and, 205–
      207
dress codes, 77–79, 80–81,
   122

E
eating, in offices, 80
education and training
   programs, 47–48, 265–266

Elements of Style, The (Strunk and White), 144
e-mail, 92–93, 96
  writing skills and, 144–145
employee assistance programs (EAPs), 83–84, 255
employees
  anger of, 251–254
  concerns of, when managers change, 2–3
  education and training of, 47–48
  encouraging productivity of, 38–41
  expectations of, 49–56
  failing, signs of and how to help, 207–212
  handling problems between, 52–53
  maintaining distance from, 13
  making daily contact with, 7–9, 137–139
  manager's expectations of, 61–63, 124–126
  managing former coworkers, 16–19
  retaining good, 43–45
Equal Employment Opportunity Commission (EEOC), 218

equal opportunity, *see* diversity
Equal Pay Act, 225
evaluations, *see* performance standards and evaluations
"exempt" employees, 224

F

Fair Labor Standards Act (FLSA), 224–225
fairness, *see* diversity
Family and Medical Leave Act (FMLA), 229
family matters, 228–230
favoritism, avoiding, 189–190
feedback, *see* communication; performance standards and evaluations
firings, 212–215
flextime, 72
friendships, in workplace, 237–241

G

gender diversity issues, 181–184
generational diversity issues, 179–181

glass ceilings, 67–68
goals, encouraging employees', 43
"good" manager, tips for replacing, 22–23

H

harassment, 184, 223–228
hiring, *see* promotion and hiring

I

inappropriate behaviors
  handling of, 45–46
  list of, 80–81
information security, 84
interviews, 196–202
intranet, 95

J

job descriptions
  employee's refusal to exceed, 129–132
  hiring and, 192, 194–195
job offers, extending, 202
job sharing, 73–77

L

layoffs, *see* downsizing
leadership role, 3–6
legal issues

firings, 212–214

promotion and hiring, 192–193, 201

regulations, 217–231

workplace romances, 244–245

see also diversity

licensure, importance of, 265

limitations, knowing own, 11–12

listening, importance of, 135–137

loyalty, to and from company, 59–60

M

manager

anger of, 255–256

career path and, 263–274

employees' expectations about, 51–53

expectations of, 57–63

expectations of employees, 61–63, 124–126

personal accountability of, 41–42, 230–231

personality issues of, 249–251

roles and responsibilities of, 1–14, 28–36, 65–67

success and, 64–65, 68–69

upper management's expectations about, 5–6, 13–14, 37–38

manipulation, managing employee's, 127–129, 234–235

mediator, manager as, 34–35

meetings, 147–160

agenda for, 151–153

basics of running, 148–150

ending of, 156

follow up to, 160

managing employee interaction at, 155, 156–159

presenting self at, 153–155

starting on time, 153–153

who should attend, 148, 150–151

mentors, 7, 29–30, 64

differ from enablers, 209–210

mergers and acquisitions, effects of, 270–273

modeling, of behavior, 3–5

music, in offices, 79–80

N

National Institute of Occupational Safety and Health (NIOSH), 221

O

Occupational Safety and Health Administration (OSHA), 221

office politics, 234–236

open door policy, 139–140

overloads of work, 104–105

P

parent, manager in role of, 32–34

parties, 245–247

passive-aggressive behavior, of former coworkers, 18

Patton, George S., 30

performance standards and evaluations, 124–126, 127, 161–175

follow-up to, 174–175

identifying performance issues, 168–170

job performance coaching, 170–174

relationship between performance and evaluation, 162–164

structures for, 162, 165–168

personality conflicts, 116–118

Peter Principle, 62

posture, *see* body language

potential, recognizing employees', 187–188

privacy issues, 95–96

productivity

comfort and, 77–79, 122–123

creativity and, 98–99

encouraging employees', 38–41

technology and, 87–88

telecommuting and, 73

professional organizations, importance of joining, 265

promotion and hiring, 191–202

applications and resumes, 195

interviews, 196–202

job descriptions, 192, 194–195

legal issues of, 192–193, 201

offers, 202

references, 196, 201–202

R

rebuilding process, in work group, 23–24

recognition

for employees, 63

for managers, 59

references, 196, 201–202

regulations, legal, 217–231

equal opportunity and, 222–228

family matters and, 228–230

importance to workplace, 218–221

personal accountability and, 230–231

safety and, 221–222

restructuring, downsizing and, 205–207

resumes, 195

romance, in workplace, 241–245

rumors, handling, 236

S

safety issues, 81–84, 221–222

salary and benefit issues

employees' expectations about, 53–54

job sharing and, 74, 75

managers' expectations about, 58

performance standards and, 126, 164

security issues, information and, 84. *See also* safety issues

sense of humor, meetings and, 159

sexual harassment, 184, 227–228

shadowing, 30

silent treatment, at meetings, 159

social interactions, 233–247

as employee expectation, 50

friendships and cliques and, 237–241

office politics and, 234–236

parties and after-hours events and, 245–247

romance and, 241–245

setting limits on, 236–237

spam, 93

"star players," 190

stress management

personal, 257–259

in work group, 259–261

structure of jobs, 101–105

success
of employees, 107–108
of managers, 64–65,
68–69

T

teacher, manager as, 30–32
teams, 112–114
technology, *see* workplace
issues
telecommuting, 72–73,
89–91
titles, using person's
correct, 139
tone, setting of, 3–5

V

violence, in workplace,
81–84, 253
viruses, computer, 93

W

web surfing, 93–95
women, in workforce,
181–184
"work at will" positions, 212
workaholics, 105–107

work group
dynamics of, 111–120
handling promotion
within, 16–19
rebuilding of, 23–24
stress management in,
259–261
system versus people
problems, 116–118
traits of effective, 115–116
workplace issues, 71–96,
121–132
behaviors and, 79–81
comfort and productivity,
77–79, 122–123
confidentiality and, 95–96
e-mail and, 92–93, 96,
144–145
flextime, 72
individual growth and,
126–127
intranet, 95
job descriptions and,
129–132
job sharing, 73–77
managing manipulation,
127–129

performance standards
and, 124–126, 127
safety and, 81–84
technology decisions
and, 86–89
telecommuting, 72–73,
89–91
web surfing, 93–95
see also diversity
work styles, 97–110
creativity and, 98–102
employee success and,
107–108
influence of manager's,
108–110
structure and, 101–105
workaholics and, 105–107
written communication,
143–145

THE EVERYTHING SERIES!

BUSINESS & PERSONAL FINANCE

Everything® Accounting Book
Everything® Budgeting Book
Everything® Business Planning Book
Everything® Coaching and Mentoring Book
Everything® Fundraising Book
Everything® Get Out of Debt Book
Everything® Grant Writing Book
Everything® Home-Based Business Book, 2nd Ed.
Everything® Homebuying Book, 2nd Ed.
Everything® Homeselling Book, 2nd Ed.
Everything® Investing Book, 2nd Ed.
Everything® Landlording Book
Everything® Leadership Book
Everything® Managing People Book, 2nd Ed.
Everything® Negotiating Book
Everything® Online Auctions Book
Everything® Online Business Book
Everything® Personal Finance Book
Everything® Personal Finance in Your 20s and 30s Book
Everything® Project Management Book
Everything® Real Estate Investing Book
Everything® Robert's Rules Book, $7.95
Everything® Selling Book
Everything® Start Your Own Business Book, 2nd Ed.
Everything® Wills & Estate Planning Book

COOKING

Everything® Barbecue Cookbook
Everything® Bartender's Book, $9.95
Everything® Chinese Cookbook
Everything® Classic Recipes Book
Everything® Cocktail Parties and Drinks Book
Everything® College Cookbook
Everything® Cooking for Baby and Toddler Book
Everything® Cooking for Two Cookbook
Everything® Diabetes Cookbook
Everything® Easy Gourmet Cookbook
Everything® Fondue Cookbook
Everything® Fondue Party Book
Everything® Gluten-Free Cookbook
Everything® Glycemic Index Cookbook
Everything® Grilling Cookbook

Everything® Healthy Meals in Minutes Cookbook
Everything® Holiday Cookbook
Everything® Indian Cookbook
Everything® Italian Cookbook
Everything® Low-Carb Cookbook
Everything® Low-Fat High-Flavor Cookbook
Everything® Low-Salt Cookbook
Everything® Meals for a Month Cookbook
Everything® Mediterranean Cookbook
Everything® Mexican Cookbook
Everything® One-Pot Cookbook
Everything® Quick and Easy 30-Minute, 5-Ingredient Cookbook
Everything® Quick Meals Cookbook
Everything® Slow Cooker Cookbook
Everything® Slow Cooking for a Crowd Cookbook
Everything® Soup Cookbook
Everything® Tex-Mex Cookbook
Everything® Thai Cookbook
Everything® Vegetarian Cookbook
Everything® Wild Game Cookbook
Everything® Wine Book, 2nd Ed.

GAMES

Everything® 15-Minute Sudoku Book, $9.95
Everything® 30-Minute Sudoku Book, $9.95
Everything® Blackjack Strategy Book
Everything® Brain Strain Book, $9.95
Everything® Bridge Book
Everything® Card Games Book
Everything® Card Tricks Book, $9.95
Everything® Casino Gambling Book, 2nd Ed.
Everything® Chess Basics Book
Everything® Craps Strategy Book
Everything® Crossword and Puzzle Book
Everything® Crossword Challenge Book
Everything® Cryptograms Book, $9.95
Everything® Easy Crosswords Book
Everything® Easy Kakuro Book, $9.95
Everything® Games Book, 2nd Ed.
Everything® Giant Sudoku Book, $9.95
Everything® Kakuro Challenge Book, $9.95
Everything® Large-Print Crossword Challenge Book
Everything® Large-Print Crosswords Book
Everything® Lateral Thinking Puzzles Book, $9.95
Everything® Mazes Book

Everything® Pencil Puzzles Book, $9.95
Everything® Poker Strategy Book
Everything® Pool & Billiards Book
Everything® Test Your IQ Book, $9.95
Everything® Texas Hold 'Em Book, $9.95
Everything® Travel Crosswords Book, $9.95
Everything® Word Games Challenge Book
Everything® Word Search Book

HEALTH

Everything® Alzheimer's Book
Everything® Diabetes Book
Everything® Health Guide to Adult Bipolar Disorder
Everything® Health Guide to Controlling Anxiety
Everything® Health Guide to Fibromyalgia
Everything® Health Guide to Thyroid Disease
Everything® Hypnosis Book
Everything® Low Cholesterol Book
Everything® Massage Book
Everything® Menopause Book
Everything® Nutrition Book
Everything® Reflexology Book
Everything® Stress Management Book

HISTORY

Everything® American Government Book
Everything® American History Book
Everything® Civil War Book
Everything® Freemasons Book
Everything® Irish History & Heritage Book
Everything® Middle East Book

HOBBIES

Everything® Candlemaking Book
Everything® Cartooning Book
Everything® Coin Collecting Book
Everything® Drawing Book
Everything® Family Tree Book, 2nd Ed.
Everything® Knitting Book
Everything® Knots Book
Everything® Photography Book
Everything® Quilting Book
Everything® Scrapbooking Book
Everything® Sewing Book
Everything® Woodworking Book

Bolded titles are new additions to the series.
All Everything® books are priced at $12.95 or $14.95, unless otherwise stated. Prices subject to change without notice.

HOME IMPROVEMENT

Everything® Feng Shui Book
Everything® Feng Shui Decluttering Book, $9.95
Everything® Fix-It Book
Everything® Home Decorating Book
Everything® Home Storage Solutions Book
Everything® Homebuilding Book
Everything® Lawn Care Book
Everything® Organize Your Home Book

KIDS' BOOKS

All titles are $7.95

Everything® Kids' Animal Puzzle & Activity Book
Everything® Kids' Baseball Book, 4th Ed.
Everything® Kids' Bible Trivia Book
Everything® Kids' Bugs Book
**Everything® Kids' Cars and Trucks Puzzle
& Activity Book**
Everything® Kids' Christmas Puzzle
& Activity Book
Everything® Kids' Cookbook
Everything® Kids' Crazy Puzzles Book
Everything® Kids' Dinosaurs Book
**Everything® Kids' First Spanish Puzzle and
Activity Book**
Everything® Kids' Gross Hidden Pictures Book
Everything® Kids' Gross Jokes Book
Everything® Kids' Gross Mazes Book
Everything® Kids' Gross Puzzle and
Activity Book
Everything® Kids' Halloween Puzzle
& Activity Book
Everything® Kids' Hidden Pictures Book
Everything® Kids' Horses Book
Everything® Kids' Joke Book
Everything® Kids' Knock Knock Book
Everything® Kids' Learning Spanish Book
Everything® Kids' Math Puzzles Book
Everything® Kids' Mazes Book
Everything® Kids' Money Book
Everything® Kids' Nature Book
Everything® Kids' Pirates Puzzle and Activity
Book
**Everything® Kids' Princess Puzzle and
Activity Book**
Everything® Kids' Puzzle Book
Everything® Kids' Riddles & Brain Teasers Book
Everything® Kids' Science Experiments Book
Everything® Kids' Sharks Book
Everything® Kids' Soccer Book
Everything® Kids' Travel Activity Book

KIDS' STORY BOOKS

Everything® Fairy Tales Book

LANGUAGE

**Everything® Conversational Chinese Book
with CD, $19.95**
Everything® Conversational Japanese Book
with CD, $19.95
Everything® French Grammar Book
Everything® French Phrase Book, $9.95
Everything® French Verb Book, $9.95
Everything® German Practice Book with CD,
$19.95
Everything® Inglés Book
Everything® Learning French Book
Everything® Learning German Book
Everything® Learning Italian Book
Everything® Learning Latin Book
Everything® Learning Spanish Book
**Everything® Russian Practice Book with CD,
$19.95**
Everything® Sign Language Book
Everything® Spanish Grammar Book
Everything® Spanish Phrase Book, $9.95
Everything® Spanish Practice Book
with CD, $19.95
Everything® Spanish Verb Book, $9.95

MUSIC

Everything® Drums Book with CD, $19.95
Everything® Guitar Book
Everything® Guitar Chords Book with CD,
$19.95
Everything® Home Recording Book
**Everything® Music Theory Book with CD,
$19.95**
Everything® Reading Music Book with CD,
$19.95
Everything® Rock & Blues Guitar Book
(with CD), $19.95
Everything® Songwriting Book

NEW AGE

Everything® Astrology Book, 2nd Ed.
Everything® Birthday Personology Book
Everything® Dreams Book, 2nd Ed.
Everything® Love Signs Book, $9.95
Everything® Numerology Book
Everything® Paganism Book
Everything® Palmistry Book
Everything® Psychic Book
Everything® Reiki Book
Everything® Sex Signs Book, $9.95
Everything® Tarot Book, 2nd Ed.
Everything® Wicca and Witchcraft Book

PARENTING

Everything® Baby Names Book, 2nd Ed.
Everything® Baby Shower Book
Everything® Baby's First Food Book
Everything® Baby's First Year Book
Everything® Birthing Book
Everything® Breastfeeding Book
Everything® Father-to-Be Book
Everything® Father's First Year Book
Everything® Get Ready for Baby Book
Everything® Get Your Baby to Sleep Book, $9.95
Everything® Getting Pregnant Book
**Everything® Guide to Raising a
One-Year-Old**
**Everything® Guide to Raising a
Two-Year-Old**
Everything® Homeschooling Book
Everything® Mother's First Year Book
Everything® Parent's Guide to Children
and Divorce
Everything® Parent's Guide to Children
with ADD/ADHD
Everything® Parent's Guide to Children
with Asperger's Syndrome
Everything® Parent's Guide to Children
with Autism
Everything® Parent's Guide to Children with
Bipolar Disorder
Everything® Parent's Guide to Children
with Dyslexia
Everything® Parent's Guide to Positive Discipline
Everything® Parent's Guide to Raising a
Successful Child
Everything® Parent's Guide to Raising Boys
Everything® Parent's Guide to Raising Siblings
**Everything® Parent's Guide to Sensory
Integration Disorder**
Everything® Parent's Guide to Tantrums
Everything® Parent's Guide to the Overweight
Child
Everything® Parent's Guide to the Strong-Willed
Child
Everything® Parenting a Teenager Book
Everything® Potty Training Book, $9.95
Everything® Pregnancy Book, 2nd Ed.
Everything® Pregnancy Fitness Book
Everything® Pregnancy Nutrition Book
**Everything® Pregnancy Organizer, 2nd Ed.,
$16.95**
Everything® Toddler Activities Book
Everything® Toddler Book
Everything® Tween Book
Everything® Twins, Triplets, and More Book

PETS

Everything® Aquarium Book
Everything® Boxer Book
Everything® Cat Book, 2nd Ed.
Everything® Chihuahua Book
Everything® Dachshund Book
Everything® Dog Book
Everything® Dog Health Book
Everything® Dog Owner's Organizer, $16.95
Everything® Dog Training and Tricks Book
Everything® German Shepherd Book
Everything® Golden Retriever Book
Everything® Horse Book
Everything® Horse Care Book
Everything® Horseback Riding Book
Everything® Labrador Retriever Book
Everything® Poodle Book
Everything® Pug Book
Everything® Puppy Book
Everything® Rottweiler Book
Everything® Small Dogs Book
Everything® Tropical Fish Book
Everything® Yorkshire Terrier Book

REFERENCE

Everything® Blogging Book
Everything® Build Your Vocabulary Book
Everything® Car Care Book
Everything® Classical Mythology Book
Everything® Da Vinci Book
Everything® Divorce Book
Everything® Einstein Book
Everything® Etiquette Book, 2nd Ed.
Everything® Inventions and Patents Book
Everything® Mafia Book
Everything® Philosophy Book
Everything® Psychology Book
Everything® Shakespeare Book

RELIGION

Everything® Angels Book
Everything® Bible Book
Everything® Buddhism Book
Everything® Catholicism Book
Everything® Christianity Book
Everything® History of the Bible Book
Everything® Jesus Book
Everything® Jewish History & Heritage Book
Everything® Judaism Book
Everything® Kabbalah Book
Everything® Koran Book
Everything® Mary Book

Everything® Mary Magdalene Book
Everything® Prayer Book
Everything® Saints Book
Everything® Torah Book
Everything® Understanding Islam Book
Everything® World's Religions Book
Everything® Zen Book

SCHOOL & CAREERS

Everything® Alternative Careers Book
Everything® Career Tests Book
Everything® College Major Test Book
Everything® College Survival Book, 2nd Ed.
Everything® Cover Letter Book, 2nd Ed.
Everything® Filmmaking Book
Everything® Get-a-Job Book
Everything® Guide to Being a Paralegal
Everything® Guide to Being a Real Estate Agent
Everything® Guide to Being a Sales Rep
Everything® Guide to Careers in Health Care
Everything® Guide to Careers in Law Enforcement
Everything® Guide to Government Jobs
Everything® Guide to Starting and Running a Restaurant
Everything® Job Interview Book
Everything® New Nurse Book
Everything® New Teacher Book
Everything® Paying for College Book
Everything® Practice Interview Book
Everything® Resume Book, 2nd Ed.
Everything® Study Book

SELF-HELP

Everything® Dating Book, 2nd Ed.
Everything® Great Sex Book
Everything® Kama Sutra Book
Everything® Self-Esteem Book

SPORTS & FITNESS

Everything® Easy Fitness Book
Everything® Fishing Book
Everything® Golf Instruction Book
Everything® Pilates Book
Everything® Running Book
Everything® Weight Training Book
Everything® Yoga Book

TRAVEL

Everything® Family Guide to Cruise Vacations
Everything® Family Guide to Hawaii

Everything® Family Guide to Las Vegas, 2nd Ed.
Everything® Family Guide to Mexico
Everything® Family Guide to New York City, 2nd Ed.
Everything® Family Guide to RV Travel & Campgrounds
Everything® Family Guide to the Caribbean
Everything® Family Guide to the Walt Disney World Resort®, Universal Studios®, and Greater Orlando, 4th Ed.
Everything® Family Guide to Timeshares
Everything® Family Guide to Washington D.C., 2nd Ed.
Everything® Guide to New England

WEDDINGS

Everything® Bachelorette Party Book, $9.95
Everything® Bridesmaid Book, $9.95
Everything® Destination Wedding Book
Everything® Elopement Book, $9.95
Everything® Father of the Bride Book, $9.95
Everything® Groom Book, $9.95
Everything® Mother of the Bride Book, $9.95
Everything® Outdoor Wedding Book
Everything® Wedding Book, 3rd Ed.
Everything® Wedding Checklist, $9.95
Everything® Wedding Etiquette Book, $9.95
Everything® Wedding Organizer, 2nd Ed., $16.95
Everything® Wedding Shower Book, $9.95
Everything® Wedding Vows Book, $9.95
Everything® Wedding Workout Book
Everything® Weddings on a Budget Book, $9.95

WRITING

Everything® Creative Writing Book
Everything® Get Published Book, 2nd Ed.
Everything® Grammar and Style Book
Everything® Guide to Writing a Book Proposal
Everything® Guide to Writing a Novel
Everything® Guide to Writing Children's Books
Everything® Guide to Writing Research Papers
Everything® Screenwriting Book
Everything® Writing Poetry Book
Everything® Writing Well Book

Available wherever books are sold!
To order, call 800-258-0929, or visit us at *www.everything.com*
Everything® and everything.com® are registered trademarks of F+W Publications, Inc.